The Black Family

THE
BLACK
FAMILY

Strengths, Self-Help, and Positive Change

edited by

Sadye L. Logan

University of Kansas

 WestviewPress
A Division of HarperCollins*Publishers*

To my Guru
who is the root of all action

Copyright © 1996 by Westview Press, Inc., A Division of HarperCollins Publishers, Inc.

Published in 1996 in the United States of America by Westview Press, Inc., 5500 Central Avenue, Boulder, Colorado 80301-2877, and in the United Kingdom by Westview Press, 12 Hid's Copse Road, Cumnor Hill, Oxford OX2 9JJ

Library of Congress Cataloging-in-Publication Data
The Black family : strengths, self-help, and positive change / edited
  by Sadye L. Logan
    p.   cm.
  Includes bibliographical references and index.
  ISBN 0-8133-2576-5 (hc). — ISBN 0-8133-2577-3 (pbk.)
  1. Social work with Afro-Americans.   2. Family social work—United
States.   3. Afro-American Families—Social conditions.   4. Afro-
American families—Services for.   5. Afro-American children—
Services for.   I. Logan, Sadye Louise, 1943–   .
HV3181.B54   1996
362.84´96073—dc20   96-10328
                                                                      CIP

The paper used in this publication meets the requirements of the American National Standard for Permanence of Paper for Printed Library Materials Z39.48-1984.

10   9   8   7   6   5   4   3   2   1

Contents

Foreword

Sadye Logan and her colleagues are to be commended for this very important new addition to the growing body of literature on strengths of the Black family. Every student, scholar, policy maker, teacher, and professional concerned with African American families from an academic or programmatic perspective will find this collection of essays and studies a valuable new resource. It combines insightful theoretical and conceptual analyses with advice, counsel, and recommendations that will be useful to practitioners working in many areas related to the health and well-being of Black families.

In the three decades since Daniel Patrick Moynihan published his highly controversial report entitled *The Negro Family: A Case for National Action* (1965), African American scholars have led the way in amassing evidence and providing alternative interpretations to dislodge and discredit the "deficit model" of Black families popularized by the Moynihan report. Moynihan's declaration that African Americans are caught in a "tangle of pathology" caused by the "deteriorating" structure of the lower-income family spurred an entire generation of scholars to challenge his formulations and interpretations.

A number of these scholars focused on documenting the historical and continuing strengths of African American families, who faced racism and discrimination in employment, education, housing, health care, and every other social sector that affects family life. Andrew Billingsley's *Black Families in White America* (1968) and Robert Hill's *The Strength of Black Families* (1971) were pioneering efforts in this regard. Significant and lasting contributions to this genre were also made, beginning in the 1970s, by Charles Willie, Robert Staples, Carol Stack, Walter Allen, Harriette and John McAdoo, and others.

The work of Sadye Logan and her colleagues builds on this tradition: In addition to documenting the strengths of Black families, it proposes "strength-oriented solutions to the problems impacting the quality" of the lives of their members. The contributors tackle many difficult problems facing Black families, including violence, disease, and homelessness, with the aim of not only explaining these phenomena but intervening and improving the lives of those challenged by them.

Not surprisingly, the contributors all recognize the importance of *values* in the change process; they draw on the heritage of Africa as well as the history of the Black church in advocating certain family values that help to socialize children and serve the needs of entire families. Their suggestion that an "African-centered perspective" can strengthen programs that serve African American families and youth deserves serious consideration as we build and revise models for improving family functioning and delivering family services.

Too often in the area of Black family studies, African American scholars end up talking to each other while scholars in the majority academic community ignore their findings and interpretations of Black family life. So too with those responsible for public policies and family services. Most of these practitioners continue to base their programs on analyses and perspectives that have been impugned for years. One hopes that this new book by Logan and her colleagues, which makes a very important contribution to theory and practice in the area of African American family studies, will not languish on library shelves or serve only as a citation in bibliographies on the Black family. It deserves to become a much-used reference and resource for all of those who consider themselves in the "mainstream" of policy-making and scholarship on African American families.

Niara Sudarkasa

Acknowledgments

This book could not have been written without the commitment and support of numerous players. It is a synergistic product reflected in the theme "the one in many." Therefore, I welcome this opportunity to thank everyone who has contributed to the successful completion of this project. I especially thank Edith Freeman for her support and encouragement as a colleague and friend and Valerie Loeschen, a Masters of Social Work student, for reviewing and commenting on the manuscript. A special thank you goes to the University of Kansas School of Social Welfare for support services and to Marian Abegg for her tireless efforts in typing this document. Deep appreciation also goes to all the contributors to this volume who are committed to knowledge building and to providing quality service and care to Black families and children. Finally, I thank my family for their unconditional love and support during the development and production of this project. It is in their love and caring that I find strengths, support, and the courage to grow and change.

Sadye L. Logan

Introduction

Despite the widespread agreement that families have undergone massive structural and functional change, families continue to be the major institution for sustaining and shaping human destinies. There is no doubt, however, that families are under severe stress. They struggle with everyday problems-in-living that are compounded by issues of teenage pregnancy, child care, family violence, the aged, unemployment, and substance abuse, among others. Available statistics, general observations, and self-reports indicate that Black families[1] and other families of color are disproportionately affected by these systemic issues and concerns.

These are complex issues and relate in part to a range of economic, social, and political factors. It is becoming increasingly evident that the American family never existed as it was portrayed four decades ago on the national television show *Father Knows Best*, and it is little like today's popular shows *Roseanne* and *The Cosby Show*. What we had then and now are families that are in transition and change—families that are confronted with problems-in-living, as well as with opportunities that are numerous, complex, and unique. Further, it is evident that the future of this country and perhaps the world depends on how well each of us—social service institutions, businesses, government—work to strengthen families. This is the challenge.

This book is a response to the challenge. It represents a movement away from the deficit model toward an empowering, strength-oriented perspective. The intent is to provide a positive, broader framework for conceptualizing and implementing services to Black families and children. Within that context, this text specifically provides content in which readers would be able to:

1

- Gain a culturally specific focus on Black families and children
- Better understand how societal issues create vulnerable Black families and children
- Surface as well as reframe problems that impact the quality of life of Blacks
- Find strength-oriented solutions to problems that impact the quality of life of Black families.

The expanded perspective reflected in this content attempts on some level to be responsive to the profound question raised by Somé (1994): Why is it that the modern world cannot deal with its ancestors and endure its past? Implicit in this query is the West's ongoing search for solutions to the numerous life problems that threaten the very foundation of our existence. This search, however, is not rooted in the knowledge and wisdom of our forebears and our history. Not unlike other critical thinkers on this topic, Somé (1994) asserts that the apathy, restlessness, and feelings of alienation that seem endemic to our society are an outgrowth of unhealthy or dysfunctional relationships with our ancestors. In Somé's view, in Dagora country in Africa and many other non-Western cultures, the ancestors are intimately and vitally connected with the world of the living. Their role includes guide, teacher, and nurturer. In this capacity the ancestors serve as a conduit between the physical world and the spirit world, thereby providing the living ancestors with guidelines for successful living. But what has all this to do with African American families?

Essentially, it serves as an affirmation of the strong emphasis throughout this book on an African-centered[2] value system—a system that places emphasis in the moment and on hope, in a better world where all people have dignity, equal respect, an equal voice, and equal influence in shaping the world in which they live. These values are derived from the collective unconscious of the wisdom bearers of the past and the present. Further, these values are available to provide powerful guidelines in successful living for contemporary African American families. These guidelines are reflected in four assumptions about people and their lives (Logan, 1995).

1. That an inherent inner strength or life force exists within each human being
2. That when people are affirmed and adopt a positive mind-set about their worth and value as human beings an inner and outer transformation occurs

3. That empowerment is a process that must be moved from outside to inside (to be owned by person or persons) for permanent healing to occur
4. That when problems are viewed as friends and as teachings about life it brings about personal growth and helps in finding solutions to life concerns.

The chapters in this volume may be viewed as the effort of a group of critical thinkers who are committed not only to build families' strengths through self-help and innovation but also to assist families in overcoming obstacles (Part One) and to create and promote change (Part Two).

Overall, this volume serves a three-fold purpose. One, it provides an expanded, strength-oriented perspective on Black families, thereby extending a small but growing body of literature on empowerment. Two, it serves as a frame of reference for everyone involved in working with Black families and children. More specifically, this book of readings will be a beneficial resource for community leaders, agency administrators, social work practitioners, classroom and practicum instructors, and students. The target audience may also include other disciplines such as nursing, psychology, and counseling. Finally, this text can be used as supplemental or required reading for courses in clinical practice, family treatment, the Black family, social policy, practice-based research, human behavior and the social environment, and field instruction. In addition to serving as a resource guide, this text provides clear, concise, and practical strategies for supporting families in addressing everyday problems-in-living, as well as those seemingly intractable issues and concerns.

Notes

1. The terms *Black families* and *African American families* are used interchangeably throughout this book.
2. The terms *African-centered* and *Afrocentric* are used interchangeably throughout this book.

References

Logan, S. (1995, January). Wholistic healing and an expanded perspective for working with inner city families. Paper presented at the First International Conference on Social Work in Health and Mental Health, Jerusalem, Israel.

Somé, M. R. (1994). *Of water and the spirit: Ritual, magic, and initiation in the life of an African shaman.* New York: G. P. Putnam's Sons.

PART ONE

Building Strength Through Self-Help and Innovations

Part One of this volume emphasizes strength within Black families and their communities through self-help and innovations. Six chapters constitute the first part of this book.

The emphasis on self-help is in large part a reminder to the professional community that our emphasis in offering help must be not only on the provision of services but also on helping clients to become self-sufficient through taking responsibility for their lives. Further, self-help and innovative strategies have seemed to assist families in overcoming obstacles and to create change of a lasting nature.

With the recognition that families have been impacted by numerous economic, social, and political forces and have undergone tremendous change, Logan takes a broad-brush approach in her chapter and paints a useful and insightful picture of the historical underpinnings of the Black experience. Once she has established this framework, she outlines a plan of action that encourages Black Americans to rekindle their strengths in kinship bonds; role fluidity, religious spiritual practices, achievement orientation, and work orientation. Although her message, in part, is not new, it serves to challenge Black families and children and all helping professionals to commit themselves to building and supporting strength within the individual, as well as within the environment.

Coupled with the aforementioned recognition is the realization that emphasis on a deficit perspective limits the search for solutions to only an internal focus. The reawakening interest in strengths and self-help offers new possibilities and focuses on internal as well as external change.

In this regard, Smith provides a stimulating discussion of the contemporary Black family in what he describes as the context of postindustrial enlightenment. Smith advances the theme that the contemporary African American family is more informed, advanced, self-reliant, and capable of sustaining institutional racism and discrimination. Emphasis is placed on empowerment through creative and disciplined self-development. Case examples are presented as illustrations of this development. The social work and education communities are strongly encouraged to join forces with African American families and communities in finding creative solutions to those intransigent problems-in-living.

Advances in medical technology have prolonged the life spans of chronically ill persons, and rising medical costs have led to a shift from institutional to home health care for the sick. This shift in response to illness, however, is not new for Black families and children. Likewise, available support and information about sickle cell anemia, a serious blood disorder unique to African Americans, were nearly nonexistent approximately three decades ago. Black families are still unserved or underserved by the medical and helping professions for a variety of reasons. As a result, Black families have taken on greater responsibilities in caring for their sick members. Such developments have created a conflictual set of dynamics between the families and service delivery systems. Despite such conflictual relationships, Black families as a group still consistently seek professional help over time for a variety of problems-in-living. Hill's chapter is an elaboration on the help-seeking behavior and survival strategies of Black families. She poignantly describes the issues and concerns that impact those families and children struggling with the management of health care needs of children chronically ill with sickle cell disease.

As families like those described by Hill move toward fuller community participation and control of their lives, they are often unexpectedly confronted by menacing social ills such as homelessness, Acquired Immune Deficiency Syndrome (AIDS), and youth violence. These and other problems-in-living continue to dissipate the strengths of these striving families. In their chapter, Logan and Joyce are concerned with the impact of AIDS on Black American families. According to available data, the numbers of reported AIDS cases are not only disproportionate but are increasing among Black Americans. For example, a recent report on gay Black men and gay and heterosexual Black male drug users spoke of the extreme difficulty involved in preventing the spread of AIDS among Black men (Hodgkinson, 1989). The difficulty is in part a result of the general attitude of the Black community regarding homosexuality and drug use and of the financial constraints connected to health care. Logan and Joyce's chapter focuses not only on such front-end issues as treatment and prevention, but their primary concerns are the caregivers of persons with AIDS. Often, families of persons with AIDS are without financial or social support. In part, this neglect is the result of an exclusive focus on helping persons with AIDS deal with feelings of helplessness and on the role of service providers. Families and other caregivers have not been a focus of helping professionals. The authors strongly suggest that service providers meet the challenge of developing effective strategies to support families and caregivers of persons with AIDS.

Homelessness is one of the most insidious problems-in-living. Available evidence suggests that the fastest-growing homeless group is families with children, of which Black families constitute a disproportionate number. Freeman, in her chapter on homelessness among Black American families, dispels the stereotypes of homeless persons as bums and vagabonds hopping railroad cars or as "skid-row alcoholics" with no family ties. On the contrary, a recent study showed that one-third of the homeless in Washington, D.C., were Black families with children with one full-time worker. The full-time worker, however, was working at a fast-food job paying $3.80 an hour (Hodgkinson, 1989). In addressing the issues and concerns of the homeless, Freeman discusses the need for differentially based service planning that addresses macro- and micro-level needs. She also describes solution-focused strategies for alleviating this insidious problem at the educational, service delivery, and community levels.

The influence of youth gangs is increasing. In the late 1970s there were 225 gangs in Los Angeles County; today there are more than 1,000. According to local law enforcement officials, African American membership in these gangs totals 46,000. The conditions that create gangs in big cities like Los Angeles, New York, and Chicago also exist in smaller cities like Denver, Kansas City, and Shreveport. As a result, smaller cities are witnessing a tremendous growth in gang activity. Although it is a rarely cited fact, young women are being recruited into gangs in increasing numbers. Mitchell and Logan, in the final chapter in Part One, acknowledge the complexity, as well as the general destructiveness, of this expanding systemic problem. They also underscore the critical need for African Americans to remain diligent in implementing pro-youth programs that are community centered.

1

A Strengths Perspective on Black Families: Then and Now

SADYE L. LOGAN

> If you do not know where you are or where you have been, you cannot
> know where you are going; any road will take you there.
> —**West African proverb**

It appears that people's lives and environments are being transformed throughout the world. These changes generally reflect movement from a stance of hopelessness to one of hopefulness. A similar trend is reflected in the literature. Those groups and situations that have traditionally been viewed and discussed in pejorative terms are being revisited from a more hopeful, strength-oriented perspective. Interestingly, within this context two major popular magazines, one that serves a predominantly white audience and the other that serves a predominantly Black audience, ran special reports on the state of the Black family in the same month. One report was extremely pessimistic, whereas the other was fairly optimistic. The optimistic report described Black families as diverse, determined, and dynamic. The pessimistic reporting perpetuated the condition that suggests that Black families are endangered and need to be saved.

An astute observer of Black family life once challenged a group of helping professions to stop saving the Black families. Then he related an old scenario: "Tony, God, you look bad. Let me get you a chair. Sit down here. Do you need an aspirin?" How long, he asked, is it going to take Tony to start feeling bad? He concluded, "Not long!" and the reason is that you are "saving" Tony. The bottom line is that Tony did not need saving until he started to be saved. The emphatic point to the audience was that Black families did not need to be saved but needed to be strengthened, empowered, and utilized as resources.

This proclamation is not new. It has become the common language of the day. But the struggle is over how we truly convince ourselves to stop trying to save Black families, as well as to convince many Black families that they do not need to be saved.

As a careful student of Black family life, I contend that answers can be found in the historical past and current strivings of Black families. The historical past referred to here extends beyond slavery to the African heritage. It is in this remembrance that a people will begin to reconnect with their innate capacities, with their ability to break out of the current vicious cycle of human suffering. The cycle incorporates seven perspectives that can be grouped into four views: the historical period, the traditionalist period, the revisionist period, and the contemporary period (see Figure 1.1).

Periods of Black Family Life

The Historical Period

Scholars generally focus on West Africa when attempting to date and describe the transmission of Africa's influence on African Americans. Chief among the West African states that carried this influence were ancient Ghana, Mali, Songhay, and the Mossi States, currently known as Burkina-Faso.

Ghana, known as the "Land of Gold" because of the abundance of this precious metal, has a history that extends back as far as the seventh century B.C. Ghana was a land rich not only in natural resources but also in agricultural products and great and talented craftspeople. Although this great kingdom declined as a result of external invasions, internal conflicts, and climatic changes, the family was and remains a central focus (Bennett, 1987; Franklin, 1956; Washington, Burns, & Vas, 1992). Scholars of Black family life have identified several African family patterns that with some variation have survived the slavery holocaust (Bennett, 1987; Franklin, 1956; Sudarkasa, 1981).

1. *Blood ties.* Blood ties take precedence over all types of relationship.
2. *Extended family orientation.* Extended family takes precedence
   over nuclear family.
3. *Childrearing.* Children are viewed as the responsibility of parents
   and the extended family.
4. *Respect and reverence.* Great respect and reverence are shown to
   family elders and others.
5. *Reciprocity.* Mutual aid and reciprocity exist among family members.
6. *Restraint.* Family needs take precedence over individual needs.
   Therefore, self-restraint with regard to emotions and personal
   wishes is practiced.
7. *Cooperation.* Shared responsibility for the well-being of others is
   practiced.
8. *Marriage.* Polygynous marriages are practiced.

Studies of ancient Africa describe a civilization rich in precious met-
als, agriculture, and culture and highly evolved spiritually with a great
emphasis on home and family life. According to the view of family systems theory, many of these processes have not been lost but have been
transmitted through the family's emotional process over space and time.
Given the right circumstances, these values will emerge again (Bowen,
1988).

The Traditionalist Period

This period extends from approximately 1870 to 1975 and overlaps with
the revisionist period. Here, the primary emphasis was on home and
family life. This period also reminds us that the existence of Africans in
the United States began with indentured servants. The body of scholarship during this period addressed nearly all aspects of Black life in
pathological terms (Guthrie, 1976; Jones, 1973; Kamin, 1974). The only
disagreement among the scholars studying the Black family during this
period was about causality. Some argued that the so-called pathology
that characterized Black family life was the result of genetics; others argued that it was environmental. The view that Blacks were an inferior
species extended from approximately 1870 to 1930 and was replaced by
the environmental perspective (Frazier, 1939).

Figure 1.1   Views and Perspectives of Black Family Life

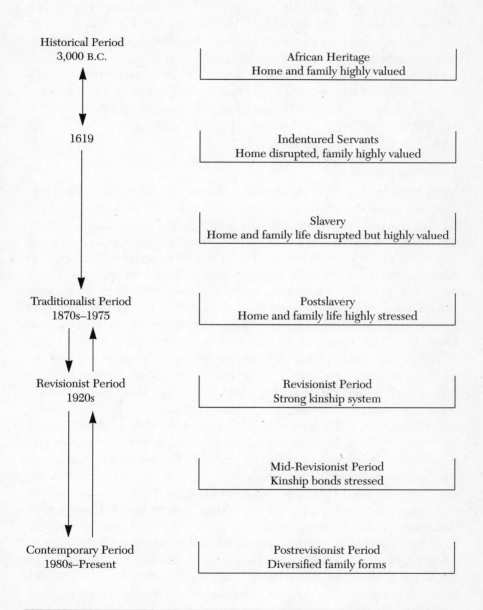

E. Franklin Frazier (1939), an African American sociologist, argued that if traces of African heritage did exist, they had been obliterated by the experience of U.S. slavery. His work, viewed as the definitive history of Black family life, confirmed the thinking of his contemporaries that the personal lives of poor Blacks were dysfunctional and characterized by pathology. Melville Herkovits (1941), a Caucasian anthropologist, argued with equal force—but with fewer believers—that most Black American social and cultural patterns were African in origin. The view presented by Frazier (1957) and perpetuated by others (Glazer & Moynihan, 1963) went unchallenged until the 1960s.

The Revisionist Era

In addition to anthropological studies that found sufficient evidence to date and place the oldest complete skeleton of a human ancestor (3–5 million years old) in Africa (Leakey, 1977, 1994), molecular biologists, chemists, and geneticists revolutionized the study of human evolution. These scientists verified the finding of paleontologists with respect to Africa as the "cradle of civilization" (Tierney, Wright, & Springer, 1988). According to available information, these scientists, through the process of examining all structures over time, were able to trace the evolution of modern human beings from the present generation back in time to more than 200,000 years ago to a female ancestor in Black Africa (Cann, Stoneking, & Wilson, 1987). These findings, in addition to refuting the thesis of one race as more superior or advanced than another, have affirmed earlier thinking regarding Africa as the seat of civilization.

Complementing these findings, social scientists were forging a different perspective on Black family life. For example, Robert Hill's research on the strengths of Black families is perhaps the first well-publicized indication that scholars had begun to challenge the established pathological theory regarding Black family life (Hill, 1972). Several other researchers extended Hill's thesis and in concert moved toward dispelling the myth that the U.S. slave experience destroyed the Black family (Blassingame, 1972; Genovese, 1974; Gutman, 1976). These "revisionist" historians are credited with affirming a Black kinship system that was resilient, intact, and adaptive from enslavement until a few years before the Great Depression of the 1930s. Not only Black families but all families were derailed by the impact of a failed economy. Therefore, much, if not all, of what was described as pathological was an expression of living below the poverty level and not having basic human needs fulfilled.

The Contemporary Period: An Era of Innovation and Change

In the early 1980s the University of Michigan completed the first nationally representative sample of Black adults. The study provided data on the feelings, attitudes, and behaviors of 2,107 adult respondents on all aspects of the Black experience. It especially provided new insights into understanding the complexity of Black family life (Jackson, 1991). In many ways this major study extended the thinking of those social scientists whose research consistently described a viable, functional Black family system (Billingsley, 1968; Gary et al., 1983; McAdoo, 1977).

There is no doubt that the Black family has experienced a great deal of external and internal change dictated by a rapidly transforming environment and lifestyles. These evolutionary changes that result in diverse family forms are frequently referred to in the literature as "endangered," "changing," or "dying." Despite the overemphasis on deteriorating family forms, the traditional Black family, consisting of a married couple and children, is still the most prevalent family form (Billingsley, 1992). Actually, current data show that despite the marked increase in single-person households, the actual number of married-couple families in the United States increased from 3.3 million in 1970 to over 3.8 million by 1990 (Massaqui, 1993). Massaqui (1993) also reports that significant numbers of Black married couples are opting to remain childless, whereas a smaller percentage (5 percent of Black adults) are living together in relationships that are stable and economically sufficient.

According to Billingsley (1992), the largest group of stable Black families is the "nonpoor working class," which is made up of families whose combined income ranges from $10 thousand to $25 thousand annually. This group is viewed as the economic, social, spiritual, and political backbone of the Black community. Moreover, despite the stressors and numerous systemic problems that impact Black families, the evidence suggests that on the whole Black families are strong, viable, and resilient systems.

Coupled with this view is the ongoing battle against the pervasive scholarship that asserted Black Americans did not have a historical or cultural background to help define their cultural selves. These studies concluded that "the Negro is only an American and nothing else. He has no history or culture to guard and protect" (Glazer & Moynihan, 1963). Despite such overwhelming reports, a few scholars maintained with equal conviction that most Black Americans' social and cultural patterns were African in origin (Herkovits, 1941).

Movement Toward Making a Difference

Numerous solutions have been proposed for addressing the needs and problems that impact Black families. These have ranged from suggestions that everyone of African descent should return to Africa to advocating a declaration of war on poverty. Somewhere between these measures, or perhaps beyond them, lie the hope, desire, and strength that will propel Black people into the twenty-first century. This hope is reflected in a rekindling of the traditional Black value system and in the gradual unfolding of an awareness that we create our own realities, which we experience as our life (Shulman, 1992).

The Black Value System

It seems evident that the time has come for U.S. Blacks to move to a different level of awareness regarding self, family, community, and society (Billingsley, 1992). In its predominantly outward focus, the experience of Blacks in this society has transformed persons and environments. However, during this process Blacks have forgotten many of the precepts that gave strength and meaning to their existence. A general theme of cooperation and support appears in the current striving of Black families. This theme also resonates at the centers of ancient African family life (Hilliard, Williams, & Damali, 1987) and the Black value system (Baraka, 1969; Oliver, 1989; Salaam, 1974), which include

1. *Unity.* To strive for and maintain unity in the family, community, nation, and race
2. *Self-determination.* To define, name, and speak for ourselves instead of being defined and spoken for by others
3. *Collective work and responsibility.* To build and maintain our community together and to make our brothers' and sisters' problems our problems and solve them together
4. *Cooperative economics.* To build and maintain our own stores, shops, and other businesses and to profit together from them

5. *Purpose.* To make as our collective vocation the building and developing of our community to restore our people to their traditional greatness
6. *Creativity.* To always do as much as we can, in the way we can, to leave our community more beautiful and beneficial than when we inherited it
7. *Faith.* To believe with all our heart in our parents, our teachers, our leaders, our people, and the righteousness and victory of our struggle

These seven principles were proposed by Maulana Ron Karenga and further developed by Baraka as guideposts for liberating the soul, mind, and body of Black people (see Chapter 7). However, Karenga also saw all people as benefiting from these principles. These values are intended to serve as the foundation upon which Black people build their entire lives; they will frame how families live and also in what manner and with what purpose. There is a common thread running through and connecting these seven principles. This thread is spirituality—a belief in the wholeness of what it is to be human, a belief that relates to a person's or a people's search for a sense of meaning and a morally fulfilling relationship with the universe. An important factor in this value system is that it is spiritual without being religious. In this way everyone is included, and it moves to the highest level of human aspirations but involves no ritual or dogma. This freeing perspective creates the necessary arena for the construction of different individual and group realities.

Creating New Realities: Toward an African-Centered Perspective and Wholeness

There is a basic assumption that how we understand our world is based on a combination of observations, the language we inherit, and the cultural assumptions and historical precedents that shape who we are (Wilkins, 1989). Therefore, the concepts and beliefs we use to describe who we are and how we live are as much products of the period and culture in which we live as they are by-products of several generations over time (Bowen, 1988). It is this socially shaped understanding that justifies our current mode of behavior and interaction with others. For most, if not all, Black Americans, this level of understanding has not created environments that have been psychologically nurturing and growth enhancing. However, as is evidenced in the broader society, Black Americans are also assuming a greater voice in defining their identities and agendas. This empowering stance became evident during the civil rights movement of the 1960s and continues to be reflected in situations that cover all facets of life.

Examples of such situations are reflected in the David Duke incident in Louisiana. Billingsley (1992) points out that Blacks in Louisiana were described as representing an insignificant minority of the voting electorate that could not possibly defeat Duke, who was campaigning on a racist platform for U.S. senator and later for governor. According to Billingsley (1992), "Most commentators did not anticipate that a unified, Black minority would lead a coalition that [would defeat] Duke both times" (p. 18). In explaining why this so-called insignificant minority was successful, Billingsley underscores a very significant life principle: that each individual has the personal power to create his or her own realities. In this instance, the Black voters chose not to define or to view themselves as an insignificant minority. Instead, they chose to identify with their strength and their belief that a racist platform was distasteful to all people, especially to Blacks and other people of color. This is a profound and very powerful movement toward positive change.

Other examples of this movement toward the creation of new and more nurturing environments for Black families and children can be seen from small towns to major urban centers. For instance, in Washington, D.C., such activities include an after-school male project and a church-sponsored rites-of-passage program. These programs are designed to help Black males and females with the transition into responsible adulthood. In Atlanta, Georgia, two men have started Fathers Foundation, Inc., a group working to involve more Black men in raising their children. Similar programs are scattered all over the United States. Included among these are church-sponsored senior citizen programs, literacy programs, food and clothing programs, housing programs, and parenting programs (Billingsley, 1992).

For some observers of Black family life, the impact of these examples might be compared to spitting in an ocean. However, the emphasis here is that the full-scale change that is proposed must occur on many levels. Critical to this process is change on the spiritual and psychological levels. This internal change represents a new level of consciousness. For many African Americans this emerging consciousness is fueled by a variety of orientations. Perhaps the most visible and effective approach is found in African-centered beliefs and teachings (Asante, 1992; Asante

& Welsh-Asante, 1985). This perspective captures the essence of a strength-oriented empowering stance. According to Covin (1990), five measures or principles characterize this perspective (pp. 127–128):

1. People of African descent share a common experience, struggle, and origin.
2. Present in African culture is a nonmaterial element of resistance to the assault on traditional values caused by the intrusion of European legal procedures, medicine, political processes, and religions into that culture.
3. African culture takes the view that an Afrocentric modernization process would be based upon three traditional values: harmony with nature, humaneness, and rhythm.
4. Afrocentricity involves the development of a theory of an African way of knowing and interpreting the world.
5. Some form of communalism or socialism is an important component of the way wealth is produced, owned, and distributed.

Overall, this powerful perspective is about commitment, reconstruction, and transformation. At the center of these three processes is the Black family. As families become more connected to these processes, they will become more capable of defining and creating their own worldviews and defining their experiences of the world. These processes also provide the context for families to create new behaviors and modify old and self-defeating ones. Inherent in this progenerative approach to life and living is the potential for eventually transcending all perspectives and living only from the center where Truth resides.

Finally, along with the collective, each individual must work for and sustain external and internal change. To sustain change, however, one must be prepared to accept the change and make it multiply. As McCall (1993) suggests, if you change your self-perception you can change your behavior, and if you can change your behavior you can change your attitude, and if you can change your attitude you can change your life, and if you can change your life you can change the world.

Summary and Conclusion

There is no doubt that a great deal of work lies ahead for all involved in working toward improving the quality of life of all Black families but especially for struggling Black families. It is generally agreed that the impetus for this advancement must start with the Black community, but it is by no means a responsibility that belongs solely to Black Americans. For the serious student of Black family life, solutions must be multifaceted, targeted toward the development of an effective national economic policy and a major commitment by the federal government to work toward repairing all of the damages sustained by Black Americans during centuries of exploitation and mistreatment (Swinton, 1987).

Despite this vision, some nationally recognized observers of Black family life believe the nation is only at the dialogue stage (Chideya et al., 1993). However, we cannot and must not forget that we are dealing with a situation that involves everyone in this society. This means that everyone is affected not only by the success of our efforts but also by the struggles of the least among us. The bottom-line implication is that we must do more than posture ourselves to begin a useful debate on the situation. We must act now with deliberate speed to create environments that are nurturing and growth-enhancing for everyone.

References

Asante, M. K. (1992). Afrocentricity. Trenton, NJ: African World Press.

Asante, M. K., & K. Welsh-Asante (1985). *African culture: The rhythms of unity*. London: Greenwood.

Baraka, I. (1969). The Black value system. *The Black Scholar, 21*(3), 54–60.

Bennett, L. (1987). *Before the Mayflower: A history of Black America* (rev. ed.). New York: Penguin.

Billingsley, A. (1968). *Black families in white America*. Englewood Cliffs, NJ: Prentice-Hall.

Billingsley, A. (1992). *Climbing Jacob's ladder: The enduring legacy of African-American families*. New York: Simon and Schuster.

Blassingame, J. (1972). *The slave community*. New York: Oxford University Press.

Bowen, M. (1988). On the differentiation of self. In M. Bowen, *Family therapy in clinical practice* (2d ed.) (pp. 467–528). Northvale, NJ: Jason Aronson.

Cann, R., M. Stoneking, & A. Wilson (January 1987). Mitochondrial DNA and human evolution. *Nature, 25*(6), 31–36.

Chideya, F., M. Ingrassia, V. Smith, & P. Wingert (August 30, 1993). Special report: A world without fathers: The struggle to save the Black family. *Newsweek, 122*(9), 16–29.

Covin, D. (1990). Afrocentricity in O movimento negro unificado. *Journal of Black Studies, 21*(2), 126–144.

Franklin, J. (1956). *From slavery to freedom.* New York: Knopf.

Frazier, E. F. (1939). *The Negro Family in the United States.* Chicago: University of Chicago Press.

Frazier, E. F. (1957). *The Negro in the United States* (rev. ed.). New York: Macmillan.

Gary, L., L. Beatty, G. Berry, & M. Price (1983). *Stable Black families: Final report.* Mental Health Research and Development Center, Institute for Urban Affairs and Research. Washington, DC: Howard University Press.

Genovese, E. (1974). *Roll, Jordan, roll.* New York: Pantheon.

Glazer, N., & D. Moynihan (1963). *Beyond the melting pot: The Negroes, Puerto Ricans, Jews, Italians, and Irish of New York City.* Cambridge: M.I.T. Press.

Guthrie, R. V. (1976). *Even the rat was white.* New York: Harper and Row.

Gutman, H. (1976). *The Black family in slavery and freedom, 1750–1925.* New York: Pantheon.

Herkovits, M. (1941). *The myth of the Negro past.* Boston: Beacon Press.

Hill, R. (1972). *Strengths of Black families.* New York: Emerson Hull.

Hilliard, A., L. Williams, & N. Damali (Eds.) (1987). *The teachings of pathology: The oldest book in the world.* Atlanta: Blackwood Press.

Hodgkinson, H. L. (1989). What ever happened to the Norman Rockwell Family? In D. Bishop (Ed.), *The Changing American Family.* Providence, RI: Manisses Communication Group.

Jackson, J. (Ed.) (1991). *Life in Black America.* Newbury Park, CA: Sage Publications.

Jones, R. (1973). Proving Blacks inferior: The sociology of knowledge. In J. A. Ladner (Ed.), *Death of white sociology* (pp. 28–33). New York: Random House.

Kamin, L. (1974). *The science and politics of I.Q.* Potomac, MD: Earlbaum.

Leakey, R. E. (1977). *Origins: What new discoveries reveal about the emergence of our species and its possible future.* New York: Dutton.

Leakey, R. E. (1994). *The origin of humankind.* New York: Basic Books.

Massaqui, H. (1993). August special issue: The new Black family is determined, dynamic and diverse: The Black family nobody knows. *Ebony, 47*(10), 28–31.

McAdoo, H. (December 1977). *The impact of extended family variables upon the upward mobility of Black families.* Final Report, submitted to the Department of Health, Education, and Welfare, Office of Child Development, Contract no. 90-C-631(1).

McCall, N. (July–August 1993). From a dying generation. *The family therapy networker, 17*(4), 47–49.

Oliver, W. (1989). Black males and social problems. *Journal of Black Studies, 20*(1), 15–39.

Salaam, T. (1974). Practice the values and love revolution. *Black Books Bulletin, 2*(3–4), 40–49.

Shulman, L. (1992). *The skills of helping: Individuals, families and groups* (3rd ed.). Itasca, IL: F. E. Peacock Publishers.

Sudarkasa, N. (1981). Interpreting the African heritage in Afro-American family organizations. In H. P. McAdoo (Ed.), *Black families* (p. 40). Beverly Hills, CA: Sage Publications.

Swinton, D. (1987). Economic status of Blacks in 1986. In J. Dewort (Ed.), *The state of Black America* (pp. 49–74). New York: National Urban League.

Tierney, J., L. Wright, & K. Springer (January 11, 1988). The search for Adam and Eve. *Newsweek,* 46–52.

Washington, E. B., K. Burns, & V. Vas (October 1992). Land of gold: Ghana. *Essence, 25*(6), 89–103.

Wilkins, S. (March 1989). The implications of social constructionism for social work education. Paper presented at the Annual Program Meeting of the Council on Social Work Education, Chicago, Illinois.

2

Building on the Strengths of Black Families: Self-Help and Empowerment

HARRISON Y. SMITH

[We] must not obscure the valiant and multiple efforts we are finding in Black communities across the country that are beginning to rally together to recapture our youth and families.
—**Marian Wright Edelman**

A well-known African American philosopher and theologian, euphorically reminiscing about his family ties to Ethiopia and the grand ritual ceremonial experiences of recent times, reflected on several questions: "What is my relation to my African heritage and Ethiopian house? How do I understand my African American tradition and sense of Black homelessness in America? Who is the I or me that emerged out of a particular Black family, church and neighborhood, a white academy, a multicultural American mass communication network, and set of progressive political organizations? And, to put it bluntly, why do I have the urge to leave America and live in Ethiopia? Is this the urge of an émigré, an expatriate, or an exile?" (West, 1993, p. x). In a kind of cynical fashion, Cornel West goes on to say:

> As I reflect on these complex questions, I realize that they sit at the core of my intellectual vocation and existential engagement: a profound commitment to what I call a prophetic vision and practice primarily based on a distinctly Black tragic sense of life. On the one hand, this commitment

21

looks the inescapable facts of death, disease and despair in the face and affirms moral agency and action in our everyday, commonplace circumstances. On the other hand, it is rooted in a certain view of the Christian
tradition that is so skeptical about our capacity to know the ultimate truths
about our existence that leaps of faith are promoted and enacted because
they make sense out of our seemingly absurd conditions. (1993, pp. x–xi)

West's perception of self as occupying "a distinctly Black tragic sense
of life" and a quest for "the ultimate truths" about his place in the
United States has been, and will continue to be, a painful dilemma for
all African Americans as a population. Like most African Americans, his
is a perpetual dilemma and zeal for enlightened self-development and
self-reliance in an overwhelming hostile environment. Merriam Web-
ster's *Collegiate Dictionary* defines "enlightenment" as "a philosophic
movement of the eighteenth century, marked by a rejection of traditional social, religious and political ideas and an emphasis on rationalism" (p. 384). Correspondingly, "nihilism" is defined as "a doctrine or
belief that conditions in the social organization are so bad as to make
destruction desirable for its own sake, independent of any constructive
program or possibility" (p. 784). What do these concepts and Cornel
West's concerns have in common, especially in relation to the state of
the African American family's quality of life?

Historically, the African American family has been placed in the middle of these conflicting dogmas of social thought West ponders. On the
one hand, there is the temptation to reject traditional dominant Eurocentric cultural orthodoxy in favor of the right to exercise individual will
and socioeconomic self-reliance. On the other hand, there is the socializing evolutionary attraction to Eurocentric values, religious fidelity, and
the Western welfare ethic that puts the responsibility of life outside the
body and soul of an African-centered self. That is, African Americans
have generally been taught to expect eternal saving grace through hu-
mility, spiritual compliance, and submission to the will of the welfare
state for the expected reward of heavenly transcendence beyond earthly
oppression and hardship. Yet because of endless oppression and social
injustice, there is a growing critical mass of African Americans who reject historically imposed debilitating conditions of the status quo in exchange for enlightened self-reliance and the grand feelings of competence that accompany such reliance.

Advanced technology, increased benefits of modern education, and
African-centered family solidarity have created a variety of resistive
strains of African American survival patterns. The long historical evolu-

tion of the African American family through a labyrinth of oppression and denigration has caused the emergence of postmodern "African American family enlightenment." The family is a more informed, advanced, self-reliant social unit, whose bonded fabric reflects phenomenal resiliency of the human spirit and the incredible will to survive and prosper. Drawing from a history of unrelenting oppression, educational advances, increased economic leverage, and modern insights brought on by global communications, the African American family has become much more enlightened, rational, self-reliant, and future-oriented.

This chapter is written to emphasize, encourage, and capitalize on the strengths and challenges of African American families. Major strengths and positive social, cultural, and economic changes are illustrated through case examples, which provide evidence of an increasing rejection by African Americans of dependence on the dominant society. Likewise, there is an emphasis on empowerment through disciplined self-reliance and a corresponding compassion for the well-being of all African Americans. More modern approaches to social work thinking and intervention are encouraged. Recommendations are made to stimulate the social work profession to move beyond traditional boundaries in finding more effective approaches to working with African American families.

The most positive aspect of writing about the strengths of Black families within a self-help and empowerment context is the theme's tendency to generate instant excitement, fervor, enthusiasm, and scintillation. The mere thought of the topic brings instant gratification and hope for a renewed life. Self-help and empowerment to the powerful majority and disenfranchised minority may appear to be an oxymoron or a contradiction to the quest for an improved quality of life. To the contrary, self-help and empowerment are necessary ingredients for survival of a people. As there is a need for oxygen, food, and water, a people have an insatiable need to recognize themselves and to be recognized. This is *especially* true in the face of discrimination and oppression. Unless this need is completely fulfilled, the validation of one's existence as a people can never be realized.

Profile of the Modern-Day African American Family

The "enduring legacy of African American families" can best be viewed by A. Billingsley, who is noted for his seminal work *Black Families in White America* (1968). Billingsley (1968) presented both weaknesses and strengths of African American families but argued that their strengths were far greater than given credit through their phenomenal adaptive and regenerative powers. Twenty-four years later Billingsley (1992) followed with *Climbing Jacob's Ladder*, exploring theoretical propositions in which he argued that the whole of African American families is greater than its parts.

Billingsley's holistic perspective describes particular sources of strength within the African American family as impacted by U.S. geopolitical history. Billingsley (1992) defines the African American family as "an *intimate association* of persons of African descent who are *related to one another* by a variety of means, including blood, marriage, formal adoption, informal adoption, or by appropriation; sustained by a history of common residence in America; and deeply embedded in a network of social structures both internal to and external to itself. Numerous interlocking elements come together, forming an extraordinarily resilient institution" (p. 28, italics added).

The Black Helping Tradition

Running the gauntlet of institutional racism, discrimination, and bigotry is a way of life for African American families. This seemingly eternal struggle has come to be expected as part of the rite of passage to, at best, a marginalized existence with regard to the greater scheme of American life as set forth by the majority's structuralist-functionalist orientation of status quo. Martin and Martin (1985) refer to the "Black helping tradition as the largely independent struggle of Blacks for their survival and advancement from generation to generation" (p. 4). Survival, although humanly instinctual, is a natural prerequisite for advancement, which, of course, is a perquisite to enlightenment that further stimulates the need for increased self-development. It is simply a case of "the psychology of rising expectations." This is a unique human quality, regardless of race, creed, ethnicity, or national origin.

The seminal work of Robert Hill (1972) continues to hold up as the standard hallmark of the strengths inherently exhibited by African American families. Hill's five strengths of Black families are adaptability of family roles, strong kinship bonds, strong work orientation, strong religious orientation, and strong achievement orientation. Hill's strengths typology provides a vivid and solid structure for the helping professions to use as a basic foundation and framework for interventions. The synergistic qualities of these strengths are more vibrant and dynamic today than ever. Yet many in the helping professions continue to focus on narrowly defined research and make assumptions that characterize the African American family as dysfunctional. Of course, it would be naive to assume that the overall African American population is void of maladies. Clearly, a great deal of diversity exists in terms of social, economic, and educational statuses.

Katz and Bender (1976) eloquently state that people "need to live, to be valued, to experience, to give, to share with others, to transcend the boundaries of their own egos—to give and take in social communion. Many must fight for a place in the world, to reshape a society that cannot see their value" (p. 3). Richardson (1994) insists "African-Americans must turn inward to find the needed strength to define their own economic destiny through self-help programs and cooperative partnerships and initiatives" (p. 113). Wallace-Benjamin (1994) poses a challenging question for African American parents: "What characteristics and qualities must the adults have which will enable them to provide the support young people need to reach the academic and character standards for the 21st century?" (p. 195). Her assertion is that several qualities will be needed: openness to new ideas; ability to think globally; personal sacrifice; continuous learning and development; high ethical standards; entrepreneurship; commitment to cooperation and collaboration with colleagues, friends, and neighbors; ability to write and speak English; a focus on something greater than self; a control of ego; more principled interactions with others; and membership and active participation in the activities, goals, and mission of local community organizations. Such qualities will create an environment in which our children can grow, learn, and reach the next century (pp. 195–196).

From an enlightened self-development perspective, social work and other helping professions are particularly suited to complement and enrich the lives of African American families. Wallace-Benjamin's characteristics and qualities cited here present clear challenges for human-service practitioners to replace traditional Eurocentric-oriented group socialization strategies of behavior modification with modern, proactive collaborative learning strategies, especially in the area of fostering African American family preservation.

Although most writers generally extol the virtues and attributes of African American self-development, Martin and Martin (1985) are more typologically cryptic, identifying positive and negative social forces. On the positive side, they propose that a "pattern of Black self-help was spread from the Black extended family to institutions in the wider Black community through fictive kinship and racial and religious consciousness" (p. 5). Martin and Martin's (1985, pp. 4–5) profile of African American enlightened self-development is presented through these behaviorally recurring key concepts.

- *Black helping tradition* refers to the largely independent struggle of Blacks for their survival and advancement from generation to generation.
- *Black extended family* consists of a multigenerational, interdependent kinship system held together basically by a sense of obligation to the welfare of members of the kin network.
- *Mutual aid,* a dominant element in extended family life, involves a reciprocal effort of family members to pool the resources necessary for survival and growth.
- *Social class (status-group) cooperation* is the endeavor of family members of different income, educational, and social class levels to downplay class distinctions in giving and receiving aid.
- *Male-female equality* is the adherence of Black men and women to certain conventions that promote the welfare of the family through an emphasis on sexual equality and a deemphasis on matriarchy and patriarchy.
- *Prosocial behavior* involves the attitudes and practices of cooperation, sharing, and caring that Black adults consciously strive to instill in Black children so the tradition of Black self-help will be passed on to future generations.
- *Fictive kinship* is the caregiving and mutual-aid relationship among nonrelated Blacks that exists because of their common ancestry, history, and social plight.
- *Racial consciousness* is the keen awareness by many Black people of their history and condition as a people and their overwhelming desire to uplift their race to a state of dignity and pride.
- *Religious consciousness* refers to deliberate attempts by Blacks to live according to those religious beliefs that call for acts of charity and brotherliness and neighborliness toward one another as a means of coming closer to God and carrying out God's will.

Martin and Martin (1985) credit these concepts with helping to explain the major forces responsible for African American family self-help, survival, and overall growth and development.

On the negative side, Martin and Martin (1985) identify *racism,* the *bourgeoisie ideology* (suburban African American "buy-in" to mainstream U.S. structural-functionalist ideologies), *street ideology* (lower-class urban-based deviant culture), and *patriarchy* (male-centered/male-dominated family and society) as four major elements that have impeded the development of the Black helping tradition. It becomes apparent that Martin and Martin view the African American struggle as having two opposing social forces: one that positively reinforces enlightened self-development and one that creates barriers to progressive social change. These opposing forces reflect West's (1993) dilemma in his search for the ultimate truth about the status of African American existence and Katz and Bender's (1976) eloquent axiom that people need to live, to be valued, to give, to share, and often have to fight for a place in this world.

Like all other American families, African Americans have been, and are being, affected by all the major social systems of our society, most notably economic, political, health care, welfare, housing, educational, criminal justice, military, transportation, communication, and religious systems. Clearly, the African American family's survival reflects its high degree of adaptability to the many vagaries of these systems and their many changes. The African American family continues to display astounding regenerative qualities. Billingsley's message is that "one cannot understand contemporary patterns of African American family life without placing them in their broad historical, societal, and cultural context" (1992, p. 22). Upon such understanding, human-service practitioners can begin where the consumer is, therefore placing themselves in a more strategic position to become enlightened about the actual and real needs of African American families.

Inasmuch as African American family life has been structurally segregated from the U.S. mainstream since this country was founded, it was natural for African Americans to develop their own institutions, including the Black church, colleges and universities, social service agencies, fraternal and civic organizations, and civil rights organizations, to list a few. Albeit fairly small, African American entrepreneurship has had a profound impact on its own communities, particularly in regard to family owned businesses and Black economic development.

From a human-service perspective, it is critical for practitioners to engage in professional self-examination and determine the status of their knowledge gaps about the African American family's connectedness to its contemporary community and what its needs are. This requires a paradigm shift in regard to how practitioners implement individual, group, and community assessments. The enlightened African American family is much more capable than the unenlightened family of articulating the quality-of-life issues that surround its existence. Practitioners' use of community participatory action research that involves primary inputs from African American families should be a fundamental requisite to new ways of providing human-service intervention.

It is Billingsley's belief that self-help is the key to the future progress of African American families. He identifies "promising signs" of existing African American self-help initiatives. Under *individual initiatives* Billingsley identifies responsible parenting and parenting of the children of others. *Personal crusades* have been taken on by celebrities, and *advocates and mentors* have emerged to help disadvantaged youth. *Institutional initiatives* are too numerous to count. Their presence reflects the beginning of time to preslavery to postslavery to current postmodern times of high technology.

Neighbors, Elliott, and Gant (1990) identify five characteristics or conditions in their definitive construction of Black self-help: There is (1) repeated emphasis on economic development and political empowerment; (2) a strong tradition of church-based social support; (3) the presence of community uplift projects and resource-mobilization efforts, many organized by women's groups; (4) a deep concern for, and active involvement in educational achievement; and (5) the development of social and political groups ideologically grounded in racial consciousness, Black pride, and group solidarity (pp. 192–193). Neighbors, Elliot, and Gant emphasize the fundamental role of the Black church in the historical development of Black self-help and the development of Black-owned schools, universities, and businesses as a major achievement in the evolution of the Black self-help tradition.

Neighbors and colleagues' most significant contribution was their treatise on "the functional utility of Black self-help" and its "empowerment" qualities. They developed a theoretical taxonomy of African American self-help organizations that covered the entire social fabric of African American life. Neighborhood and church-based social organizations, political and economic institutions, Black family and youth-oriented groups, Black female-oriented organizations, groups of Black professionals, mainstream membership organizations, and special-interest groups were the most prevalent examples of enlightened Black self-development. The authors focused primarily on identification of specific organizations with single-line descriptions. Their major emphasis was a self-debate exercise about the "structuralist viewpoint" of victim blaming versus individual efforts to eradicate the causes of African American disenfranchisement.

From a constructivist perspective, it seems important that Neighbors and his colleagues avoid the pitfall that West (1993 p. x) describes as "a distinctly Black tragic sense of life" in search of "the ultimate truth" about African American existence. Rather, it is best to focus on the obvious strengths of Black families vis-à-vis enlightened self-development and future prosperity.

African American Family Enlightenment: Empowered Self-Development

Empowered self-development of African American families refers to a process of collectively creating strategic ways of developing, increasing, exercising, and maintaining high-functioning interpersonal and intrapersonal social and intellectual skills and performance of valued social roles (Solomon, 1976; Williams & Wright, 1992). There is another reality: African Americans have resolved that "past is prologue" in regard to historical experiences of social injustices and what to expect for the future. It is fairly clear to African Americans that there is the need to move forward into a more *enlightened realm of existence through disciplined self-reliance and industry.*

African American family enlightenment and resulting coping strategies take on an "African-centered orientation" (Daly et al., 1995), which is discussed in detail in Chapter 7. This worldview combines compassion with rational thought within the context of facilitating same-race system maintenance. The net result is a shared concern not only for the well-being of the rank-and-file disenfranchised but for an equitable quest to assure the continued psychosocial, economic, cultural, and educational development of mainstream African American citizens. For example, countless social, fraternal, and civic African American organizations provide annual college scholarships. These same organizations conduct perennial cultural and civic events that are focused on African American self-development. Discipline-specific educators routinely hold national conferences designed to enrich and enlighten themselves, students, and the general African American public. Black Church organizations continue to take profound leadership in spiritual and commu-

nity social service provisions, economic development, and overall quality-of-life enhancement (see Chapter 11).

Not unlike the church program described by Brashears and Roberts
in Chapter 11, other programs are emerging (Billingsley, 1992). These
programs illustrate classic examples of the Black Church's dominant
role in building on the strengths and empowerment of Black families
through disciplined and rational self-development; African American
family enlightenment also assumes the position that its racial group has
been, is, and will continue to be an integral part of the American landscape. It is inextricably interwoven into the fabric not only of Western
society but is also figured into the foundation of Third World development, emphasizing social justice and planned prevention, and thus
should be proactive in social change. Emphasis on strengths transcends
previous preoccupation with blame, self-pity, acceptance of dominant
society's labeling and control, and in-group conflicts. Instead, there is a
synergistic thrust and thirst for dialogue, membership, and empowerment through self-help and, when strategically important, an indul-
gence in mainstream cooperation.

Mainstream cooperation is especially important with regard to African
American families and the various health care delivery systems, which
historically have been egregiously hostile to African Americans. Early
segregation enforced segregated health care delivery, which forced
African American families to resort to home-based self-treatment.
Harper (1990, p. 240) provided this historical relationship between
African American families and mainstream health care delivery systems:

- Blacks have always cared for the sick at home, yet it was never labeled "home care."
- Blacks have been dying at home and receiving care in the process,
  yet it was never called "hospice care."
- Blacks have relieved each other from the caring and curing
  processes, yet it was never seen as "respite care."
- Blacks have cared for each other in their homes, in their neighborhoods, and throughout their communities, yet it was never referred to as "volunteerism."

Today, institutional racism has caused Black families to continue to
underutilize mainstream health care facilities (Weddington & Gabel,
1992). Urban disenfranchised communities are beginning to address

this problem with the installation of proactive health care delivery systems that encompass both mainstream technology and a comprehensive care philosophy of total community caregiving. This case example describes a very successful African American community-based comprehensive health care system. Although it is African American community-based with a predominantly African American client population, the Swope Parkway Health Center in Kansas City, Missouri, serves all community constituents regardless of ability to pay:

Comprehensive Care That Benefits the Whole Family . . . and the Entire Community. Swope Parkway is a non-profit organization with a staff of licensed certified professionals dedicated to the treatment and prevention of physical and mental illness. Many efforts are made to reach out to our neighbors, including those who are not patients. One of the most far-reaching examples is health education. The Health Center, through its clinic at Southeast High School, offers not only medical and mental health treatment, but health education as well. We are involved in many outreach programs. Our Community Health Project focuses on combating infant mortality and [providing] low birthweight service assistance, nutrition education and free transportation to participating prenatal and well-baby care sites. Our Health Care for the Homeless Program addresses the health needs of this population through a mobile team which visits shelter sites in the community, in our medically equipped Mobile Health Care van. Our Elderly Services Project offers health screenings, individual and group counseling, social service assistance and activity therapy to senior citizens at a number of senior residential complexes. Our HIV/AIDS Program provides comprehensive health and social services to persons affected by HIV disease, as well as risk reduction programs designed to reach individuals in churches, schools, shelters and on the streets of the city. Our Health Ministry Project works with inner city churches; each minister designates volunteer health coordinators who are then trained to assist those in the congregation needing help in securing health services themselves or for their families. These things we do above and beyond our Comprehensive Medical Services Program for all ages, our Comprehensive Mental Health Services Program, and Associated Health Care Support Services and Special Programs. (Swope Parkway Health Center, 1992, n.p.).

Clearly, this case illustration encompasses a relevant, contemporary, and meaningful holistic approach to health care delivery for African American families. It is characterized by definitive, well-developed, and comprehensive caregiving that is responsive to the wide range of human service needs of an urban disenfranchised community. When this program was evaluated, the role of the social worker was determined to be vital to the overall caregiving strategy. The social work department was sufficiently undergirded with resources to allow it to provide both clinically related and general case management services at all levels of intervention (individuals, families, and the community). Social services included a "continuum of care" of outreach–high-risk case finding, preadmission services, discharge planning, and a wide range of community social work tasks.

Self-Development for African American Children

Billingsley (1992) emphasizes that "children are the centerpiece of African-American family life" (p. 65). Survival as an African American people rests with the primary affective and instrumental functions of the family as a social unit. This means it is important not only to provide food, clothing, and shelter for the family but also that a nurturing environment is in place to assure that a quality of life is achievable.

This is especially critical in regard to childrearing. Yet African American children as an "affected class" are one of the most vulnerable and at-risk groups in the United States (Comer & Poussaint 1992). African American parents are acutely aware of this dilemma. They are also inherently cognizant of the importance of the role the Black child will play in the future survival of African Americans as a race. According to Billingsley (1992) African American parents are compelled to socialize their children to have a "double consciousness" in order to survive in an ever-more-hostile environment; that is, parents sense the need to "model and teach their children that they are not just Black, and certainly not just American, but both simultaneously" (p. 224). This means African American parents must actively combat negative messages of racism while teaching their children to succeed in a white-dominated culture.

Institutional racism has particularly placed the Black child in jeopardy with respect to the U.S. child welfare system (Day, 1979; Edelman, 1980; see Chapter 8). Despite the inequities of this system, Black parents—including foster care, extended families, and fictive kin—have come to the rescue with highly creative and courageous efforts, providing a network of social and child welfare services (Billingsley & Giovannoni, 1972). African American parents, grandparents, and fictive kin have also done a magnificent job of meeting the needs of children who are subject to adoption. Nearly 16 percent of all Black children are informally adopted (U.S. Bureau of the Census, 1990).

Kinship care of children in the African American community assumes the attributes of extended family far beyond the normal definition. In addition to blood lineage, kin is a bond that is honored through "in-law" status and through shared history and common worldviews. In regard to the latter, Carol Stack (1974) refers to this relationship as "fictive kin" in which identified persons external to the family are treated with the same deference and respect accorded blood relatives, and the ties and obligations to the family are just as strong. Formal social service institutions have begun to capitalize on this phenomenal strength as a natural and strategic opportunity to place African American children who are without nuclear-based family homes. This case situation provides an example of how kinship services stabilized a family and helped to promote permanence for an at-risk African American child:

Julie, a 10 year old African American female, was placed in a licensed foster care home due to abandonment. Julie came to the attention of the Michigan Department of Social Services (MDSS) in early February, 1994, when her father abandoned her in search of new employment. The assigned MDSS Protective Service Worker found that Julie and her father had been living in a rooming house. Prior to his abandoning Julie, the father sent her to live with a friend from his job for a period of six weeks. Julie's school reported that she was frequently absent or late, and she often arrived hungry and unsanitary. Julie was made a temporary ward of the court and placed in foster care. Later, Julie was placed with an older sister. The social worker determined Julie's sister to be under severe stress; she was employed full time and was a part-time student, caring for two small children of her own. Julie was also rebellious with her older sister and hostile to her little niece and nephew. The social worker conducted an extensive genealogical study of the family, identifying branches within Michigan and in other States. Lines of communication were opened between family units in Michigan and several other States. Based on family inputs and court-ordered home studies, several permanent placement options were developed. Ultimately, with the consent of the family and the social worker's recommendation, the decision was made to place Julie with one of her paternal aunts who was determined to be the "best fit." Julie now lives in another state. She has begun to settle into a state of normalcy. At the urging of her aunt, Julie routinely communicates with her father and sister. (Mills & Usher, 1995, p. 10)

The African American extended family involved in this scenario desired no change of relationship through formal adoption. The provision of support services served to promote family involvement in decision-making and case planning. One of the difficulties was the lapse of time without services to Julie's family, causing sufficient strain that Julie had to be removed. The wisdom of the original plan to place Julie with her sister without adequate preplanned supportive services is also questionable. Nonetheless, preliminary results suggest that the final solution provided under the kinship model, both extended and biological, was directly helped in a variety of ways.

A significant amount of mainstream professional child welfare thinking favors "family preservation services," in which the aim is to prevent out-of-home placement of children. Family preservation services are currently receiving much public and professional support, because such programs emphasize keeping families together. It is also believed that these programs are much more cost-effective than institutional care and are in concert with prevailing public-policy mandates (Wells & Biegel, 1991; see also Chapter 9). Although research studies have shown that there has been measured success with intensive family preservation programs, it is difficult to determine if the concept of "success" is fact or was merely configured to reflect a specific program's expected outcomes. Wells and Biegel (1991) found no empirical evidence (1) that services provided assured safety of children when left at home, (2) of the proportion of children approved for out-of-home placement who met established criteria for entrance into intensive family preservation services, and (3) that clinical hypotheses underlying these services were generally valid. In the case of Julie and for African American families, the definition of "home" extends beyond Eurocentric thinking of the immediate family as the best place for the child. "Kinfolk" is also a valued sanctuary for continued attachment and nurturance; it is also home. In this case, it becomes important for human-service practitioners to become more enlightened about what is truly valued within the context of African American family life.

Summary and Conclusion

Whether one is Black, white, Hispanic, or of Oriental descent, if the person is a professional human-service practitioner or university educator she or he is perceived as *an intervention force outside the commu-*

nity. Nearly all that is written and done on behalf of the African American community (or any other community of color) is accepted within the context of "detached paternalism." The basic issue or question is: How does social work (and other helping professions) build on the strength of African American families and communities in such a manner that the perception of "outsider" is minimized or nonexistent? Perhaps a more fundamental question is: Is this possible? The answer to the latter question is yes.

For example, I am reminded of a Black church in Kansas City, Missouri, in which the dearly loved and admired minister is a white man who was born and raised in Mississippi. He is totally acculturated and immersed into the African American culture. He lives and breathes African centrism. He has a double consciousness in regard to his Eurocentric racialism and associated dominant culture, but he takes advantage of it only on behalf of his Black church constituency and its community. However, building on the strengths of African American families may be possible only if the helping professions are willing to step outside their sanctuaries and become totally immersed in the African American community. This challenge is particularly pertinent to Black professionals who have decided to "escape" from the center city "because it is not the place to raise and educate their children." The challenge is theirs to make, and it should be measured against their professional deeds.

Social work and other helping professions have either lost or never had authentic *connectedness, attachment, and loyalty* to African American communities. Without these three requisite *identity attributes,* it is virtually impossible to have *influence* with African American families. One can teach and rhetorically espouse the need to demonstrate social work ethics, purposes, and values, but it is an entirely different matter when it comes to *living the ethics* through professional deeds of intervention. Perhaps a beginning would be to develop more meaningful "communal and participatory action research" (Harkavy & Puckett, 1994, p. 313), linking professional social work educators and practitioners with existing urban community organizations. Johnson (1994) refers to this participatory process as a scholar-advocate approach in which problems, needs identification, and related research development are conceived and driven by community constituents in collaboration with social work researchers and practitioners.

Smith advocates a "community management and comprehensive quality leadership approach." He insists that *social work scholars, practition-*

ers, and related professionals must actually live in the African American community (Smith, forthcoming, pp. 1, 5). They should slowly begin to develop connectedness, attachments, and loyalties as requisites of influence. Ultimately, this interprofessional team should begin to develop community management programs that integrate and parallel Afrocentric and Eurocentric knowledge and skills for training key community constituents to become more effective urban leadership role models (see Chapter 7). Additionally, new culturally competent and gender-sensitive curriculum models need to be developed that literally pull social work educators and practitioners out of their conventional orthodoxies to meet the challenges of the twenty-first century (CSWE, 1995).

As a parallel process, the profession needs to revisit its admissions standards with regard to its ability to select prospective students who would be "best fits" for the social work profession. It is not unusual to find many students who easily enter the profession because of "coaching" to be able to say the right things regarding social justice and oppression on their applications. Once admitted, many struggle with addressing issues of racism and homophobia and with predisposed notions of becoming private clinical practitioners for a Eurocentric client population. The challenge to the practice and to education communities is to begin influencing African American families to *collaboratively* develop programs and services that would address the various needs of all ethnic-group families.

References

Billingsley, A. (1968). *Black families in white America.* Englewood Cliffs, NJ: Prentice-Hall.

Billingsley, A. (1992). *Climbing Jacob's ladder: The enduring legacy of African-American families.* New York: Simon and Schuster.

Billingsley, A., & J. M. Giovannoni (1972). *Children of the storm: Black children and American child welfare.* New York: Harcourt Brace Jovanovich.

Comer, J. P., & A. F. Poussaint (1992). *Raising Black children.* New York: Plume.

Council on Social Work Education (CSWE) (1995). Commission on educational policy outlines millennium project work plan. *Social Work Education Reporter, 43*(1), 1–6.

Daly, A., J. Jennings, J. O. Beckett, & B. R. Leashore (March 1995). Effective coping strategies of African Americans. *Social Work, 40*(2), 240–248.

Day, D. (1979). *The adoption of Black children.* Lexington, MA: Lexington Books.

Edelman, M. W. (1980). *Portrait of inequality: Black and white children in America.* Washington, DC: Children's Defense Fund.

Harkavy, I., & J. L. Puckett (September 1994). Lessons from Hull House for the contemporary university. *Social Service Review, 68*(3), 299–321.

Harper, B.C.O. (1990). Blacks and the health care delivery system: Challenges and prospects. In M. L. Logan, E. M. Freeman, & R. G. McRoy (Eds.), *Social work practice with Black families* (pp. 239–256). White Plains, NY: Longman.

Hill, R. (1972). *The strengths of Black families.* New York: Hall Publishers.

Johnson, A. K. (1994). Linking professionalism and community organization: A scholar/advocate approach. *Journal of Community Practice, 1*(2), 65–86.

Katz, A. H., & E. I. Bender (Eds.) (1976). *The strength in us : Self-help groups in the modern world.* New York: New Viewpoints.

Martin, J. M., & M. P. Martin (1985). *The helping tradition in the Black family and community.* Washington, DC: National Association of Social Workers Press.

Mills, C. S., & D. Usher (February 10, 1995). *Project to promote permanence in kinship care—Evaluation report year II.* Training Grant no. 90CO0600. Washington, DC: U.S. Department of Health and Human Services.

Neighbors, H. W., K. A. Elliott, & L. M. Gant (1990). Self-help and Black Americans: A strategy for empowerment. In T. J. Powell (Ed.), *Working with self-help* (pp. 189–217). Silver Spring, MD: National Association of Social Workers Press.

Richardson, W. F. (1994). Mission to mandate: Self-development through the Black church. In B. J. Tidwell (Ed.), *The state of Black America 1994* (pp. 113–126). Washington, DC: National Urban League.

Smith, H. Y. (Forthcoming). Community management: A comprehensive quality leadership approach. *Journal of Progressive Social Work.*

Solomon, B. B. (1976). *Black empowerment: Social work in oppressed communities.* New York: Columbia University Press.

Stack, C. (1974). *All our kin: Strategies for survival in a Black community.* New York: Harper and Row.

Swope Parkway Health Center (1992). *The neighbor who cares.* Kansas City: Swope Parkway Health Center.

U.S. Bureau of the Census (March 1990). *Current Population Reports, Household Family Characteristics.* Washington, DC: U.S. Bureau of the Census.

Wallace-Benjamin, J. (1994). Organizing African American self-development: The role of community-based organizations. In B. J. Tidwell (Ed.), *The state of Black America 1994* (pp. 189–196). New York: National Urban League.

Weddington, W. H., & L. L. Gabel (1992). Quality of care and Black American patients. *Journal of the National Medical Association, 84,* 569–575.

Wells, K., & D. E. Biegel (Eds.) (1991). *Family preservation services: Research and evaluation.* Newbury Park, CA: Sage Publications.

West, C. (1993). *Keeping the faith.* New York: Routledge.

Williams, S. E., & D. F. Wright (1992). Empowerment: The strengths of Black families revisited. *Journal of Multicultural Social Work, 2*(4), 23–34.

3

Caregiving in African American Families: Caring for Children with Sickle Cell Disease

SHIRLEY A. HILL

> I just made up my mind that I had to get control of this situation, or I'd
> be in a psychiatric ward.
>
> **—43-year-old mother of a son with SCD**

For the first 12 years of her life Elsie Jenkins experienced debilitating pains, aches, fevers, and occasionally an inability to walk. Her mother's numerous efforts to obtain medical care for Elsie at a local children's hospital resulted in various diagnoses, including poor posture, growing pains, and laziness. Finally, a concerned junior high school teacher—convinced that his student was seriously ill—intervened, and Elsie was correctly diagnosed as having sickle cell anemia, a sickle cell disease (SCD) that now affects approximately 80,000 African Americans.

Sickle cell anemia was first diagnosed in 1910; still, by the early 1960s, when Elsie was diagnosed, African Americans knew little about the disease, and it frequently went undetected. Genetic screening for sickle cell anemia was almost nonexistent, diagnoses were difficult to obtain, medical treatment was limited, and persons diagnosed with the disease were often told to expect an early death. During the 1960s, however, the work of Black civil rights activists, coupled with medical advances in technology, helped transform SCD into an important health care issue. Broad support was garnered for the implementation of SCD education and screening programs, and in 1972 Congress responded by passing the National Sickle Cell Anemia Control Act "for the purpose of establishing a national program for the diagnosis, control, and treatment of, and research in, sickle cell anemia" (Rosner et al., 1982, p. 1527).

Despite the attention devoted to education and screening for sickle cell anemia during the past two decades, researchers have only recently begun to assess the psychosocial impact of the disease on people who have it and their families. Further, virtually no research has been done on how African American families manage the medical and home care of children with the disease. This scarcity of research reflects both a failure to view SCD as a serious disease that requires family caregiving work and a general tendency to define family and caregiving issues in ways that exclude many African American families. The family is often tacitly seen as a nuclear, two-parent, affluent unit, and family caregiving studies have focused on how childhood chronic illness affects marriage quality, spousal support and communication, and the parental sharing of caregiving work (see Barbarin, Hughes, & Chesler, 1985; Lansky et al., 1978; Patterson, 1985). Although these marriage-related issues do affect many African American families with chronically ill children, the organization of the Black family and the social context of inequality give rise to additional challenges. African American families are often composed of single mothers and their children and are characterized by early parenthood, extended family relations, low income, and nontraditional gender roles (see Billingsley, 1992; Nobles, 1985; Stack, 1974). These family characteristics, along with racial and economic inequality, shape family responses and adjustment to illness and caregiving work.

This chapter examines the psychosocial impact of SCD on Black people and their families and how families manage demands of caring for children with SCD. The data were drawn from in-depth interviews with 32 low-income Black mothers of children with SCD, who were solicited from a large, urban comprehensive care clinic for children with SCD. They were contacted by mail and paid a $10 honorarium for participating in the study. Interviews were conducted in the homes of mothers and were recorded on audiotape. Of the 32 mothers interviewed, 29 were biological mothers; one was an adoptive mother, one a great-aunt, and one a grandmother. All had custody of the child with SCD and were the primary caregivers, and all were referred to as mothers. They ranged in age from 21 to 72, with an average age of 34.9. Fourteen mothers had a high school education or less; 18 had a high school education and additional education, including one with a bachelor's degree. A slight majority of mothers, 17 of the 32, were employed, mostly in low-paying jobs. Eight of the mothers were married, 10 were single, 8 were divorced, 5 were separated, and one was widowed. The 32 mothers had a total of 36 children with SCD, 16 males and 20 females. The children ranged in age from 2 months old to 22 years old, with an average age of 10.4. Twenty-nine of the children had sickle cell anemia, and 7 had other types of SCD.

Sickle Cell Disease

SCD is a group of blood disorders marked by the presence of sickle cell hemoglobin, which causes normally round red blood cells to assume the shape of a "sickle." This obstructs the flow of blood through the vessels and causes a pain crisis—a relentless, repetitive, gnawing pain in the bones and joints (Linde, 1972). Pain crises are the most frequent manifestations of the disease, although SCD also can cause gallstones, urinary and bladder problems, damage to bodily organs, destruction of bones, stroke, and early death (Whitten, 1992).

Sickle cell anemia is the most common SCD among African Americans; it is genetically transmitted when both of the parents have the sickle cell trait and pass it on to a child. One in every 12 Black Americans carries the sickle cell trait, and one in every 600 is born with sickle cell anemia (Whitten, 1992). People with sickle cell anemia are treated primarily with narcotics administered after the onset of pain symptoms. Treatment strategies also include daily dosages of prophylactic penicillin for young children with SCD, as they are especially vulnerable to infections and pneumococcal septicemia (Gaston et al., 1986). Fetal hemoglobin, which helps suppress pain crises, can be increased through intravenous infusions of butyrate (a fatty acid) and the use of hydroxyurea (*Kansas City Star*, January 14, 1993). Gene therapy and bone marrow transplants are considered risky and experimental but may be used in severe cases of the disease.

The Diagnosis Experience

Research on the psychological impact of being diagnosed with SCD is of recent origin and has focused on a tendency among Blacks to deny the diagnosis or feel stigmatized by it. African Americans often misunderstand the nature of the disease and are concerned that having a race-specific genetic disease might lead to further racial discrimination and exclusion (France-Dawson, 1986; Wright & Phillips, 1988). The initiation of SCD education and screening programs during the 1970s alerted many Blacks to the existence of the disease, but these programs were often hastily implemented, and they perpetuated myths and misconceptions about sickle cell anemia (Bowman, 1977; Reilly, 1977) and raised concerns about the consequences of universal screening (Wilkinson, 1974). In many cases, the SCD information provided was erroneous or incomplete, and there was little follow-up for those diagnosed with the trait.

The majority of the mothers in this study grew up during the 1970s and had learned about SCD, been screened for the sickle cell trait, or both before having a child with the disease. However, they often received insufficient information about the reproductive implications of having the sickle cell trait. One mother who had been identified during childhood as having the trait said:

> I didn't know that if you came into contact with another person with sickle cell, and you and him had the trait, you had a 25 percent chance of having a baby with it. I didn't know that until afterward. Nobody told me by having the trait you have to watch who you come into contact with. Nobody ever explained that to me.

The need to educate African Americans about SCD continues, as the transmission of the disease can be prevented through genetic screening and selective reproduction. A recent study found that 60 percent of African American college students still did not understand that SCD could be controlled by reproductive choices (Ogamdi, 1994). Education about SCD can help demystify the disease and in the process eliminate the stigma and fear associated with sickle cell anemia.

The lack of information about SCD and its consequences made obtaining a diagnosis difficult for the mothers in this study, as neither they nor their physicians suspected the presence of SCD—even when a child was experiencing classic symptoms of the disease. Most infants were not screened at birth for the sickle cell trait, and they commonly experienced a prolonged period of sickness before being accurately diagnosed with SCD. The difficulty in diagnosing the disease increased the stress mothers experienced. One young mother had sought medical care for her infant son on many occasions before finally challenging the physician's diagnosis of a cold and a hip infection:

Every time he would get a cold he would get real sick and just cry all the time. And when he got big enough to walk, when he got a cold he would stop walking. . . . So I took him to the doctor, and they told me it was a hip infection because the cold had settled in his hip and caused him to stop walking. So I let that go and treated it as a hip infection. About a month later he caught a cold again and stopped walking on his legs and just cried constantly. I went and told [the doctor] that something else was wrong. . . . I started complaining that I thought something else was wrong, and he did a series of tests. That's when they found SCD.

In 1987 the American Medical Association recommended universal screening of all newborns for SCD, citing "indisputable evidence that rates of morbidity and mortality can be significantly reduced" by early detection (Consensus Conference, 1987, p. 1206). At least 40 states have laws requiring newborn screening for SCD, but many states have not funded these programs (Whitten, 1992), and there is widespread dissatisfaction among Black parents with the quality of programs that do exist (Rao & Kramer, 1993). Sickle cell anemia can also be detected pre-natally, although inadequate and late prenatal care often precludes this possibility.

Denial, disbelief, and guilt were common among these mothers when they learned their children had SCD. Fathers, who were even less likely than mothers to know they had the sickle cell trait, were especially likely to deny their contribution to the illness. Mothers experienced feelings of fear and helplessness as a result of the diagnosis, as most were given few instructions on how to care for their children. Some mothers actively sought information from libraries, but much of the literature they found was outdated and provided no medical advice on home care. Mothers said they received little information from doctors on how to care for their children. For the most part, they were told to watch for a reoccurrence of the symptoms that led to the diagnosis of SCD and, should these symptoms recur, to seek professional medical care. A 32-year-old mother, whose 5-year-old daughter was diagnosed with SCD at age 2, was told nothing about how to care for her child: "No. I mean nothing. They said when she gets a fever, take her temperature and bring her in. And make sure she gets lot of fluids, and that's it. And that she might have pain. Usually I know when she's sick, I can always tell. But they really don't tell you anything, you know."

The failure to obtain medical care instruction at the time of the diagnosis generated uncertainty and fear among mothers. They were typically told to beware of probable but unpredictable health consequences and responded by continually seeking medical care for minor fevers and colds. Their primary defense against having minor illnesses turn into major medical crises was to develop a readiness stance, or a continual state of alertness and vigilance in monitoring the child's health status. In the process, they saw illness episodes that evoked feelings of fear, helplessness, and vicarious suffering. One 33-year-old mother, describing the pain experienced by her 9-year-old daughter, said: "I can't take it. The pain feels like it's going through your body, because it's your child. And it's hard to see somebody hurt like that."

Gradually, however, mothers began to discern their children's illness patterns; they related specific activities, events, and diets to the onset of illness symptoms and learned to take early steps to prevent or control pain crises. Despite the absence of medical advice, these mothers developed competency in caregiving that gave them more confidence in their ability to control the disease and helped alleviate the stress and uncertainty of having a child with SCD.

The Caregiving Experience

Mothers gained first-hand, experiential knowledge through the necessity of providing care for children who experienced myriad fevers, colds, infections, and pain crises as a result of SCD. Their caregiving strategies included efforts to prevent and manage pain crises by administering medications, controlling food and fluid intakes, helping their children avoid stress, and restricting their children's activities. The mother of a 10-year-old said:

> You have to watch their diets, you force fluids, that's any kind of fluids. Sometimes you have to force-feed, you know, children aren't big on just drinking, drinking, drinking. [During fevers and colds] you constantly give them Tylenol and penicillin three or four times a day. They gave me a big container [of penicillin], and I mix it myself.

Other mothers, understanding SCD to be a "blood disease," connected the onset of pain crises with diets: "I can tell when she's getting sick; her eyes start to get yellow, and I try to make her eat a lot of liver, stuff good for her blood. But she doesn't like milk, so I give her a lot of ice cream and cheese, to keep her diet right." And mothers were also attuned to the role stress might play in causing SCD medical crises: "A headache can trigger a crisis, because it's stress. Stress kicks off sickle cell. Arguments kick off sickle cell. The pain don't just start naturally. Something triggers it off."

Avoiding SCD pain crises also meant mothers monitored their children's activities to prevent overexertion and protect the child from temperature extremes. The mother of a 10-year-old son said: "You don't let them get too tired. You try to keep them inside in the winter; you keep them real warm and out of the cold weather as much as possible. In the summertime, you keep them as still as possible—which is almost impossible—and you keep them out of heat as much as you can."

With time, mothers developed caregiving strategies with their children that seemed to work in preventing and managing pain crises, and they became confident in their ability to provide good care for their children during most illnesses. No amount of competent home care, however, completely eliminated the need for professional medical care.

Obtaining Medical Care

Typically, the mothers interviewed for this study provided 12 to 24 hours of continuous home care, depending on the child's age and severity of symptoms, before resorting to medical care. One mother of a 10-year-old explained that she takes her son to the hospital only after the pain crisis gets

> Worse and worse, and then he just can't walk anymore, and he's bedfast . . . he tosses, you know, and he tumbles and slides . . . he's really a miserable person when he's in a crisis. I deal with it until I can't deal with it, and then we go to the hospital. And they always end up keeping him, because when I take him to the hospital there's no point in them sending him back home, because I have exhausted every way to deal with it.

Medical care for pain crises usually consisted of pain treatment, on either an inpatient or an outpatient basis, but it could mean blood transfusions and in some cases surgeries. One issue faced by these low-income mothers was their reluctance to go to the hospital because they were uninsured and could not afford the medical bills: "I didn't have insurance. I had insurance, but I lost it because I was laid off from work . . . so more or less you're scared to go [to the doctor], because they're going to charge you and you ain't got the money."

Chronic illness increases the need for medical care; Hurtig and White (1986) found that children under five years old with SCD were hospitalized an average of more than two times a year. Mothers with no or inadequate medical insurance were especially reluctant to seek medical care, and when they did they often had to turn to a variety of state or community organizations or both for financial help, with no assurance that they would receive it.

Mothers also expressed many concerns about the medical care their children were given. There was concern that SCD continued to be a disease doctors did not understand. A mother with two children who have SCD has dealt with the disease for nearly 20 years and noted, "It's been a chore trying to maintain the right physician or someone really knowledgeable about their disease." In other cases, mothers simply doubted the medical technologies that were used and were especially skeptical of daily dosages of penicillin, blood transfusions, and surgeries.

The greatest amount of dissatisfaction over medical care expressed by mothers was directed toward the nursing staff. When mothers insisted their children could not be left unattended during stays in the hospital, they typically said it was because of the way nurses treated their children. What they generally described were patterns of neglect and insensitivity, which some mothers viewed as racially motivated. One 52-year-old mother who felt she had to stay in the hospital with her child described incidents in which nurses scolded her sick child for bed-wetting, although he was under heavy medication, and refused to give the doctor-prescribed amount of medication, saying it would cause addiction. Another mother of a 5-year-old daughter said:

> [The] only thing I don't like is the nurses. They act like they're scared of minority people [laughing]. I mean, really, they're scared of Black kids. When all the white kids are there, like the ones with cancer, they're hugging them and everything. And as soon as they see a Black face they put the gloves on. When they're with the white patients, they hold them and stuff.

Thus, hospitalization provided little respite from caregiving for these mothers.

The Impact of SCD on Families

The diagnosis of SCD results in pain, increased dependency, emotional distress, and fear among children with SCD and imposes on parents the management of severe and unpredictable pain attacks that may interfere with their performance of household and job responsibilities and create inconvenience and hardship (Whitten & Nishiura, 1985, p. 251).

Moreover, the fact that the disease is incurable and unpredictable heightens the stress experienced by families (Graham et al., 1982). Still, researchers have found that parents of children with SCD often deny that the disease has affected their lives (Burlew, Evans, & Oler, 1989). I found that mothers focused instead on their ability to manage the disease. One mother of two sons with SCD, ages 8 and 10, said: "Really, it hasn't messed up my life, since I know how they got it. I don't think anything would be different. It's about the same to me, really . . . because I know how to deal with them, just like I know how to deal with [my daughter] who doesn't have SCD."

The extent to which families are disrupted by caring for a child with SCD depends on factors such as family structure, social support, economic status, coping strategies, and characteristics of the child with SCD (Midence, Fuggle, & Davies, 1993). Blacks in the United States are overrepresented among those who live in single-mother families and in poverty, and these factors may adversely influence the family's caregiving capabilities. Brody and colleagues (1994) found that the lack of economic resources increased depression and pessimism among the parents of children with SCD, and this may be implicated in the behavioral problems experienced by children with SCD. Studies comparing children with SCD to those without the disease have found that SCD children are more likely to have behavioral problems (Kumar et al., 1976; Thompson et al., 1993) and emotional distress or psychological morbidity (Barbarin, Whitten, & Bonds, 1994; Bennett, 1994; Iloeje, 1991), although low social class might account for some of these problems (Lemanek et al., 1986). Single mothers perceive behavioral problems in children with SCD more than two-parent families (Evans, Burlew, & Oler, 1988). The siblings of children with SCD may experience psychological distress, as they often receive less attention and are expected to be more independent and responsible than their stricken siblings (Trieber, Mabe, & Wilson, 1987).

The age and sex of the child with SCD are the major variables that affect adjustment to the disease: Girls adjust better than boys, and younger children adjust better than adolescents. Whereas the mothers of young children in this study rarely reported adjustment problems in their children, those with older children—especially sons—were likely to have experienced problems. The mother of a 15-year-old reported a recent suicide attempt by her son, and another with a teenage son described a pattern of withdrawal and hostility:

He just doesn't talk like he used to. And the pictures that he's been draw-ing in the last year—it's [always about] just killing somebody. I don't like to see him do this. There is something wrong somewhere, and I really think he needs to have counseling. . . . And he's gotten to the place where he just wants to fight all the time.

Researchers have argued that older children may experience poor self-esteem, hypochondria, depression, and embarrassment over the physical signs of the disease (Wright & Phillips, 1988) and have greater problems because they are facing the task of identity formation (Mor-gan & Jackson, 1986) and realizing the limitations imposed by the dis-ease. It has also been suggested that males may simply be more vulner-able to psychological disruption and react more negatively to growth retardation than females (Hurtig, Koepke, & Park, 1989; Hurtig & White, 1986). Boys may find it difficult to fulfill the "masculine role," which often pivots on physical aggressiveness and participation in sports, especially among low-income African American males (Hill & Zimmerman, 1995). Although age and sex influence adjustment to SCD, family climate is the major factor in a child's ability to adjust to the disease. Children adjust better in families that emphasize high achievement and those "characterized as committed, helpful, support-ive, and encouraging of open, direct expression of feelings" (Hurtig & Park, 1989, p. 175).

Coping with Childhood SCD

With time, the mothers in this study moved from denial and distress over the diagnosis of SCD to effective coping with the disease. They fo-cused on their ability to manage SCD and on the positive aspects of the illness experience. As one mother noted: "Having a disease is never good, but I think learning to deal with it and accept it can be. I don't pamper it; that's the best remedy you can do. . . . I feel like if you look at it and know it can't beat you, you still got it made." Mothers also coped by maintaining high expectations for their children, as seen in this mother's view of her 13-year-old son: "I always feel like he can do any-thing he wants to do, that he can be anybody he wants to be. I don't feel like there is any difference between him and my oldest son [who doesn't have SCD]: Whatever he feels he can do, he can do."

Social support is a crucial factor in successful coping. In two-parent families of children with SCD, caregiving work is shared (Slaughter &

Dilworth-Anderson, 1988), and parents provide a ready source of social support for one another. Although some research has suggested that single-parent families receive limited support from relatives (Dilworth-Anderson, 1989), nearly all of the single mothers in this study had reliable sources of support. Almost 30 percent of the mothers lived in extended families, and most of the others had family members living nearby. A mother of three, asked if there was anyone who helped during her son's pain crises, said: "My mother. She lives right down the street. My mother keeps these two [younger children] a lot, while I go to the hospital with my son. During crises I have to rub him up [massage him], but sometimes my mother just tells me to leave him at her house, and she'll rub him up." A divorced mother said:

> We're a real close family. I have sisters, I have brothers—there's eight of us. So we're like I said, a real close family. And whenever [my daughter's] sick—she's everybody's favorite—so whenever she's sick or anything everybody just drops whatever they're doing to see about her and make sure I'm doing what I'm supposed to be doing.

A few mothers also participated in formal SCD support groups, which were especially valuable in providing medical information and support during illness crises. Sickle cell support groups have been formed in many cities across the United States, and the support they provide has been shown to increase SCD knowledge, improve patient-doctor relationships, and help those with SCD resolve psychosocial issues associated with the disease (Butler & Beltram, 1993).

Summary and Conclusion

African American families that provide caregiving for children with chronic illnesses experience an array of challenges, all of which are complicated by economic and racial inequality. Black families are often characterized by poverty, single-mother families, lack of access to medical care, and an uneasy relationship with health care professionals, and these factors influence the strategies families use to care for chronically ill children.

Despite the fact that Black families are often seen as weak and ineffectual, especially when dealing with crises, interviews with these mothers clearly challenge the image of Black families as overwhelmed by the task of providing adequate home and medical care for children. The mothers in this study demonstrated high levels of activity and competency in caring for their children. They actively sought SCD information that was not provided by doctors, devised caregiving strategies based on the experiences of their own children, and made the sacrifices necessary to obtain medical care for illnesses that could not be managed at home. They coped with SCD by focusing on their ability to control the disease, having high expectations for their children's futures, and relying on the support available from both family members and formal organizations.

References

Barbarin, O. A., D. Hughes, & M. Chesler (1985). Stress, coping, and marital functioning among parents of children with cancer. *Journal of Marriage and the Family, 47,* 473–480.

Barbarin, O. A., C.F. Whitten, & S. M. Bonds (1994). Estimating rates of psychosocial problems in urban and poor children with sickle cell anemia. *Health and Social Work, 19*(2), 112–119.

Bennett, D. S. (1994). Depression among children with chronic medical problems: A meta analysis. *Journal of Pediatric Psychology, 19*(2), 149–169.

Billingsley, A. (1992). *Climbing Jacob's ladder: The enduring legacy of African-American families.* New York: Simon and Schuster.

Bowman, J. E. (1977). Genetic screening programs and public policy. *Phylon, 38,* 117–142.

Brody, G. H., Z. Stoneman, D. Flor, & C. McCrary (1994). Financial resources, parent psychological functioning, parent co-caregiving and early adolescent competence in rural two-parent African American families. *Child Development, 65*(2), 590–605.

Burlew, K. A., R. Evans, & C. Oler, (1989). The impact of a child with sickle cell disease on family dynamics. In C. F. Whitten and J. F. Bertles (Eds.), *Sickle cell disease* (pp. 161–171). New York: New York Academy of Sciences.

Butler, D. J., & L. R. Beltram (1993). Functions of an adult sickle cell group: Education, task orientation, and support. *Health and Social Work, 18*(1), 49–56.

Consensus Conference (1987). Newborn screening for sickle cell disease and other hemoglobinopathies. *Journal of the American Medical Association, 258,* 1205–1209.

Dilworth-Anderson, P. (1989). Family structure and intervention strategies. In C. F. Whitten and J. F. Bertles (Eds.), *Sickle cell disease* (p. 183). New York: New York Academy of Sciences.

Evans, R. C., A. K. Burlew, & C. H. Oler (1988). Children with sickle cell anemia: Parental reactions, parent-child relations, and child behavior. *Social Work, 33*(2), 127–130.

France-Dawson, M. (1986). Sickle cell disease: Implications for nursing care. *Journal of Advanced Nursing, 11,* 729–737.

Gaston, M. H., J. J. Verter, G. Woods, C. Pegelow, J. Kelleher, J. G. Presbury, H. Zarkowsky, H. E. Vichinsky, E. R. Iyer, J. S. Lobel, S. Diamond, T. Holbrook, F. M. Gill, K. Ritchey, & J. M. Falletta (1986). Prophylaxis with oral penicillin in children with sickle cell anemia. *New England Journal of Medicine, 314*(25), 1593–1599.

Graham, A., K. G. Reeb, C. Levitt, M. Fine, & J. H. Medalie (1982). Care of a troubled family and their child with sickle cell anemia. *Journal of Family Practice, 15*(1), 23–32.

Hill, S. A., & M. K. Zimmerman (February 1995). Valiant girls and vulnerable boys: The impact of gender and race on mothers' caregiving for chronically ill children. *Journal of Marriage and the Family, 57,* 43–53.

Hurtig, A. L., D. Koepke, & K. B. Park (1989). Relation between severity of chronic illness and adjustment in children and adolescents with sickle cell disease. *Journal of Pediatric Psychology, 14*(1), 117–132.

Hurtig, A. L., & K. B. Park (1989). Adjustment and coping in adolescents with sickle cell disease. In C. F. Whitten and J. F. Bertles (Eds.), *Sickle cell disease* (pp. 172–182). New York: New York Academy of Sciences.

Hurtig, A. L., & L. S. White (1986). Psychosocial adjustment in children and adolescents with sickle cell disease. *Journal of Pediatric Psychology, 11*(3), 411–427.

Iloeje, S. O. (1991). Psychiatric morbidity among children with sickle cell disease. *Developmental Medicine and Child Neurology, 33*(12), 1087–1094.

Kumar, S., D. Powars, J. Allen, & L. J. Haywood (1976). Anxiety, self-concept, and personal and social adjustments in children with sickle cell anemia. *Journal of Pediatrics, 88*(5), 859–863.

Lansky, S., N. Cairns, R. Hassanein, J. Wehr, & J. T. Lowman (July–December 1978). Childhood cancer: Parental discord and divorce. *Pediatrics, 62,* 184–188.

Lemanek, K., S. L. Moore, F. M. Gresham, D. A. Williamson, & M. L. Kelley, (1986). Psychological adjustment of children with sickle cell anemia. *Journal of Pediatric Psychology, 11*(3), 397–410.

Linde, S. M. (1972). *Sickle cell: A complete guide to prevention and treatment.* New York: Pavilion Publishing Company.

Midence, K., P. Fuggle, & S. C. Davies (1993). Psychological aspects of sickle cell disease (SCD) in childhood and adolescence: A review. *British Journal of Clinical Psychology, 32*(3), 271–280.

Morgan, S. A., & J. Jackson (1986). Psychological and social concomitants of sickle cell anemia in adolescents. *Journal of Pediatric Psychology, 11*(3), 429–440.

Nobles, W. W. (1985). *Africanity and the Black family* (2d ed.). Oakland, CA: Institute for the Advanced Study of Black Family Life and Culture.

Ogamdi, S. O. (1994). African American students' awareness of sickle cell disease. *Journal of American College Health, 42*(5), 234–236.

Patterson, J. M. (January 1985). Critical factors affecting family compliance with home treatment for children with cystic fibrosis. *Family Relations, 34,* 79–88.

Rao, R. P., & L. Kramer (1993). Stress and coping among mothers of infants with a sickle cell condition. *Children's Health Care, 22*(3), 169–188.

Reilly, P. (1977). *Genetics, law, and social policy.* Cambridge: Harvard University Press.

Rosner, F., L. St. Clair, G. Karayalcin, & B. Tatsis (1982). A decade of experience with a sickle cell program. *New York State Journal of Medicine, 82*(11), 1546–1554.

Slaughter, D. T., & P. Dilworth-Anderson (1988). Care of the Black child with SCD: Fathers' maternal support and esteem. *Family Relations, 37,* 281–287.

Stack, C. (1974). *All our kin: Strategies for survival in a Black community.* New York: Harper and Row.

Thompson, R. J., K. M. Gil, D. J. Burbach, & B. R. Keith (1993). Psychological adjustment of mothers of children and adolescents with sickle cell disease: The role of stress, coping methods, and family functioning. *Journal of Pediatric Psychology, 18*(5), 549–559.

Trieber, F. P., A. Mabe, & G. Wilson (1987). Psychological adjustment of sickle cell children and their siblings. *Children's Health Care, 16*(2), 82–88.

Whitten, C. F. (1992). Sickle cell anemia in the African American. In R. L. Braithwaite and S. E. Taylor (Eds.), *Health care issues in the Black community* (pp. 192–205). San Francisco: Jossey-Bass Publishers.

Whitten, C. F., & E. N. Nishiura (1985). Sickle cell anemia. In N. Hobbs, J. M. Perrin, and H. T. Ireys (Eds.), *Issues in the care of children with chronic illness* (pp. 236–260). San Francisco: Jossey-Bass Publishers.

Wilkinson, D. (May 1974). For whose benefit? Politics and sickle cell. *Black Scholar 5,* 26–31.

Wright, H. H., & L. G. Phillips (1988). Psychosocial issues in sickle cell disease. In A. F. Coner-Edwards and J. Spurlock (Eds.), *Black families in crisis: The middle class* (pp. 170–186). New York: Brunner/Mazel.

4

Helping Black Families Who Are Providing Care to Persons with AIDS

SADYE L. LOGAN
JEROME JOYCE

> I deal with this disease by looking at it as one of the best breaks I've ever had. I treat it with respect. I try to love it. I talk to it. I'll say: "You are safe with me. Do not worry. I do not hate you." I am not sure if befriending this virus within me has any healing impact. I know that it helps me to carry on. If my attitude is good and I'm happy and generous, I feel I can live with this virus within me for a very long time.
>
> **—Young person with AIDS**

Although we no longer speak about Acquired Immune Deficiency Syndrome (AIDS) or persons with AIDS (PWAs) in whispers and hushed tones, AIDS is still addressed in a negative context. Those ultimately or peripherally involved revert (at least initially) either to silence or denial. It takes a great deal of courage, compassion, and faith to stand tall and do battle with this killer disease. This is true not only for PWAs but also for their significant others (parents, siblings, friends, lovers, and children) (Raveis & Siegel, 1990).

AIDS has been viewed as endemic to the Black community and has been spoken of as the most controversial disease in modern history. According to the Centers for Disease Control (1990), AIDS taps into the fears most people harbor about dying in a dreadful way—chronically disabled and contagious. This condition is coupled with moral overtones of drug use, sexuality, sexual identity, and freedom. The observers of this epidemic either moralize about "them" deserving what "they" got or show deep compassion and caring for the extraordinary suffering of fellow human beings.

The family members of these acute sufferers often fail to receive the kind of support necessary to maintain the vigilance required in this debilitating struggle. This is especially true for Black families, which are usually underrepresented in studies and are unserved or underserved by those providing services to this client group (Kelly & Sykes, 1989). Therefore, it is the intent of this chapter to identify and discuss those issues that will assist service providers in the delivery of more effective services to Black families that are managing the care of family members with AIDS.

Black Families and AIDS

Black Americans constitute only 12 percent of the U.S. population but account for nearly 30 percent of the reported AIDS cases (Centers for Disease Control, 1990). Available data suggest that PWAs in this country have basically been homosexual or bisexual men, intravenous drug users, and the female partners of bisexual men or intravenous drug users. Actually, the majority of women diagnosed with AIDS have been intravenous drug users or partners of intravenous drug users. According to Wingdom and Koop (1987), since a large number (30 percent) of intravenous drug users are Black or Hispanic, almost 80 percent of all children with AIDS are Black or Hispanic (Centers for Disease Control, 1988). Most of the women and children with AIDS are from families of color living below the poverty level. These are two of society's most vulnerable groups. It appears service providers will be challenged to gain knowledge and skills that will allow them to provide help to PWAs and their families across the life cycle.

Despite the helping profession's awareness of the serious psychosocial needs of family members and significant others associated with chronic fatal illnesses, service providers were slow to acknowledge the devastating impact of AIDS on the significant others involved with PWAs. Further, the original concern with the disease addressed the psychosocial aspects and ways of providing effective treatment and support.

Although numerous problems can be anticipated by the functional and biological family members of PWAs, several have been identified as the more obvious concerns (Giacquinta, 1989; Macklin, 1988; Powell-Cope & Brown, 1992):

- Social stigma and isolation
- Fear of infection
- Fear of abandonment
- Denial
- Guilt
- Anger
- Grief
- Economic hardship

These obvious concerns are not unique to the caregivers of a Black PWA, but the social and environmental contexts create a different set of realities for Black caregivers. These concerns are discussed in the context of a composite case example of the Moore family.

The Moore Family and Related Dynamics

The Moore family consists of Ben, the father (61), estranged from the family for nearly 10 years; his wife, Mae (58); and their children: Dot (35), Jeff (33), Richard (29), who is the PWA, and Molly (25). The family can be described as economically upwardly mobile. The father has two years of college education and is employed as a bookkeeper. The mother has a college degree and is employed as a mid-level manager with the state government. All of the children except Molly are college graduates and are professionally employed.

After graduating from college, Richard moved away from the Midwest. Available evidence seems to suggest that family members who are homosexual or intravenous drug users usually distance themselves from or sever ties with their families of origin before being diagnosed with AIDS (Honey, 1988). During college, Richard had become sexually active and had shared his sexual preference with his family, which caused a great deal of discord between him and his father. His mother feared what friends and extended family would say about his sexual preference. Feeling strongly about his life choice, Richard moved to the East Coast.

While living apart from his family Richard was free to live the lifestyle he chose without placing unwanted hardship on his family. His family told others he had moved for better employment opportunities. Richard returned home only for special occasions until he was diagnosed with AIDS. At this point he had become a part of the evolving social stigma that accompanies the disease. For example, a person who has AIDS or who is human immunodeficiency virus (HIV) positive will likely experience numerous forms of rejection that are fueled by prejudice, homophobia, and unrealistic fears of contamination. In Richard's case, he was fired from his job. Others have reported being ejected from apartments, shunned by neighbors and relatives, and denied a variety of services such as treatment by some dentists and physicians.

Although some families learn of a family member's intravenous drug use or confirm a member's sexual preference after learning about the AIDS diagnosis, many are not as accepting of the situation as Richard's family was. Many of these families are reluctant to have the family member return home because of the fear of becoming infected or of being ostracized by extended family members and friends. Caregiving in such situations is done by communities. Sometimes the PWA does not want to return home in hopes of preventing pain and hardship for family members. Fears of being infected are generally experienced in families that have small children. Despite the knowledge that AIDS cannot spread through casual contact, many families still fear that even casual contact can be lethal (Honey, 1988).

Some families go into a state of denial about having a family member diagnosed with HIV/AIDS, which in these instances serves as a coping device for significant others and the PWA (Grief & Porembski, 1988). Generally, the denial is connected to the inevitable loss of a loved one or simply not believing it could happen to their family. Therefore, those in denial refuse to take appropriate health precautions to protect other family members. For example, in one family the PWA was supported in his denial by an older sister. Both acted as if he were not dying of the disease. They refused to observe health precautions even in the advanced stages of the dying process. This attitude alienated other family members who were experiencing not only the tremendous suffering associated with the disease but also an overwhelming anger at the PWA and the sister.

Black families, which are already socially isolated by society, fear even greater isolation within the Black community by having an HIV/AIDS-infected member in the home. Those families that do permit HIV/AIDS-infected members to return home are often reluctant to share their knowledge even with extended family, fearing that private troubles will become public issues (Icard & Traunstein, 1987). Although there is no guarantee of how family members, friends, or colleagues might respond to such information, usually the personal benefits outweigh the risks. Caregivers have spoken of the benefits of living assertively with AIDS in terms of increased inner strength and abilities, job flexibility, help with caregiving tasks, and acknowledgment of their caregiving role (Powell-Cope & Brown, 1992).

After Richard returned home with AIDS, his mother reported that she feared negative feedback from extended family and friends. However, the fact that he had revealed his sexual preference earlier to his family made it easier for the immediate family to accept that he had AIDS. Richard's mother took the approach of her own mother in dealing with her out-of-wedlock pregnancy by not sharing it with extended family or friends until it was necessary. This approach has been described as *staging information* (Powell-Cope and Brown, 1992). In this process, information is shared over time with a select group of acquaintances and family members. This is an important strategy for dealing with the stigma connected to AIDS. Richard's extended family and friends learned of the disease after it had clearly advanced. Richard's mother's first reaction to her son returning home with AIDS was a combination of *denial* and *anger.* Her anger was directed toward her son for his lifestyle, toward the disease and the partner who may have been the source of the illness, toward society for being judgmental and unsupportive, but mostly toward herself. She felt so much *guilt* about not being able to prevent his homosexuality and, consequently, his AIDS. She and Richard's father felt they had somehow failed as parents.

The initial shock of the situation prevents clear thinking and planning regarding medical care. Honey (1988) reports that PWAs may react to the AIDS diagnosis with overwhelming depression or denial, resulting in poor medical follow-up after discharge from the hospital setting. These reactions could also influence the family members' reactions to the AIDS diagnosis. Consequently, the family does not encourage or support continued follow-up treatment.

For Black families that are living in crowded conditions and on public assistance, meeting the medical obligations of AIDS members creates extreme economic hardship. Even if the AIDS victim has health insurance, coverage is usually limited. Limited coverage creates tremendous out-of-pocket expense that remains beyond most families' means. It is out of this situation that PWAs' fear of abandonment grows.

Coupled with the stress of economic hardship in caring for her son's needs, Richard's mother was also overwhelmed by grief at the impending loss of such a young life. She said that caring for a parent dying from cancer was not nearly the challenge presented by her son's AIDS. She felt totally alone with the illness. Once extended family and friends learned of the illness, few would visit or even inquire about how the family was coping. Richard's mother reported that unlike cancer, the special health precautions for AIDS were very demanding. Once Richard's illness progressed to the point of needing assistance outside the home, lack of adequate financial support made it virtually impossible to obtain home health care. The high cost of treatment left the family nearly poverty-stricken. It is at this point that the strain of watching a loved one deteriorate becomes too overwhelming for many caregivers. Under such stress, some gradually and quietly withdraw. In Richard's situation, much of the care was assumed by his mother. She shared her feelings that having a child precede her in death was hell, particularly because he died of AIDS. However, she never considered abandoning him.

Black families, not unlike other families, often reported grieving the loss of a family member afflicted with AIDS immediately upon the family accepting the diagnosis. Awareness that AIDS has no cure is the first step in realizing that that family member is going to die. Many PWAs' families shared feelings of a profound sadness and hopelessness about the future with the family member with AIDS. Future plans of being together were set aside. As indicated earlier, families often start to shut down and pullaway to protect themselves from the pending loss. When the family prematurely pulls away from the PWA, family members may not be aware they are withholding needed emotional support. However, families that were are able to maintain emotional ties reported feeling emotionally drained after caring for a PWA. Many families reported a sense of relief after the PWA died (Grief & Porembski, 1988).

According to available literature and the experience of the authors, there is no one way that Black families respond to this chronic disease (Duh, 1991). The disruption is devastating. As indicated earlier, several factors influence the family's response to this disruption: the values and beliefs of the family members, the habitual response to stressors and the style of problem solving, the role of the infected member in the family, the family's patterns of interacting over time, the quality and nature of family environmental exchange, and the nature of the boundary between the family and the environment (organizations, agencies, and available resources). As highlighted in the composite case discussion of the Moore family, families' responses may vary from nurturance, support, and acceptance to disappointment, anger, and rejection.

AIDS, the Community, and the Black Church

Despite the reported increase of AIDS cases within the Black community, social service agencies serving that community continue to view the need for housing, employment, and crime prevention as the chief priorities. Because of poor funding and mixed feelings about AIDS within Black communities, few AIDS programs exist, and those that do exist are underfunded, with overworked volunteers and professionals who must compete with other needed social programs for funding to stay afloat. Because of poverty, high unemployment, and financial barriers to health care, many Blacks have come to tolerate poor health and inadequate health care services (Icard & Traunstein, 1987).

Some community residents are looking to the Black church for direction. As a result, in 1986 the leaderships of the Southern Christian Leadership Conference, the Urban League, and other grassroots organizations began efforts to increase awareness of AIDS among African Americans (Quimby & Friedman, 1989). Despite this proactive stance, no uniform perspective represents the views and reactions of the Black church or of all African Americans. Further, some elements of the Black community contend that the church simply has not done enough.

Some of the behaviors and attitudes of the African American community, however, are rooted in the early identification of AIDS as a disease that primarily affects gay white men. Coupled with this view is the denial of the existence of homosexuality among African Americans, many of whom do not believe AIDS is a significant problem for Black people (Duh, 1991; Hammond, 1992). Further, many African Americans separate sexual behavior and sexual orientation. In other words, individuals may engage in homosexual behavior but not view themselves as homosexual (Mays & Cochran, 1988).

Despite the mixed response of the African American community to the AIDS epidemic, traditional churches serving the Black community are very clear about the at-risk behavior contributing to contracting and spreading the AIDS virus. In some instances, the church—not unlike service agencies—views racial discrimination, poverty, and fair housing as social problems that warrant support, whereas homosexuality, intravenous drug abuse, and premarital sex are viewed as willful misconduct, which conflicts with church teachings. The dilemma faced by the church in addressing the AIDS epidemic is how to fulfill its historical civic role as community advocate without appearing to sanction the at-risk behavior that contributes to contracting the disease. One minister said, "God meant for Adam and Eve, not Adam and Steve." The church allowing homosexuals to marry in the church or to overlook drug abuse would be viewed as a "sin against God."

As social issues begin to be addressed more assertively by groups and agencies within the Black community, the church may return to its primary mission of serving the spiritual needs of that community. However, traditional Christian teachings are being questioned by some younger Blacks (Logan, 1990). Some Black youths are choosing Eastern faiths, whereas others are seeking spiritual guidance that is more accepting of their lifestyle outside the traditional church. Many homosexuals and intravenous drug users report severing ties with the church before being diagnosed with AIDS because their lifestyle was in conflict with the church's teachings (Honey, 1988). As one minister said, families returning to the church do so not always to be reunited with their religion but because of the resources the church possesses.

The church is fully aware that increasing numbers of AIDS victims are becoming infected without being involved in questionable or at-risk behavior the church would find problematic. Even though a person infected with AIDS may have engaged in such behavior, the victim's family seeking support from the church may not be in conflict with religious teachings. For many families the church is seen as the last hope in getting needed materials and spiritual guidance (Taylor, 1988). This may be why Goldman (1989) reported efforts by some Black clergy to designate a special Sunday to address the AIDS epidemic. If the church is going to be an effective agent in fighting the spread of HIV/AIDS, the clergy and laypeople will need the support of the service delivery system to become educated about the disease.

Implications for Practice

Black families in general can be a challenging population to attempt to engage in the treatment process (see the Epilogue). Those families that are caring for PWAs are even more of a challenge to service providers. The general reluctance to seek help is compounded by the stigma attached to AIDS. Therefore, many families' first contact with treatment providers comes after they have been caring directly for PWAs for an extended period of time. Many other Black families never come in contact with treatment providers. This lack of contact results from a variety of factors, some of which are related to the location of the services, lack of outreach, insufficient funds, and insufficient or unavailable service staff (Kelly & Sykes, 1989).

Intervention Strategies

As indicated throughout this chapter, a tremendous need exists for mental health services and support services for Black families and significant others who are providing care for or living with a PWA. Evidence suggests that these families need help not only in dealing with AIDS but also in dealing with their own feelings and the PWA's feelings about AIDS. With this in mind, as well as the tremendous personal suffering and emotional pain experienced by PWAs and their families, the discussion provides practice guidelines for helping professionals.

It is important to begin with the awareness that intervention with PWAs and their families is equally stressful for the service provider. This is a complex situation that requires preparation on the intellectual, emotional, and spiritual levels. Therefore, in addition to being knowledgeable about current treatment issues and about AIDS as a disease, practitioners must also be in touch with their own values and beliefs concerning this disease. Of equal importance is the practitioner's sensitivity to the Black community's response to AIDS and to the impact of negative stereotypes that are associated with AIDS and the Black community. Beyond adopting a knowledgeable and compassionate stance, professional helpers must also be able to identify, create, and refer families to appropriate services.

Research has shown that an effective service for families and significant others is the support group. These groups help families to help themselves as well as each other (Kelly & Sykes, 1989). As a modality of choice, the group context not only supports families in dealing with loss, grief, and related issues but also helps to demystify the experience. Facilitation of this process requires not only appropriate skills but also awareness about the impact of culture on the grieving process. Little has been written about the dynamics of loss and grief among African Americans; however, available research and experience affirm that

African American men in general express grief and loss differently than African American women. Men are more stoic in expressing their pain and believe they must be strong for other family members. They further believe faith in a higher power and prayers will provide the necessary relief (Freeman, 1984; Manns, 1981; Secundy, 1991).

Relief for families and PWAs may also come through culture-specific services. These services may include music, church services, contemplative readings, and other coping strategies such as imagery, meditation, select readings from the Bible, talking about the impending loss or the actual loss with the survivors, or simply sitting and being still (Dossey, 1993).

Another thorny area in working with PWAs and their families concerns denial. The evidence suggests that not only is an individualized approach needed based on a thorough assessment of the needs of all parties involved, but care and great sensitivity are also required. Much skill is required in balancing and respecting the needs and wishes of the PWA to not share information that could place significant others in less healthful situations. It is also important to provide information in a manner that does not construe factual data but is appropriate to the PWA's level of emotional acceptance (Grief & Porembski, 1988).

Other helpful ways of managing treatment issues may take place within the group context or within the family as a unit. These issues include the provision of anticipatory guidance within a cultural context. On the first level, guidance is given to the family: Keeping in mind the meaning and significance of the disease for Blacks in general and for the family in particular, the preparation is directed toward sharing information with others about the AIDS diagnosis of the family member. On the second level, guidance is provided to the family as a means of responding more effectively to the demands of home health care. These demands may escalate stress and tension and could result in severe family conflict.

A sometimes neglected but critical area of focus in family work concerns the increasing numbers of women and children infected with the disease. Many of these women are parenting alone, but in some instances both parents are involved. The issue of planning for the future care of the children is critical, not only because of the trauma associated with the loss of a parent, but also because as a result of their ethnicity and the disease, children will fit into the hard-to-place category. In addition, parents must be aided in confronting issues related to living wills and powers of attorney to handle business and financial concerns.

The work with the family as a unit may take the form of what is considered to be nontraditional practice. For example, home visitation may be required, as well as ongoing collaborative contacts with other professionals, extended family members, the clergy, and other agencies serving the PWA's family. In addition to employing a nontraditional approach, the practitioner must also be willing to engage in aggressive outreach to this client population. It is commonly acknowledged that African Americans are reluctant to seek help outside of traditional helping structures, but they are no less in need of effective services than is the general population. The committed practitioner will not only provide services in the home but will also visit Black churches to describe available services for this client population, give educational talks at parent-teacher meetings and at fraternal and civic organizations, and write articles on AIDS for the local newspaper.

An Approach to Implementing a Family Service Plan: Wraparound Services

It is important to note that not all resources are needed by all PWA clients at the same stage of the illness. Different resources become important at different stages to different PWA clients. Knowing this, care providers and PWAs need an effective tool in providing services that are needs-driven, that are consistent and uninterrupted. One such tool is developing a tailor-made care process that wraps services around (wraparound) PWAs and their families. Such services are needs-driven by the PWA client as opposed to being limited by a given agency resource. Wraparound is not a state or federal program. It is a process that works with PWA clients and their families with the value base of unconditional commitment to create services for those clients with complex needs.

Wraparound grew out of the 1980s social case work with families wishing to keep children and youths who are severely challenged with emotional, physical and often legal problems at home rather than having them institutionalized. Such an approach has proven to be more cost-effective both to service deliverers and to the youths' families. An added bonus has been a greater sensitivity to the clients' needs. Community agencies and family support workers, friends, clergy, and other identified resources pooling together and developing a wraparound process has ensured greater linkage between the PWA and the identified services needed, with more consistency and fewer interruptions in service delivery.

The wraparound approach is family centered and needs-driven. The process is based on the belief that each individual is endowed with an inherent strength. Positive reframing of the PWAs assets and the desire to help him or her to have a normalized life are key elements in the wraparound process. Wraparound focuses on normalization of the PWA, recognizing that many PWA clients desire to be with loved ones and to engage in activities of daily living as long as their health permits.

Wraparound is a two-step process that constitutes two interrelated working teams: the family team and the community support team. First, a family-based team of individuals is needed to develop the needs-driven agenda. This team should be made up of extended family members, supportive friends within the community, clergy, PWA advocates, and others as deemed necessary. The family team's primary focus is to develop a comprehensive needs-driven agenda that focuses on the PWA client's life domain areas, which include the family; the living situation; social, recreational, psychological, emotional, medical, and legal needs; a crisis intervention plan; and educational and vocational needs.

At the same time, a community support team is being developed. This team is made up of persons who have flexible funding, the ability to break down barriers, and the willingness to try new things in helping PWA clients. This team is made up of health care professionals and paraprofessionals, counselors, case managers, lawyers, clergy, and others as deemed necessary.

The two teams are brought together in collaboration with a single purpose of providing unconditional care and service to PWA clients and their families. Ground rules for working together are:

- To include all family members, care providers, and community support agencies deemed of benefit to the PWA
- To be respectful of PWA clients and their families by maintaining a nonjudgmental approach
- To be culturally sensitive to the PWA
- To tailor a program that addresses the individual's needs
- To have access to a natural support network as a resource
- To develop a means for monitoring the wraparound plan
- To meet whenever necessary

Both the PWA family team and the community support team will need to identify a facilitator, an integrated administrative team, a place to meet, and flexibility in developing funding and resources for the PWA client.

Wraparound services can be a powerful tool in providing the needed care and resources to PWAs who have limited knowledge about obtaining the necessary help for themselves and their families. The wrap-around approach gives ownership to all participants while continuing to empower PWAs to self-direct their lives as they struggle with an illness that is debasing and that will continue to deteriorate their well-being.

Summary and Conclusion

Working with the PWA family may be the greatest challenge for any practitioner. The stigma, hostility, and fear that accompany this disease constitute a great burden for any family but especially for families that are already dealing with racism and other forms of oppression on a daily basis.

It is important, however, for Black families not to become complacent regarding the AIDS crisis. Stopping the spread of HIV/AIDS means making AIDS a priority in the Black community. Increased education of Blacks, the clergy, and youth is essential if prevention is to be effective. It is generally believed that the family plays a key role in education, prevention, and attitude change regarding AIDS (Macklin, 1988).

Practitioners and social service agencies must work diligently to assure that cultural, economic, and sociopolitical factors do not become barriers to developing effective strategies for serving all segments of the Black community.

References

Centers for Disease Control (January 18, 1988). *AIDS Weekly Surveillance Report*. Atlanta, GA: Centers for Disease Control.

Centers for Disease Control. (October 1990). *HIV/AIDS Surveillance Report* (pp. 8–11). Atlanta, GA: Centers for Disease Control.

Dossey, L. (1993). *Healing words: The power of prayer and the practice of medicine*. San Francisco: Harper San Francisco.

Duh, S. (1991). *Blacks and AIDS: Causes and origins*. Newbury Park, CA: Sage Publications.

Freeman, E. (1984). Loss and grief in children: Implications for school social workers. *Social Work in Education, 6*, 241–258.

Giacquinta, B. J. (1989). Researching the effects of AIDS on families. *American Journal of Hospice Care, 28*, 31–36.

Goldman, S. L. (June 1989). Blacks pause to consider AIDS peril. *New York Times*, pp. B1, B9.

Grief, G. L., & E. Porembski (1988). AIDS and significant others: Findings from preliminary explanation of needs. *Health and Social Work, 13*, 259–264.

Hammond, E. (1992). Race, sex, AIDS: The construction of "other." In M. Anderson and P. Collins (Eds.), *Race, class and gender: An anthology.* Belmont, CA: Wadsworth.

Honey, E. (1988). AIDS and the inner city: Critical issues. *Social Casework, 6,* 365–370.

Icard, L., R. F. Schilling, N. El-Bassel, & S. Broadnax (1992). Preventing AIDS among Black gay men and Black gay and heterosexual male intravenous drug users. *Social Work, 57*(5), 440–445.

Icard, L., & D.M.B. Traunstein (1987). Black, gay, alcoholic men: Their character and treatment. *Social Casework: The Journal of Contemporary Social Work, 68*(5), 267–272.

Kelly, J., & P. Sykes (1989). Helping the helpers: A support group for family members of persons with AIDS. *Social Work, 34*(3), 239–242.

Logan, S. (1990). The Black Baptist Church: A social-psychological study in coping and growth. Dissertation Abstracts International, 41/06A.

Macklin, E. D. (April 1988). AIDS: Implications for families. *Family Relations, 37,* 141–149.

Manns, W. (1981). Support systems of significant others in Black families. In H. P. McAdoo (Ed.), *Black families* (pp. 238–251). Beverly Hills, CA: Sage Publications.

Mays, V. M., & S. D. Cochran (1988). Issues in the perceptions of AIDS risk and risk reduction activities by Black and Latina/Latino women. *American Psychologist, 43,* 949–957.

Powell-Cope, G. M., & M. Brown (1992). *Social Science and Medicine, 34*(5), 571–580.

Quimby, E., & S. Friedman (1989). Dynamics of Black mobilization against AIDS in New York City. *Social Problems, 36*(4), 403–415.

Raveis, V., & K. Siegel (1990). Impact of caregiving on informal or familial caregivers. In *Community-based care of persons with AIDS: Developing a research agenda* (pp. 17–28) (DHHS Publication no. PHS 90-3456). Rockville, MD: Agency for Health Care Policy and Research Publications and Information Branch.

Secundy, M. G. (Ed.) (1991). *Trials, tribulations and celebrations: African-American perspectives on health, illness, aging and loss.* Yarmouth, ME: Intercultural Press.

Taylor, R. J. (1988). Structural determinants of religious participation among Black Americans. *Review of Religious Research, 30,* 114–125.

Wingdom, B. E., & C. E. Koop (1987). *No-nonsense AIDS answers.* Chicago: Blue Cross/Blue Shield Association.

5

A Perspective on Homelessness Among African American Families

EDITH M. FREEMAN

> Homelessness "hit home" for me when, for more than a year and a half, drug and alcohol abuse left my uncle without a place to call his own. I imagine there were times during this period when people passed him on the streets and thought, *What a bum, why doesn't he get a job?* But it's not so simple.
> —**Kimberly Aiken, Ms. America, 1994**

Recent estimates suggest that the homeless population includes approximately 736,000 persons on any given night and that from 1.3 to 2 million individuals in this country were homeless at least one night during 1987 (National Alliance to End Homelessness, 1988). Other data indicate the annual homeless population is 1.5 million persons (Fischer, 1991). Although these escalating statistics are alarming, it must be recognized that homelessness is both an old and a new problem. In the past, homeless individuals were primarily older, skid row, male alcoholics. Today, 30 to 40 percent of homeless persons have a problem with other drugs such as crack cocaine and heroin (Harris, Mowbray, & Sclarz, 1994; Milburn, 1989). Weinreb and Bassuk (1990) note that substance abuse problems cut across many segments of the homeless population such as families with children, single parents, adolescents, and all of the various racial and ethnic groups.

This means the homeless population today is more diverse in terms of age, ethnicity, and gender and that many in this group are polyaddicted rather than addicted to alcohol only. Thus, the new problem of homelessness is more complex than in the past: It cannot be viewed in isolation from interrelated factors such as substance abuse and racism. Among African Americans in particular, poverty and racial discrimination may increase the risk of homelessness, as well as a pattern of coping with racial stress by abusing substances. A multicausal analysis and a multilevel problem-solving approach are necessary for addressing such a complex problem within this segment of the homeless population (Freeman, 1994; McChesney, 1990; Tessler & Dennis, 1989).

The purpose of this chapter is to discuss a framework for analyzing the many factors that affect homelessness among African Americans through an application of relevant theories and the use of specific family examples. A multilevel prevention, intervention, and treatment approach to the problem is included in the discussion. This approach emphasizes a culturally sensitive, strengths-oriented perspective.

A Conceptual Framework for Analysis

A number of theories are useful for analyzing and determining the needs of homeless African American families. These include theories of loss and grief, cultural adaptation, and systems. Each of the theories

Figure 5.1   Conceptual Framework: Analyzing the Ecological Field
of Homeless African American Families

contributes an important element to the total sphere shown in Figure 5.1, which illustrates the family's ecological field. These three theories build upon the knowledge base practitioners typically apply to families in their clinical practice, including personality, communications, group, family life cycle, and intergenerational theories.

Theories of Loss and Grief

During the transition to homelessness, families have often experienced an entire series of losses, either as individual members or as a total unit. These include loss of employment or financial stability, familiar surroundings and possessions, status, complementary roles, significant relationships, and a loss of control, as well as diminished self-esteem (Freeman, 1984). Such losses affect the family in very important ways. First, they are cumulative, often occurring in a relatively brief time period and increasing the overall negative impact on the family's functional level. Second, African American and other families of color may be affected in a manner that is unique to those families. If they perceive themselves as having a devalued status because of racism and discrimination, a type of chronic loss may be experienced over time prior to the point when they become homeless (Willie, Kramer, & Brown, 1983). The cumulative losses identified earlier are then "piled on top of" this type of chronic loss, which may simply exacerbate the family's diminished functioning and inability to utilize its existing strengths.

Alcohol and other drug abuse in the family present yet another potential loss experience, whether this represents a preexisting addiction or a newly adopted mechanism for coping with homelessness or other stresses such as racism. An additional loss of both control and nurturing relationships may be experienced by all family members as the substance abuse becomes the central organizing theme of the unit (Freeman, 1993). Ironically, with these families intervention and treatment can create other losses that are incurred during the recovery process based on Kübler-Ross's (1968, 1983) stages of loss and grief (see Figure 5.2). This loss process is complicated by the range of roles adopted by other family members that must also be relinquished for the system's recovery process to occur: the family hero, enabler, mascot, or scapegoat (Wegscheider-Cruse, 1985).

Families may not be completely aware of the series of losses they have experienced or of the possible positive and negative effects those changes can have on the unit. Therefore, when they are referred to a

70

Figure 5.2   Kübler-Ross's Loss and Grief Theory:
The Recovery Process in Chemically Dependent Families

Denial   Anger and   Bargaining   Depression   Acceptance
and Shock   Irritability

Denial and Shock: The addicted person and family members respond with denial even when confronted by external evidence of dysfunctions in one or more major life domains as a result of chemical dependency. Their responses cushion the initial shock that results from the loss of control, but the responses can become dysfunctional when prolonged because they can prevent or disrupt substance abuse treatment.

Anger and Irritability: The family recognizes that additional losses have occurred other than the loss of control: the loss of nurturing family relationships, subsequent dysfunctional family roles (e.g., family hero), and cultural drug and drinking networks. The anger may be directed toward those viewed as responsible for such losses, including professional helpers, other family members, and the majority group or large systems that are the sources of racial stress.

Bargaining: The addicted member attempts to bargain or trade reducing his or her abuse of substances for the opportunity to use again, whereas family members may bargain to reduce complaining about the old substance abuse for the uncertainty and stress of recovery.[a] The bargaining often leads to unsuccessful efforts to use lesser amounts of substances or to reassume old family roles.

Depression: The family's beginning recognition that the addicted member cannot control his or her substance use and that the family roles are truly dysfunctional leads to a stage of profound grief and mourning. The resulting depression includes sadness about a required change of lifestyle *and* the lack of resources for achieving this goal, including resources for resolving homelessness and racial stress.

Acceptance: The family acknowledges that substance abuse and the dysfunctional roles and communication patterns must be given up for recovery to occur. The stage involves increased awareness of how substances function in the family's life and the need for culturally relevant, nonabusing social networks in recovery. Substance abuse–related behaviors such as avoidance of pain and conflicts are replaced by presocial behaviors including the ability to cope with stress without substances and developing planning and problem-solving skills (e.g., solving the problem of homelessness). This lifelong stage requires more effort and time than the other stages.

Recovery is a lifelong process involving different problems at each stage of loss and grief. A person can skip stages, go back to an earlier stage, or stay "hung up" in one stage for a long period. The recovering family member needs to know what stage he or she is in and the signs and triggers of relapse during that stage. Other family members should be aware of the roles they have assumed and how the loss of those roles during recovery can also trigger relapse in the recovering family member. Such losses can exacerbate losses from homelessness.

[a]Adapted from Elizabeth Kübler-Ross, 1982. *Living with Death and Dying* (New York: Macmillan).

shelter or to a social agency for other services, they may not initiate a discussion about those events. There is both a societal *and* an ethnic-group taboo about discussing loss, particularly with those outside the social support system such as helping professionals (Johnson, 1992; Manns, 1981). Yet attempts to serve these families without providing education and counseling for helping them to manage their losses are likely to be ineffective. Loss and grief theories such as those of Kübler-Ross (1968, 1983) highlight the long-term effects of loss on a family's functioning, especially on the members' process of cultural identity and adaptation.

Theories of Cultural Adaptation and Coping

African American families are less able to address their concerns about cultural maintenance and supports if they are either at risk for homelessness or actually homeless. All of their energies may be directed toward physical survival rather than cultural survival. Cultural survival means families of color are able to maintain a positive ethnic identity, engage in meaningful cultural traditions and customs such as celebrating Juneteenth Day, and call attention to situations in which they are discriminated against. Yet as noted by Willie, Kramer, and Brown (1983), to maintain good mental health in an ethnically relevant manner, African American families cannot ignore issues of cultural maintenance and identity. In essence, homelessness robs these families of the opportunity to make choices: choices about how to cope, adapt, and identify themselves within the ethnic group and in relation to the dominant culture (Atkinson, Morten, & Sue, 1983; Cross, 1987; McRoy, 1990). Figure 5.3 reflects a continuum of the identity and adaptation choices available to African American families based on cultural adaptation theory (Logan, Freeman, & McRoy, 1987).

In effective work with homeless African American families, some focus must be directed toward barriers to maintaining the desired stage of cultural adaptation while homeless. Often, meeting families' basic needs for shelter, food, clothing, and health care must come first. However, their needs for cultural supports and nurturance should not be ignored as part of the work to increase the family's movement out of homelessness and address dysfunctional coping patterns that can negatively affect its ethnic identity. Cultural supports include the availability of African American–oriented magazines, newspapers, and music; positive Black role models and mentors for providing emotional resources and advice; knowledge of African and African American history and traditions; peer acceptance and approval; and an understanding of the eth-

Figure 5.3 Continuum of Ethic Identity and Adaptation
Choices Available to African American Families

Continuum	Complete assimilation within the dominant society	Biculturalism or adoption of a dual perspective	Cultural immersion within the African American culture
Benefits	Greater acceptance by and blending in with larger society	Increased ability to function in both cultures and to use resources from both	Increased group support and cultural maintenance; decreased racial rejection
Limitations	Loss of African American culture and group support	Emotional stress from adapting to two conflicting sets of expectations	Limited access to resources of society and positive aspects of diversity

Stages

Conformity: Acceptance of the dominant view of African Americans

Dissonance: Development of a conflicting perspective

Resistance and immersion: Movement toward the African American culture and away from the dominant one

Introspection: Developing a more balanced basis for interaction with whites and African Americans

Synergetic articulation and awareness: Conflicts resolved and the emergence of new pluralistic perspectives

Source: E. M. Freeman, 1990. "The Black Family's Life Cycle: Operationalizing a Strengths Perspective." In S. M. Logan, E. M. Freeman, and R. G. McRoy (Eds.), *Social Work Practice with Black Families: A Culturally Specific Perspective* (White Plains, N.Y.: Longman); and D. R. Atkinson, G. Morton, and D. W. Sue (Eds.), 1983. *Counseling American Minorities: A Cross Cultural Perspective* (2d ed.) (Dubuque, Iowa: William C. Brown).

nic identity process as applied to themselves. Families should be encouraged to discuss the benefits and limitations at each point on the continuum or stage of adaptation included in Figure 5.3 (McRoy, 1990).

Systems Theory

Homeless African American families can also be analyzed in terms of the multiple systems that interact within their ecological field or life space (see Figure 5.1). Systems theory provides a practical framework for identifying ethnically relevant support systems that are important to families of color that may be overlooked in traditional assessments. Freeman and Landesman's (1992) adaptation of Ziter's (1987) cultural ecomap goes beyond traditional ecomap assessments to help identify culturally relevant support systems for addicted African American families. The cultural ecomap is equally useful in assessment of nonaddicted African American families.

This ecomap focuses on supports and barriers in a number of interlocking life-space areas. It is even more important in assessing the homeless in terms of supports and barriers: within the family, within the African American minority group world, within the interracial world related to sources of meaningful contacts and exchanges between the dominant culture and the family, and within the white world or larger environment involving sources of powerlessness—media, social policies, and large institutions (Freeman & Landesman, 1992). Systems theory is useful for helping African American families recognize and acknowledge the impact of this larger environment on their homelessness and in health care, education, employment, legal, social, and political areas (Bassuk, Rubin, & Lauriat, 1986; McChesney, 1990). This process of analysis can discourage the type of self-blame and guilt homeless families often experience while helping them to understand and problem-solve around the impact of these multiple interacting systems on the family (Kerr, 1982; Rhodes, 1986).

Homeless Families: Strengths and Problems

Overview of Homeless Families

The conceptual framework described in the previous section provides practitioners with an approach to helping African American families understand the many factors that affect their condition of homelessness. These factors can be summarized in the following questions: What types of African American families become homeless? What consequences do they experience as a result of being homeless? Do they have special needs and strengths that should be the focus of assessment and intervention when using the identified framework? How have environmental conditions influenced the prevalence and resolution of homelessness among African Americans?

In response to these questions, research has shown that the largest numbers of homeless families are of two types: single-parent and underemployed or unemployed two-parent families, with 75 percent of the children in these families belonging to a racial minority group (Bassuk, Rubin, & Lauriat, 1986; Miller & Lin, 1988; Wood et al., 1990). Statistics on African American families are either not distinguished from those of white families or are included in the overall category of the nonwhite homeless population.

The primary consequences for these families can be seen in problems with mental health (depression and anxiety), education (learning difficulties and attendance problems), and health (lack of needed immunizations, failure to thrive, and substance abuse), with the greatest impact experienced by the children (Bassuk & Rubin, 1987; Fox et al., 1990; Miller & Lin, 1988; Timberlake & Sabatino, 1994). Therefore, these areas, along with housing needs, may represent the primary needs that should be addressed during assessment. They are consistent with the loss, cultural adaptation, and systems impact analyses related to mental health that were discussed in the previous section.

Finally, McChesney (1990) and Wood and colleagues (1990) report that in addition to poverty, the overall low-income housing ratio is the most important environmental condition that influences homelessness. Moreover, two-thirds of Bassuk and colleagues' (1986) sample of homeless families (N=80) reported that housing and social welfare agencies had not been helpful in addressing these environmental conditions. Thus, whereas research has been useful in clarifying the systemic problems of homeless families in general, insufficient attention has been devoted to clarifying their strengths or the special needs of African American families. Two examples of homeless African American families are useful for providing a more balanced perspective on such families.

The Taylor Family

This family consists of Mr. and Ms. Taylor and their four children under 6 years of age. Both Mr. and Ms. Taylor are high school dropouts; they supported their family through employment and resources from their extended families prior to becoming homeless. In fact, they lived with Mr. Taylor's brother for eight months after the former lost one of his two part-time jobs and used up his unemployment compensation. The Taylor family had been living in public housing previously, but they could no longer afford to pay even the subsidized rate they were being charged. Mr. Taylor is in the 18- to 25-year-old African American male population group that has the highest unemployment rates, in this case as a result of his education background and institutionalized racial discrimination.

These chronic and recent losses have taken their toll on the family's problem-solving activities. Ms. Taylor had tried to work to supplement the family's income from time to time, but the cost of child care and her family helping out with child care only periodically made it impossible for her to work regularly. While living with his brother, Mr. Taylor, who had been a heavy drinker previously, gradually became an alcoholic. This meant less of Mr. Taylor's income from his other part-time job was available to buy food. The parents argued about his drinking openly at home, but Ms. Taylor did not want people outside the family to know about the problem, particularly Mr. Taylor's employer. After eight months they were evicted, along with Mr. Taylor's brother, when the latter lost his job in the automobile industry.

At that point, the family applied for food stamps but were told they were not eligible without a permanent address and that there was a waiting list for emergency housing. During the first six months of being homeless, they spent most of their nights in the park or occasionally stayed with other relatives. The cultural ecomap indicates that they are now cut off from most family members who have helped as much as possible but who are also struggling to maintain themselves. Eventually, the Taylors began to spend some nights in the city's two homeless shelters for families when they were able to get there before the maximum number had been admitted. They speak of having little energy to become involved with the other homeless families in the shelters, including the African American families. This lack of ethnic connections has diminished the family's self-esteem and self-value, which indicates that they are not coping adaptively in terms of their cultural needs.

In spite of these problems, the family has many strengths. The parents still nurture and support their children. Mr. Taylor admits he has a drinking problem but feels he can eliminate the problem once the family is stable again. Although extended family resources have been exhausted, these family members are emotionally supportive of the Taylors. Ms. Taylor has tried to send their oldest two children (5 and 6 years of age) to school several days per week. The principal has warned the family that he will refer the oldest child to court, based on the state's compulsory attendance law, if attendance does not improve. The parents blame themselves for the family's plight and consequently tend to ignore how they have become caught between the many environmental systems—including education, housing, public welfare, and health care—that were designed to help families. These same systems are also affecting the family's cultural supports and have made it difficult for those supports to continue to provide resources they made available in the past.

The Simmons Family

Ms. Simmons is a single parent with three children: 6-month-old Derrick, 14-year-old Alice, and 16-year-old Alvin. Ms. Simmons has supported her family with Aid to Families with Dependent Children (AFDC) and part-time employment in the past. She has not returned to work since Derrick's birth because of a lack of low-cost child care. Also, Alvin was able to find a job through a summer youth employment program this past year, which supplemented the family's income. Ms. Simmons has learned that this program will not be funded for the coming summer. Mr. and Ms. Simmons separated one and a half years ago, but he pays child support only periodically, even though he is the father of the youngest child. The prosecutor's office that handles support payments is backed up with similar cases, and it is unlikely it will get around to enforcing these payments soon. These systemic barriers are frustrating to the family as a unit and particularly to Alvin, who sees the system as indifferent to African American families and especially to males.

Ms. Simmons was raised in an alcoholic family, and because of the physical and emotional abuse she experienced in her family she has remained abstinent. This is a strength for her; however, she has recently discovered that Alvin uses marijuana and alcohol. He has several friends who use crack cocaine, and she is fearful Alvin will be tempted to use that drug, too. Alvin sometimes stays out late or all night with his friends and has not been attending school regularly. He is embarrassed about the family being homeless. Ms. Simmons has reacted by denying the multiple losses they have experienced and by saying things will soon be the way they were previously. She has threatened to make Alvin leave their home if he starts using crack, because she does not want him to influence Alice to start using drugs also. Alice has sickle cell anemia, which requires regular medical care. The loss of the family's medical card has made it more difficult for Ms. Simmons to continue to follow the medical regimen necessary for Alice. This had been one of the family strengths in the past, along with Ms. Simmons's efforts to maintain regular employment as a factory worker.

Ms. Simmons lost her AFDC entitlement after she admitted that Mr. Simmons is Derrick's father and that he sometimes spent the night with the family. At that time, the family moved in with Ms. Simmons's aunt, but after several months she asked them to move because of Alvin's substance abuse and late hours. The family has been placed in a former hotel now used as transitional housing for homeless families. It is located in an outlying suburban area away from the central city where the Simmons family lived formerly. A cultural ecomap conducted with the family reveals that this area is mostly white, with only a few Hispanic and African American families, who live mostly in the hotel. The move has caused the Simmons family to be cut off from its family and social support network, along with the culturally oriented, no-cost events available in the neighborhood where they lived previously. The needs and the strengths of the two families that have been described here must be considered in approaches to resolving the interrelated and systemic problems confronting them.

A Multilevel Approach to Serving Homeless Families

Homeless African American families obviously require a comprehensive systems-oriented approach to addressing their needs in general and specific needs based on the two previous examples and discussion. Figure 5.4 represents such an approach, which contains five major components: (1) culturally specific substance abuse treatment, where appropriate; (2) multiple housing options, ranging from transitional to permanent, for families at different stages of the program; (3) survival skills training for improving environmental deficits, such as education, employment, and health care; (4) cultural social supports for enhancing cultural adaptation and ethnic identity; and (5) psycho-education around loss and grief and cultural patterns of coping (Freeman, 1992; Phillips et al., 1988; Phillips, Kronenfeld, & Jeter, 1986). These components could be available as a menu of services, with families receiving only those components that are appropriate to their needs and strengths at a given time.

Some aspects of this approach are noteworthy. First, it is consistent with the ecological perspective illustrated in Figure 5.1 along with the related loss and grief, cultural adaptation, and systems theories that have been discussed. Second, it can be applied to total family units, as well as to individual at-risk members of families. For example, given the current strains within the Simmons family (the second family vignette in the previous section), it may be more effective to serve Alvin, the 16-year-old son, separately from his family—with a group of other unattached and homeless teenagers who could be housed together. The range of program components reflected in Figure 5.4 could be adapted for this population group to a small-group, supervised living situation implemented jointly by the Salvation Army, public schools, and public welfare. The purpose would be to eliminate substance abuse as a developmental and peer-group coping mechanism. Survival skills could emphasize completing high school and then making the transition from school to higher education, vocational training, or the world of work. The housing component could train the adolescents for effective small-group living and could teach them how to initially set up and maintain stable living arrangements. The social support component could emphasize developing a culturally relevant peer network to enhance positively a cultural adaptation and identity. The loss and grief component could address ways to manage the current losses and prevent future

Figure 5.4   Homeless African American Families:
A Multilevel Systemic Approach

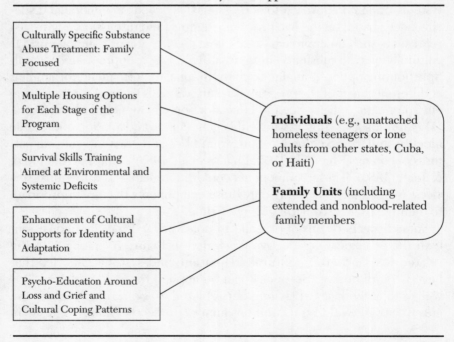

ones among children and youth (e.g., the current loss of self-esteem from discriminatory employment practices and the future loss of the drug culture as part of a successful recovery) (Freeman, 1984). Coping in a culturally relevant way with racial stress and the chronic loss that can accrue from this process is an appropriate issue for both male and female African American youth.

In using the approach with total family units, practitioners in a variety of settings could provide these comprehensive services, which must be focused systemically (McChesney, 1990). The Taylor family, for example, would require the substance abuse intervention and treatment component to handle Mr. Taylor's escalating addiction. This component would need to be culturally specific to handle the unique and common issues African American families are confronted with in comparison to other ethnic groups (i.e., coping with racial stress and cultural adaptation choices and consequences) (Wright, Kail, & Creecy, 1990). Ms. Taylor and the children would need culturally sensitive "how to cope" services designed to help the spouses and children of addicted individuals "give up" any dysfunctional roles they may have assumed in coping with the addiction (Wegscheider-Cruse, 1985).

On the other hand, Ms. Simmons has been abstinent and would require supports to remain abstinent during the current stressful period. She might need a racially mixed or African American Alcoholics Anonymous group for family members to cope with Alvin's substance abuse and any unfinished family-of-origin issues related to her parents' addiction. Such a group could offer networking opportunities, supports, and alternatives for problem solving that fit the perspective of their African American members (Hutchinson, Searight, & Stretch, 1986).

The other components of the approach would need to be provided in a similar culturally relevant way to address housing and the related needs of these families. For instance, Alice's sickle cell anemia requires comprehensive, long-term health care. Some alternative health care resources must be located to help the family in this area, or the practitioner could advocate for service at the health care organization used by the family in the past based on federal health care policies.

Moreover, practitioners must be able to engage these families in open discussion about the lifestyle and cultural issues, including diet and exercise, that can affect chronic health conditions such as Alice's. Helpers should also be skillful in helping families to identify systemic and personal barriers to their continuing access to necessary health care services (Miller & Lin, 1988).

Summary and Conclusion

The problem of homelessness in African American families can only be addressed effectively if other cultural and systemic aspects of the problem are considered. These families routinely encounter stresses that tax their cultural strengths and exacerbate problems they may develop in functioning. As the economy has worsened and become a chronic problem, the face of the homeless problem has also changed. More families of all racial and ethnic backgrounds have been affected, but African American families in particular have suffered as a result of chronic and new barriers to adequate resources. Thus, systemic aspects of the problem—such as the low-income housing ratio, inadequate health care, high unemployment, and racial discrimination—in these areas must be addressed through the approaches being used, as well as through families' personal needs for cultural adaptation and identity. Lastly, the strengths these families possess must be acknowledged and used to help bring about problem resolution and an enhanced quality of life.

References

Atkinson, D. R., G. Morten, & D. W. Sue (Eds.) (1983). *Counseling American minorities: A cross cultural perspective* (2d ed.). Dubuque, IA: William C. Brown.

Bassuk, E., & L. Rubin (1987). Homeless children: A neglected population. *American Journal of Orthopsychiatry, 57,* 279–286.

Bassuk, E. L., L. Rubin & A. Lauriat (1986). The characteristics of sheltered homeless families. *American Journal of Public Health, 76,* 1097–1101.

Cross, W. E., Jr. (1987). A two-factor theory of Black identity: Implications for the study of identity development in minority children. In J. S. Phinney and M. J. Rotheram (Eds.), *Children's ethnic socialization* (pp. 117–133). Newbury Park, CA: Sage Publications.

Fischer, P. (1991). *Alcohol, drug abuse and mental health problems among homeless persons: A review of the literature, 1980–1990.* Rockville, MD: U.S. Department of Health and Human Services, Public Health Service, Alcohol, Drug Abuse, and Mental Health Administration.

Fox, S. J., R. J. Barrnett, M. Davies, & H. R. Bird (1990). Psychopathology and developmental delay in homeless children: A pilot study. *Journal of American Academy of Child and Adolescent Psychiatry, 29,* 732–735.

Freeman, E. M. (1984). Loss and grief in children: Implications for school social workers. *Social Work in Education, 6,* 241–258.

Freeman, E. M. (1990). The black family's life cycle: Operationalizing a strengths perspective. In S. M. Logan, E. M. Freeman, and R. G. McRoy

(Eds.), *Social work practice with Black families: A culturally specific perspective* (pp. 55–72). White Plains, NY: Longman.

Freeman, E. M. (1992). Addicted mothers—addicted infants and children: Strategies for building support networks. In E. M. Freeman (Ed.), *The addiction process: Effective social work approaches* (pp. 108–122). White Plains, NY: Longman.

Freeman, E. M. (1993). Substance abuse treatment: Continuum of care in services to families. In E. M. Freeman (Ed.), *Substance abuse treatment: A family systems perspective* (pp. 1–20). Newbury Park, CA: Sage, Publications.

Freeman, E. M. (1994). Linda and her brother: The short- and long-term impact of homelessness. *Social Work in Education, 16,* 3–6.

Freeman, E. M., & T. Landesman (1992). Differential diagnosis and the least restrictive treatment. In E. M. Freeman (Ed.)., *The addiction process: Effective social work approaches* (pp. 27–42). White Plains, NY: Longman.

Harris, S. N., C. T. Mowbray, & A. Sclarz (1994). Physical health, mental health, and substance abuse problems of shelter users. *Health and Social Work, 19,* 37–45.

Hutchinson, W. J., P. Searight, & J. J. Stretch (1986). *Multidimensional networking: A response to the needs of homeless families.* Princeton, NJ: Robert Weed Johnson Foundation.

Johnson, J. (1992). Educational support services for homeless children and youth. In J. H. Strange (Ed.), *Educational support services for homeless children: Evaluating policy and practice* (pp. 153–176). Newbury Park, CA: Sage Publications.

Kerr, M. E. (1982). Application of family systems theory to a work system. In R. Sagar and K. Wiseman (Eds.), *Understanding organizations* (pp. 121–129). Washington, DC: Georgetown University Family Center.

Kübler-Ross, E. (1968). *On death and dying.* New York: Macmillan.

Kübler-Ross, E. (1982). *Living with death and dying.* New York: Macmillan.

Kübler-Ross, E. (1983). *On children and death.* New York: Macmillan.

Logan, S., E. Freeman, & R. McRoy (1987). Racial identity problems of biracial clients: Implications for social work practice. *Journal of Intergroup Relations, 15*(2), 11–24.

Manns, W. (1981). Support systems of significant others in Black families. In H. P. McAdoo (Ed.), *Black families* (pp. 238–251). Beverly Hills, CA: Sage Publications.

McChesney, K. Y. (1990). Family homelessness: A systemic problem. *Journal of Social Issues, 46,* 191–205.

McRoy, R. G. (1990). Cultural and racial identity in Black families. In S. M. Logan, E. M. Freeman, and R. G. McRoy (Eds.), *Social work practice with Black families: A culturally specific perspective* (pp. 97–112). White Plains, NY: Longman.

Milburn, N. (1989). Drug abuse among the homeless. In J. Momeni (Ed.), *Homeless in the United States,* Vol. 2. Westport, CT: Greenwood Press.

Miller, D. S., & E.H.B. Lin (1988). Children in sheltered homeless families: Reported health status and use of health services. *Pediatrics, 81,* 668–673.

National Alliance to End Homelessness. (1988). *Housing and homelessness.* Washington, DC: National Alliance to End Homelessness.

Phillips, M. H., N. DeChillo, D. Kronenfeld, & V. Middleton-Jeter (1988). Homeless families: Services make a difference. *Journal of Contemporary Social Work, 69,* 48–53.

Phillips, M. H., D. Kronenfeld, & V. Jeter (1986). A model of services to homeless families in shelters. In J. Erickson & C. Wilhelm (Eds.), *Housing the homeless* (pp. 128–148). New Brunswick, NJ: Rutgers Center for Urban Policy Research.

Rhodes, S. L. (1986). Family treatment. In F. J. Turner (Ed.), *Social work treatment: Interlocking theoretical approaches* (pp. 432–453). New York: Free Press.

Tessler, R. C., & D. L. Dennis (1989). *A synthesis of NIMH-funded research concerning homeless mentally ill individuals.* Rockville, MD: National Institute of Mental Health.

Timberlake, E. M., & C. A. Sabatino (1994). Homeless children: Impact of school attendance on self-esteem and loneliness. *Social Work in Education, 16,* 9–20.

Wegscheider-Cruse, S. (1985). *Choice-making for co-dependents, adult children and spiritual seekers.* Palo Alto, CA: Public Health Communications.

Weinreb, L. F., & E. L. Bassuk (1990). Substance abuse: A growing problem among homeless families. *Family and Community Health, 13,* 55–64.

Willie, C. V., B. M. Kramer, & B. S. Brown (1983). *Racism and mental health.* Pittsburgh: University of Pittsburgh Press.

Wood, D., B. Valdez, T. Hayashi, & A. Shen (1990). Homeless and housed families in Los Angeles: A study comparing demographic, economic, and family function characteristics. *American Journal of Public Health, 80,* 1049–1052.

Wright, R., Jr., B. L. Kail, & R. F. Creecy (1990). Culturally sensitive social work practice with Black alcoholics and their families. In S. M. Logan, E. M. Freeman, & R. G. McRoy (Eds.), *Social work practice with Black families: A culturally specific perspective* (pp. 203–223). White Plains, NY: Longman.

Ziter, M.L.P. (1987). Culturally sensitive treatment of Black alcoholic families. *Social Work, 32,* 130–137.

6

Reconceptualizing Youth Violence: Implications for Positive Change

SARAH G. MITCHELL
SADYE L. LOGAN

> When spider webs unite, they can tie up a lion.
> —Etophia

It is common knowledge that violence is increasing in the United States. But what is not so commonly known is that concerned citizens are committed to creating nurturing and healthy communities to support children and family growth. This chapter not only addresses this expanded vision of hope but also examines some of the issues connected to the current state of affairs. For example, the 1991 *Public Health Reports* state that 2.2 million Americans suffer nonfatal injuries as a result of interpersonal violence each year, homicide is the tenth leading cause of death in the United States, and the homicide rate among young males is 20 times higher than the rate in any other industrial country. Additionally, there are more gun dealers in the United States than there are gas stations, and 20,000 new guns are put on the market every day (Moyers, 1995). Violence plagues U.S. urban centers at a rate four times higher than violence in rural areas (*Statistical Abstract of the United States,* 1991). Crime within the inner city occurs at an even more alarming rate.

Since a large majority of this country's African American population resides in urban areas (*Statistical Abstract,* 1991), Blacks are much more likely to be victims of violence than are whites. In 1977 alone, more Black men died from homicides (5,734) than died in the 10 years of the Vietnam War (5,640) (Gibbs, 1988; Wilson, 1990). African American males have a 1-in-27 chance of being murdered, compared to a 1-in-205 chance for white males (*Public Health Reports,* 1991). In 1988, over half of the homicides of African Americans between the ages of 15 and 24 were concentrated in six urban centers in California, Florida, Michigan, Missouri, New York, and Washington, D.C. (Gibbs, 1994).

Adolescents in general are vulnerable to participation in and victimization by violence because of their feelings of invincibility, attraction to peer groups, and risk-taking behavior. Because of the adverse social, economic, and environmental conditions African American youth face, these teenagers are especially vulnerable to street pressures. Many of today's African American youth are turning to gangs to gain a sense of belonging and group identity, to mask feelings of alienation and devaluation, to gain protection within a highly violent society, and to obtain money and goods not available to them otherwise. Gang involvement also serves as a way for African American males and females to feel empowered. However, although the gang may meet many of its members' social needs and rebellion may be justified, its energy is often misdirected. Rather than bringing about social change, the gang's actions often involve aggressive and violent crimes against the community. Perkins cautions the African American community that "to suggest that street gangs are necessary because they do meet some of the basic needs of Black youth reflects a serious breakdown in our institutions. But until we are successful in reinforcing those strengths which still exist among most Black families and in holding institutions accountable for their services to youth, the Black street gangs will continue to prevail" (1987, p. 60).

Much national attention has been given to the issue of youth violence. Social service agencies, schools, and community groups have developed programs to prevent and deter violence. However, the increasingly conservative U.S. political climate is creating a backlash against such proactive stances in favor of reactive and punitive measures to deal with crime and violence. Government resources are being channeled away from counseling, after-school, and community-centered programs and into the criminal justice system, with its focus on social control, prosecution, punishment, and incarceration—even though there is no evidence that such tactics are effective. Forces sympathetic to today's youth, especially African American youth, must act now, for the "war on crime" is likely only to place more young African American men behind bars.

Since the government is highly unlikely to lend itself as a resource for broad-based change regarding the issue of violence, which disproportionately affects the Black community, leadership regarding youth violence must come from within the African American community itself. There is a growing movement in the Black community whose primary focus is to utilize its collective strengths and take control of the problem. Loury (1985), one of the advocates for strong community involvement, warns that depending on the government to resolve problems that concern Black Americans is dangerous, for it places the responsibility for change in the hands of "those who do not have an abiding interest in such matters" (pp. 10–11).

As indicated earlier, it is our intent to examine state-of-the-art issues regarding urban violence and adolescent participation in violence and gang-related activities. The vitality and strengths of the Black family and the Black community are highlighted, as well as strategies that have already been employed to address youth violence. Overall, emphasis is placed on reconceptualizing the growing phenomenon of youth violence. Additionally, areas of strengths within all aspects of the African American community that have potential to effect positive change regarding violence prevention are discussed.

A Perspective on Urban Violence

Numerous theories attempt to explain the prevalence of violence among African American youth in metropolitan areas. Some attribute the high rates of violence associated with Black youth (Gibbs, 1988) to poverty, limited economic opportunities, and nonnurturing families, whereas others (Grier & Cobbs, 1968) suggest that the root cause is chronic stress, which creates feelings of frustration and aggression that are then discharged onto others in the community. Environmental hypotheses (Farley, 1980, Gibbs, 1988) encompass both perspectives and also take into account demographic and structural components. From this perspective, it is believed that the overcrowded, disorganized, and isolating conditions of the inner city naturally produce high levels of stress, depression, and feelings of hopelessness, powerlessness, and social alienation among youth, who then act out their despair with violent behavior.

All three theories bring important perspectives to the understanding of urban violence as a complex phenomenon, since all of these factors undoubtedly play a significant role in the creation of this growing problem. We contend that this phenomenon is best viewed and conceptualized on a continuum. In this way, much of the complexity that is suggested by the various theories is acknowledged to some extent.

Changing Community Structures

It is evident that urban areas contain fertile ground for the creation and perpetuation of violent behavior. An especially salient feature of modern urban centers is the loss of community or of a feeling of connectedness, as occupational and residential mobility makes it difficult to maintain interpersonal ties. The individualism, materialism, and secularism of the city are rapidly replacing traditional African American values of community, collective sharing, and faith (Martin & Martin, 1978). The ensuing tenuity of human relationships, coupled with these shifts in values, has decreased the amount of respect given to all human life, which for some people (i.e., drug dealers and criminals) has become a commodity to be traded for goods and money.

Small neighborhoods, which tend to facilitate feelings of unity and commonality, have been replaced by large housing projects where thousands of people live together in a relatively small radius. It is inevitable that the lack of space and the sheer number of different personalities within such structures will generate high levels of social disorganization and interpersonal conflicts. Cloward and Ohlin (1960) found that big-city housing projects and slums "produce powerful pressures for violent behavior among youth" (in Hagedorn, 1991, p. 532).

The developmental impact on youth who grow up in violent areas further contributes to the breakdown in the sense of community. When children live in a climate of violence, they are socialized into a world of fear, aggression, and hatred. An entire generation of children is being raised that has learned, as a form of protection, to be emotionless, cold, and nonempathic (Poole, 1991). The development of these defenses against violence has a strong damaging effect on children's abilities to connect with others and form lasting relationships. Furthermore, children learn through first-hand experience about the casualness of the worth of human life (Schwartz, 1982). Children's inability to form meaningful, lasting relationships and their belief in the worthlessness of human life create a situation in which reacting violently, even lethally, is far too easy.

Other critical factors that affect healthy adolescent development relate to the availability of positive role models. The increased economic solvency of segments of the African American population has generated distance between the middle and upper income levels and the poor (Gibbs, 1988; Williams, 1990). As the more economically secure segments of the African American community leave the stressful conditions of urban life in favor of a suburban lifestyle, youths growing up in the inner city are mainly exposed to adults who are openly involved in drugs, gambling, prostitution, and other criminal behavior.

Furthermore, the declining economic base of the city has produced high rates of unemployment. The financial instability of the inner city and loss of industrial jobs, as well as racism, have led to extremely high levels of unemployment among African Americans. U.S. Department of Labor statistics from 1987 showed that whereas the national unemployment rate was 5.8 percent and the unemployment rate for all teenagers was 16.1 percent, Black youth were unemployed at the rate of 33.4 percent. During the same period, the unemployment rate for African American adolescents in urban areas was between 40 and 50 percent (Gibbs, 1989). Even when African American men are able to find work, their employment opportunities are marked by inequality (Morrisey, 1990; Williams, 1990).

The implications of the excessive unemployment common among Black adolescents are both psychological and physical. The U.S. emphasis, especially for men, on work and self-sufficiency and the subsequent devaluation of those who do not work can have detrimental effects on African American youth. The denial of access to jobs and the realization that employment will not yield the same economic rewards for them that it does for others in society may lead to low self-esteem, poor self-image, and feelings of powerlessness, frustration, and resentment. As indicated earlier, such a combination of negative feelings becomes the breeding ground for the expression of violence. May (1972) cautioned that

> As we make people powerless we promote their violence rather than its control. Deeds of violence in our society are performed largely by those trying to establish their self-esteem, to defend their self-image, and to demonstrate that they, too, are significant. Regardless of how derailed or wrongly used these motivations may be or how destructive their expression, they are still the manifestation of positive interpersonal needs. We cannot ignore the fact that, no matter how difficult their redirection may be, these needs themselves are potentially constructive. Violence arises not out of superfluity of power, but out of powerlessness. As Hannah Arendt has so well said, violence is the expression of impotence. (p. xvi)

Coser (1967) also stated that "where no social status can be achieved through socioeconomic channels it may yet be achieved in the show of violence among equally deprived peers" (p. xvii).

Since U.S. society is characterized by conspicuous consumption and bestows admiration on those who possess material goods, unemployed adolescents who do not have access to money and possession are likely not only to act out against the society that places economic barriers in their way but also to find other avenues to gain the trappings of success. The temptation to use illegitimate means to obtain material goods when legitimate means do not exist may be stronger in teenagers, who are highly image conscious. Thus, adolescents often turn to criminal activities, such as robbery or drug dealing, and participate in gangs whose expressed purpose is to acquire money and goods for their members. Wilson (1990) writes, "Much Black-on-Black violence, robbery, thievery, assault, stealing, and others, are motivated by Black males seeking to obtain or purchase these objects they have been conditioned to think of as important to their status and high regard" (p. 146). Contrary to popular belief, it is the members of the Black community, not white Americans, who are mainly affected by adolescents' predations because of their physical proximity to the teenagers. Furthermore, adolescents involved in criminal activities are also in danger of becoming homicide casualties themselves as their victims fight back during the crime or seek retaliation afterward.

Stress and Black Adolescent Development

African American adolescents, at a highly stressful developmental life stage, must confront racism, inequality, and exclusion. Within this context, many lack real opportunities to succeed. Feelings of personal impotence often result in interpersonal violence as adolescents seek to bolster their poor self-image and ward off anxious, self-contemptuous feelings. Wilson (1990) theorizes that the "violent search for power, status, material worth, excesses and comforts, hostile independence, is energized by a thousand psychological nicks and cuts" (p. 78) inflicted by a racist society.

In Erikson's (1968) view, as adolescents work to solidify an identity and develop goals for the future, their social milieu shifts from the family to society. There is a marked increase in inter- and intrapersonal conflicts as they begin to scrutinize and question the world from their expanding viewpoint. As their world is broadened, society's evaluation becomes more important and, in turn, fear of ridicule surfaces, causing adolescents to take reactionary stances whenever they feel they will be unable to perform certain tasks. For adolescents who have misgivings about their ability to measure up to society's ideas of success, the adoption of a "negative identity" may be a more appealing option than to "struggle for a feeling of reality in acceptable roles" (Erikson, 1959, p. 132).

Although it is a useful point of reference for all adolescents, it is also important to keep in mind that Erikson's perspective is geared primarily toward non-Black youths. For most African American youths the world may never expand or broaden (Logan, 1981). As Black adolescents confront U.S. racism and exclusionary practices, they may not only be deterred from attempting to meet societal expectations but also may actively reject working toward the less desirable roles they perceive the world has reserved for them. Feeling alienated from and rejected by society, and having found few traditionally accepted roads to achievement and accomplishment, Black adolescents have developed several "adaptation styles" (Gibbs, 1988). Some of these styles that are delinquency-prone include the "exploiter," the "rebel without a cause" (Gibbs, 1988; McCord et al., 1969), and the "tough guy" (Gibbs, 1988; Mancini, 1980). More recently, the embracing by young Black men of the coping style known as the "cool pose" (Majors & Billson, 1992; Majors et al., 1994) has received much attention.

The cool pose began as a coping mechanism to counter discrimination, invisibility, and the frustrations that accompany denied access to meaningful education and employment. It is a construction of masculine symbols in the form of a particular walk, stance, and demeanor underscored with clothing, hairstyles, and handshakes. For many Black youth, this combination of mannerisms and actions is "a way to act cool and show the dominant culture that they are strong, proud, and capable of survival despite their low status in society" (Majors et al., 1994, p. 247). With its emphasis on toughness, emotional detachment, and aggression, the cool pose becomes an exaggerated form of socially expected masculinity.

Although the cool pose may aid in the psychological survival of these young African American males, it also invites problems for Black youth. Young Black males who are not involved in delinquent behavior but adopt the cool pose as a self-protective measure may find themselves more often in a position to defend their tough image. Ironically, a stance developed to cope with the feelings of defenselessness, powerlessness, and fear common to residents of violent inner cities may instead invite more violence.

Equally dangerous are teenagers' narcissistic tendencies, which can have devastating effects when manifested in a violent environment (Prothrow-Stith, 1991). Not only does narcissism impair judgment, so teens may not flee dangerous situations when necessary, but the adolescents' narcissistic pride must be defended at all costs. Thus, every situation is a drama, every interaction essential, every consequence dire. The adolescent cannot back down from an insult, cannot say he or she is sorry, and must defend his or her honor. Apologizing for a mistaken nudge or a wrong word is impossible, since everything is about saving face and one's honor.

Under normal conditions, the strength of the family and secondary institutions (school, church, community center) within a community provide strong guidance for adolescents and can positively counteract the negative effects of the stressors teens experience. However, the rampant unemployment and poverty of the inner city have weakened these institutions. Historically, the African American family has been a place of shelter for its youth, who are devalued by a large part of the U.S. population. The family's vitality has enabled African American youth to develop a sense of moral values, competence, and positive self-regard through its nurturing (Chestang, 1976).

Thus, the changing structures and dynamics of some African American families are particularly detrimental to African American youth living within the violent culture of the inner city. Whereas relatively strong family organization may control youthful nonconformity, families that are underorganized may be unable to constrain youth and may unknowingly promote juvenile delinquency (Spergel, 1984). Wilson (1990) writes that the changing structure of the African American family "frequently leaves its children without a warm, caring, protective, and wise parental system with which to identify and with which they can overcome an encroaching sense of emotional and social isolation: a system which can be their ally in their embattled struggle against a hostile world" (p. 155).

The precarious viability of urban secondary institutions makes it difficult for schools, community centers, social service agencies, and police forces to meet the needs of inner-city residents and youth. Education budget cuts, along with a growing student population, have left public schools crippled and in disrepair. Outdated curricula and stressed, apathetic teachers mean students are denied a meaningful education. Dealing with financial constraints, schools have been forced to pare their offerings down to the basics. Art, music, and extracurriculars have become sparse or nonexistent, and students are left without outlets for joy and self-expression, as well as distractions from the appeal of delinquent behavior. Reductions in federal, state, and local funds to social service agencies and community centers have prevented program development, decreased present offerings, and hampered the effectiveness of existing services. Urban police forces, plagued by corruption and racism, do not inspire trust from the African American community, which may reluctantly call on the police for aid with disruptive and criminal elements within its neighborhoods. The behavior of law enforcement officials also fails to provide incentive for adolescents to believe in the goodness of law and order. Without strong family units and an effective network of secondary institutions, African American youths are left to meet their own needs and to fend for themselves within a violent world. For these adolescents, gratification of their needs, as well as protection, is often found through participation in delinquency groups and gangs.

Despite attempts to decrease the amount of urban violence and gang activity, violence within the inner city has not lessened. However, this fact should not be taken to mean that the problem is irreversible but rather to indicate that all Americans must strengthen their resolve to end this epidemic. The following sections describe the characteristics of youth gangs and discuss specific strategies and the role of the family and the community in working toward breaking the cycle of violence.

Youth Gangs

In considering the development and evolution of youth gangs, it is important to consider this process from the gang member's perspective—a perspective that is usually set against a nonnurturing family background. The following scenario is based, in part, on a real-life situation. It is a typical story, regardless of gender or ethnicity:

> Imagine being a 14 year old adolescent growing up in a deteriorating inner city. Your stepfather has raped you, he beats your mother, and family life is essentially chaotic. You have been in and out of foster care because your alcoholic mom is mostly unable to care for you. Currently you have learned that the most effective way to keep your mother sober is to beat her. It takes between 15 to 20 minutes to subdue her. After beating your mother you must calm your 3 year old sister. This tragic existence makes it

easier to physically attack others, to rob a store or to "mug" a stranger for money that you need, especially when the act of mugging is so easy; lasting for less than three minutes. (Le Blanc, 1994, p. 28)

In general, gangs are large, highly structured institutions that contain leaders and core and marginal members. Although on the national level most gangs are male-dominated, all-girl gangs are increasing both locally and nationally (Abner, 1994; Le Blanc, 1994). The age of gang members can run the gamut from preadolescence to middle-aged. Typically, in street gangs members vary in age from 12 to 20 years. Given that no prerequisite age for gang membership exists, it is not rare to find gang members at the grade school level. According to the Gang Manual of the National Law Enforcement Institute (1993, 1995), members ages 14 to 18 tend to be the most violent. Coupled with the development issue of peer acceptance, this age group is also trying extremely hard to prove itself to the older members.

Names, colors, and territories associated with gangs may last for decades. The Black Gangster Disciples, established in 1966 on Chicago's south side, are still in existence today. The Crips and Blood or Pirus in southern California generally identify themselves with the colors blue and red, respectively. Crips refer to one another as "Cuzz," and Bloods call each other "Blood." Each group may refer to another member of its set as a "homeboy" or "homie" (Gang Manual, National Law Enforcement Institute, 1993, 1995).

Gangs may engage in a variety of criminal and noncriminal activities. Narcotics trafficking, most often crack cocaine, has been identified as the predominant criminal activity of Crips and Bloods (Gang Manual, National Law Enforcement Institute, 1993, 1995). However, major objectives of gangs are the acquisition of notoriety and status, protection for members, and maintenance of turf and income-producing activities (Spergel, 1984). The gang is committed to achieving these goals through violent means. Differing somewhat from gangs, delinquent groups are small, ad hoc, and loosely knit associations of two or more youths, usually males between the ages of 10 and 17 years, who commit minor to serious crimes. These groups tend to be more expressive and less purposeful than criminal groups or gangs (Spergel, 1984; Curry & Spergel, 1992). However, the less organized delinquency groups often commit similar disturbances and also meet the needs of the adolescents and young adults who join them, just as larger gangs do.

Unfortunately, the reduced economic opportunities in depressed neighborhoods leave most teenagers with few legitimate avenues to economic success. The gang, with its offering of access to goods and money, becomes much more appealing when youths do not see other roads that will lead them to success (Abner, 1994). Indeed, Oliver (1989) theorizes that institutional racism and alienation, which place African Americans in the lower part of the socioeconomic scale, lead to greater gang involvement. For African American youth who are denied real, meaningful, and lucrative work, robbery, burglary, and drug dealing cease to be viewed as criminal activities and begin to be seen as opportunities for prosperity. For older males, gang involvement may be viewed as a means of survival. Adolescents often stay in gangs long past the age when most would suspect they would have outgrown this youthful institution. Hagedorn (1991) believes many of these young men maintain their connection with the gang since there are few jobs to which they can "age-out" (p. 530).

Past and current research indicates that gangs flourish when the needs of youth are not met by primary and secondary institutions (Fox, 1985; Hagedorn, 1991; Tannenbaum, 1938). The weakening of family values and the paucity of positive secondary institutions common to many urban areas provide fertile ground for the development of gangs. Numerous factors account for why families experience difficulties in serving as a buffer to protect children from the daily stresses and struggles of life within the inner city. Financial worries, poor mental health, and simply being overburdened with the day-to-day problems-in-living are the most common challenges for parents.

As previously mentioned, inner-city churches, community groups, and law enforcement agencies are also in a weakened state. Thus, these institutions, which normally supplement the family's care of children and adolescents, cannot meet or satisfy the youths' needs either. Under such circumstances adolescents, believing they may not be able to successfully meet societal expectations and feeling isolated from secondary institutions, frequently turn to other sources (i.e., the gang) to gratify their needs. Once it has formed, the indigenous and youthful nature of the gang makes the eradication of this institution rather difficult (Anders, 1994: Tannenbaum, 1938).

Racism also contributes to high rates of gang activity in urban areas. The existence of Black gangs is symbolic of the frustration of African American males (Majors et al., 1994) and females. Like the cool pose,

membership in gangs allows Black adolescents to defend against feelings of insignificance, alienation, and devaluation inflicted upon them
by the larger society. The gang provides an arena for these young men
and, sometimes, young women to express their independence and to
rebel against society's racist strictures and any form of authority.

Yet whereas the gang may help Black adolescents to alleviate their
immediate intrapsychic pain, this does not come without a price. Gang
membership also carries a greater exposure to violence and increases
the possibility of incarceration and death. Ironically, gangs may purport
to offer their members protection against a violent society, but their
very existence increases the need for such protection (Anders, 1994).

Nevertheless, for adolescents the benefits of gang involvement often
outweigh the costs. The gang provides disenfranchised youth with a
sense of identity, belonging, power, security, and discipline (Perkins,
1987). These are strong reinforcers for teenagers who are struggling to
form a solid identity separate from their families and to control their
conflicting impulses, drives, and hormonal shifts. Perkins (1987) writes
of adolescents who joined gangs despite the risks that accompany such a
decision: "They were willing to take the risk because the gang was the
one group that accepted them as they were" (p. 34).

As youths join gangs for a wide variety of reasons, the cycle of violence becomes entrenched in urban areas. The effects of urban violence
are far-reaching. On the individual level, the psychic toll of overexpo-
sure to violence may manifest itself in an inability to form positive
human relationships, feelings of anxiety and depression, self-destructive
behavior, and moral impairment (Garbarino, Kostelny, & Dubrow,
1991; Goleman, 1986; Prothrow-Stith, 1991; Schwartz, 1982). Families,
too, suffer from members' difficulty in forming supportive relations and
in increased domestic violence (Gibbs, 1994). Within the community
fear is common, and unity is sacrificed as various elements within the
community find themselves at odds with one another (Hagedorn, 1991).
Often, order must be restored by outside elements such as the police
and prisons, which may increase the anger of the local population. The
hostility between youth and residents, home owners, and shopkeepers
results in more violence. As businesses close and those who are able to
do so leave the neighborhood, there is a general decay in the functioning of the community (Gibbs, 1994). Indeed, violence seeps into all aspects of our society, destroying the very fabric of the nation by decreas-
ing the sense of trust and safety that holds society together (Getzel &
Masters, 1986; Prothrow-Stith, 1991).

The Family and Community as a Resource

A factor common to the Black family and community is their extraordinary resiliency. African Americans have drawn upon the vitality of their traditional African heritage and strengths of spirit, family, and community to survive and overcome the abominations of slavery, segregation, and discrimination. Norton (1976) and other Black theorists point to the enormously powerful mechanisms working in African Americans that have enabled them to function under such adverse conditions. Certainly, the Black community has a long tradition of working to improve the quality of life for itself and for its children.

The Black family has been an undying source of energy and power. Despite the challenge of surviving in the inner city, many Black families remain intact and are dynamic and vigorous groupings that provide adequately for their members. The extended family is a particularly important aspect of African American life (Billingsley, 1968; Billingsley, 1992; Martin & Martin, 1978). Black Americans have more frequent contact with their extended families than do other Americans (Hayes & Mendel, 1973; Tidwell, 1990). The significance of the extended family dates back to slavery when it was a necessity of survival to share food, clothes, lodging, and child care. Today the extended family still gives financial and material support, and it also lends emotional support during times of stress and provides a sense of history, identity, and acceptance for its members (Billingsley, 1992; Martin & Martin, 1978).

The strength of Black families is vital for the well-being of African American youth, since the family must not only shield its children from the negative evaluation placed on Blacks by racist elements within society but must also model and teach healthy characteristics that will support a strong sense of self. McRoy (1990) writes that "the Black child's significant others are to be found in the family and the Black community, not in the larger society of which his community is a part. Self-evaluation occurs largely within a comparative or relativistic framework and grows out of the child's experience in the immediate community" (p. 99).

African Americans have a strong history of pulling together with the aim of bettering the condition under which the entire community lives. From informal supportive networks of family and friends to formal national civil rights organizations, self-help initiatives have always been present within the African American community (Billingsley, 1992; Rodgers & Tartaglia, 1990). The 1960s especially were a time of great civic and political action by the Black populace. The United Black Fund was developed to ensure that proper funding went to Washington, D.C.'s African American community (Rodger & Tartaglia, 1990). The Congress of Racial Equality, the Student Nonviolent Coordinating Committee, the National Association for the Advancement of Colored People, the Nation of Islam, and the Black Panthers, along with the average citizen, promoted pride in self and in the African American culture. These massive efforts supported the fight against discrimination and segregation. The use of boycotts, sit-ins, marches, and mass demonstrations resulted in the passing of the Civil Rights Act of 1964 and a 1954 ruling in *Brown vs. Board of Education* that ended school segregation. Many of these organizations also created breakfast, after-school, tutoring, youth recreation, and voter education programs that served the community (Gibbs, 1994). These organizations, along with Black churches, clubs, fraternities and sororities, and political action groups, continue to fight and develop programs today.

Contemporary Efforts to Address Violence

Currently, many Black-oriented organizations are focusing their efforts through such vehicles as crime summits, town meetings, and special task forces on the issue of youth violence. For example, the Black Task Force on Child Abuse and Neglect has endeavored to educate social service providers and the community about the steps necessary to decrease youth violence by sponsoring several symposia dedicated to the cause. Similarly, the Black Community Crusade for Children (BCCC) seeks to mobilize the African American community on behalf of all Black children and families by educating the community on the state of crisis facing Blacks, building leadership within the community, supporting personal and organizational efforts to help Black children, and promoting initiatives and policies that will ensure that Black children are given a healthy start and stay safe throughout their lives. Much of the BCCC's work with teenagers focuses on violence prevention.

The BCCC's Northeast Coast regional office, the Rheedlen Center for Children and Families, has developed several programs to alleviate the problem of youth violence. The Beacon Program, in conjunction with other community organizations, works to educate, recreate, and provide social services to revitalize the community (Rubin, 1994). Housed in a public school because Rheedlen believes this is the most sensible place to meet the community's needs, the Beacon Program also strives to create "corridors of safety" that are free of violence for the community's residents. Another Rheedlen-sponsored community and school-based venture is the Peace Makers Program and its particularly important component, Safety Nights (Lewis, 1994). Assessing that the busiest time in New York City's Harlem Hospital's Emergency Room was Friday and Saturday nights between the hours of 4 P.M. and midnight because of the increase in violent altercations among youths at these hours, the Peace Makers now keep the school open one night per month during this time period to provide the youths with recreational activities and at least a minor respite from violence. With more funding, it may be possible to expand the amount of Safety Nights offered.

Individually, many African Americans are banding together and utilizing their strength, knowledge, and ingenuity to address the issue of youth violence. Many Black Americans are relying on an African-centered approach to guide the youth to health and well-being. They call for a return to the traditional African belief system, with its values of spirituality, truth, harmony, balance, propriety, order, and justice and its principles of the interconnectedness of all human life, respect for elders and family, and nonmaterialistic thinking (Gilbert & Tyehimba-Taylor, 1994; Harvey, 1994).

Kansas City, Missouri's, Chick Elementary School is not unlike the Milwaukee All Black Boys' School, which employs an African-centered curriculum (Majors, 1994; school principal, personal communication, 1995). Although any student who wishes can attend these schools, the classes include African and African American history along with basic subjects. Both schools focus on helping Black youngsters develop pride in self and in their culture by reclaiming historical African values and emphasizing cooperation, mutual respect, commitment, and love of self, family, race, and community.

Especially prevalent in the Black community's work to aid youths in choosing more positive life courses are mentoring, role modeling, and rite-of-passage programs. Kunjufu (1985, 1986, 1990, 1995) stresses the need for one-year rites-of-passage programs for African American males. Others call for manhood training to teach appropriate roles for fathers, husbands, sons, and brothers; to increase political awareness and commitment to community service; and to decrease the power of negative influences (Gibbs, 1994; Majors, 1994). Similar programs are also being advocated for girls.

SIMBA, which stands for "Lion" in Swahili, is such a program that was developed by Roland Gilbert. Based on the African concept that it takes an entire village to raise a child, SIMBA provides a network of

positive male role models to guide young Black males from childhood to
manhood. Integral to the vision is the belief that "people are more important than objects and each of us has power to choose our own behavior in spite of other people and circumstances" (Gilbert & Tyehimba-
Taylor, 1994, p. 34). Black men who join the program go through
intensive training before they begin to work with the young boys to
make sure they have healed their own psychic wounds and are fully prepared to take on the task of healing others. Along similar lines, Flani is a
rite-of-passage program designed especially for young Black girls.
Among other authors, Lewis's (1988) work provides the essential guidelines that can be utilized by local interest groups in designing such programs. Several less structured role-modeling programs exist in several
major metropolitan areas, where mature men and women provide
teenage boys and girls with guidance, support, and exposure to alternate
life and career choices.

Many Black adolescents themselves have also become involved in attempts to overcome youth violence. New York City's Health Watch
Players, directed by Wendell Moore, is made up of a group of teenagers
who travel to schools to enact role-plays, provide workshops, and discuss the dangers of violence with their peers. With chapters throughout
the United States, Teens on Target is another organization of young
people who teach youth with the use of role-plays, testimonials, and lec-
tures about the reality of violence. Teens on Target also offers support
groups for victims and works to make broad-based change by educating
policy-makers.

Black youths in junior and senior high schools are also becoming involved in conflict resolution and mediation programs, in which students
are trained in skills such as decisionmaking, communication, and mediation. These approaches not only reduce the potential for violence
through the resolution of individual students' conflicts with others but
also provide the participants with the opportunity to be part of something positive. Peer mediators become empowered, and their self-esteem improves as they begin to see the positive effects of their work.

A Perspective on Prevention and Change

Although the present antiviolence work of individuals and organizations
is a fine start, the magnitude of the problem of youth violence demands
a more healthful and expanded vision if the United States is to effec-

tively provide hope and growth experiences for its troubled youths. Since youth violence stems from a complex array of psychological, environmental, sociological, economic, and political factors, the scope of future violence prevention and change efforts must be broad and comprehensive. These endeavors must not only address the underlying economic and social causes of unemployment, underemployment, poverty, racism, and discrimination, which have left the inner-city Black family and community in a weakened state, but must also attempt to alleviate the poor self-esteem and feelings of alienation, depression, and hopelessness of many Black youths.

Given the complex nature of this situation, a multilevel approach to prevention and change is proposed (see Figure 6.1). We contend that change will result from enhancing the overall functioning of children and youths through strengthening the Black family and community; deterrence through fortifying existing secondary institutions and creating more community-centered programs; and achieving social change

Figure 6.1   A Multilevel Approach to Prevention and Change

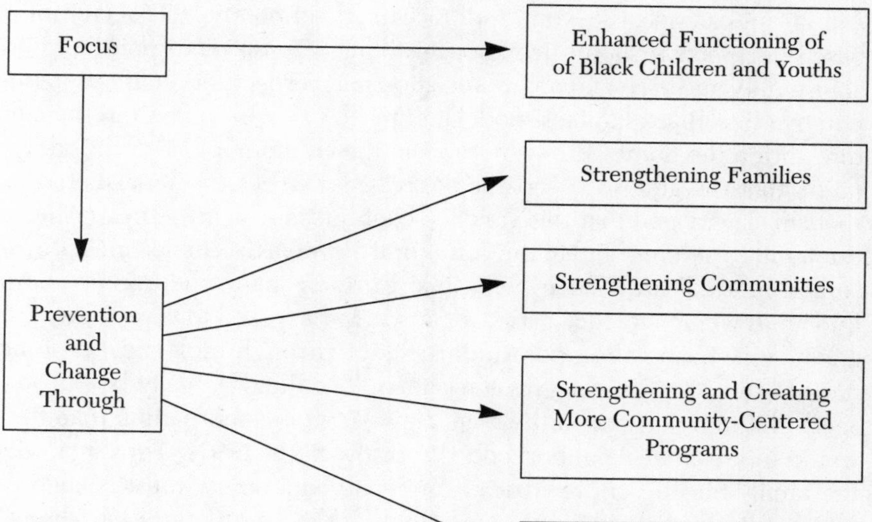

through political action, appropriations of funds, lobbying, and a re-framing of the issues.

A first step toward strengthening Black families must be psychic heal-ing (Harvey, 1994). The same detrimental conditions African American youth face are the same circumstances African American parents en-countered during their formative years and in which they continue to live today. The psychological toll on individuals has been great. Black parents must address their own pains and disappointments to lend ef-fective guidance to their children. For example, African American chil-dren frequently see that their parents are still harassed, insulted, and as-saulted by racist elements within U.S. culture despite their law-abiding behavior, solid citizenship, and hard work. Viewing these incidents, African American youths may see no reason to continue to struggle in their own lives if they believe they will be subjected to similar devalua-tion (Harvey, 1994). If African American parents have not come to terms with their own thoughts and feelings regarding their oppression, they will be unable to thoughtfully answer their children's inquiries about racism and inequities in the United States.

Harvey (1994), among others, believes education, skill development, and counseling based on an African-centered philosophy is one way Black Americans can heal the wounds of racism and oppression. This culturally based perspective should focus on instilling a sense of responsibility to community and race and an appreciation and respect for all life. It is im-perative that Black families model and teach pride in self and in the cul-ture within the home and with others in the community. With the recog-nition that the genesis of violent behavior for African Americans has its roots in slavery and that this violence continues for many African Ameri-can families at home and in the community, a proactive stance must be as-sumed in eradicating such behaviors. Further, many children are born into areas where violence exists and are never exposed to ways to express anger, upset, and disappointment except through violence. In some neighborhoods, where aggression and violence may actually be encour-aged, children may act on their aggressive impulses more often than they would in a calmer neighborhood (Prothrow-Stith, 1991). Thus, not only the family but the entire African American community must change its social attitudes toward aggression. Through the use of education, discus-sion, and challenges, Black community leaders, churches, and organiza-tions should help to lead the way because of their already powerful and respected position in the community (Gibbs, 1988).

Although parents need to take primary responsibility for their children, the entire Black community and interested individuals outside that community must make a commitment to support the efforts of parents and aid in changing the downward spiral experienced by many African American children. Black families that are functioning well need to become involved with families that are struggling by developing supportive networks, child-care associations, and food cooperatives (Gibbs, 1988). Adopt-a-family programs that would pair viable Black families with families in need of assistance is another way for African Americans to invest in their community. Retired members can reinvest in the neighborhood by providing child care, tutoring, and counseling (Gibbs, 1988). As older African Americans volunteer their time, the youth will also have access to their wisdom about life, Black history, and Black culture. It is also essential that African Americans continue to join role-modeling programs to supplement the efforts of single-parent households, which tend to have higher rates of youths involved in gangs and violence (Perkins, 1987).

Furthermore, it is vital that "people resources" stay in the community. This means the middle class and working class, as well as college graduates, need to make a commitment to remain in their communities. When these persons leave the inner city an important "social buffer" for the poor and positive role models are lost (Franklin, 1994). It is necessary for these African Americans who may have more financial and emotional strength at their disposal to create a network of strong adults that can provide a positive sense of identity, security, discipline, belonging, and self-esteem to Black youth while also lending support to the entire community.

The Black community must continue to make concerted efforts to gain financial stability and reinvest in itself economically (Gibbs, 1988; Harvey, 1994). Neighborhoods need to organize around such endeavors as the development of African American–owned businesses and movements to return African American money to the community. Presently, only five cents of every dollar stays in the Black community, whereas approximately $300 billion is spent in the white community each year (Wilson, 1990). Strides in this direction would increase the employment opportunities for African Americans and also lessen the decay of inner-city neighborhoods.

Finally, African Americans must continue in the traditions established by those families that have decided to push drugs out of their neighborhoods. Drugs account for a large part of violence in inner-city areas, as dealers protect their turf and users commit crimes while under the influence and to obtain the funds necessary to score more product (Gross, 1995).

Schools must continue to be targeted for youth gang prevention (National School Safety Center, 1990). It has been found that the better a youth's school performance, the less likely he or she is to become involved in gangs or violent activities (Perkins, 1987; Spergel, 1986). African American parents must be the catalyst for such change. Although Black parents value education and care deeply about their children's education (Freeman, 1990; Logan, Freeman, & McRoy, 1990), several factors impede their public display of support for their children within the school system. Many African American parents who are struggling to make ends meet do not have the time or money for child care and thus cannot attend school functions on a frequent basis. The National Education Association (1987) found that in urban areas, Black parents often felt alienated from educational institutions. Schools did not have outreach programs except for the Parent-Teachers Association and infrequently gave Black parents enough information to make informed decisions about their children's education (Caple, 1990).

African Americans must not only be encouraged to confront these issues to make schools true community assets and places sensitive to the needs of Black children, but they must also make efforts to join Parent-Teachers Associations, vote in school board elections, and gain positions on local school boards. Parents who are already involved in the school must reach out to other Black parents in the community to encourage more participation in their children's education. With this increased involvement, African American parents should help in planning a more diversified curriculum and push for cultural sensitivity in hiring practices. The cooperative efforts of parents, businesses, and professional and civic organizations can work to develop and support numerous projects to create and sustain more nurturing school environments. For example, large corporations should be encouraged to donate money, materials, and time to schools. With extra money, people, and raw resources in the schools, more conflict resolution and peer mediation programs, which help children learn to deal with anger and conflict without the use of verbal and physical altercations, and violence prevention curricula—which teach children to solve disputes, support each other, and build peer friendships (Prothrow-Stith, 1991)—can be initiated.

In addition to strengthening schools, other inner-city institutions need to be either fortified or reformed. To create positive change, public bureaucracies, organizations, and institutions have to become community based and controlled (Hagedorn, 1991). When social service agencies, police forces, and schools have to answer to the people they serve, accountability is greatly increased. Residents must realistically review the existing programs in their area to ascertain whether they serve the community's needs properly. If programs are judged to be inadequate, the community must fight to have funding transferred to more effective programs.

More community advisory boards and neighborhood organizations must be formed. It's imperative that youths be included on these boards; they must be part of the solution. These associations, along with the Black church, must continue to provide leadership in social change and activism within inner-city neighborhoods. Further, these organizations can strengthen their efforts through coordination, and coalition-building. The formation and development of community-based mediation groups, neighborhood patrols, watch groups, and hot-lines will also help to reduce drug-related, criminal, and violent activities in the neighborhood (Gibbs, 1988). Wilson (1990) suggests that African American males and females should be trained and paid a stipend to patrol and protect their own communities to compensate for the poor attention urban police forces give to inner-city neighborhoods.

Finally, efforts put forth by African American communities and concerned institutions need to be supported on a national level. The Black community must continue to involve itself in the political process through voter registration drives and political education campaigns. From a place of amplified political power, the African American community will be in a better position to demand commitments from federal, state, and local governments to improve the overall quality of life in the inner city. The citizenry must be encouraged to join lobbying efforts to control the manufacture and distribution of guns or to join letter-writing campaigns to express disapproval on issues ranging from food and entertainment to governmental policies that affect quality of life. Improvements should include expanded employment opportunities, better and more housing, and increased funding for schools, health care programs, and recreational facilities (Children's Defense Fund, 1986). It is also necessary for the Black community to attempt to make broad changes in the juvenile justice system, which presently, instead of reforming youths, exposes them to more violence and initiates them into a life of crime.

Summary and Conclusion

The amount of youth violence in urban areas has reached epidemic proportions. Despite feelings of futility, communities are confronting the overwhelming belief that nothing can be done to bring peace to our communities.

Although on some levels the problem seems intractable, the combination of present efforts along with the future development of resources within the African American community can greatly decrease the amount of violence over time. It is essential that families, communities, and service providers continue to expand their vision in viewing and responding to youth violence as an expression of pain, a cry for help, and an indication of the need for focus and nurturance. This view would allow all actors involved to begin constructing a new set of realities for a continued healing process.

References

Abner, A. (July 1994). Gangsta girls. *Essence, 25*(3), 64–66.

Anders, A. (1994). Gangster girls. *Essence, 25*(3), 64–66, 116–119.

Billingsley, A. (1968). *Black families in white America.* Englewood Cliffs, NJ: Prentice-Hall.

Billingsley, A. (1992). *Climbing Jacob's ladder: The enduring legacy of African-American families.* New York: Simon and Schuster.

Brown v. Board of Education of Topeka, Kansas, 347 U.S. 483, 74 S. Ct. 686 (1954).

Caple, F. (1990). The Black family and the school. In S.M.L. Logan, E. M. Freeman, & R. G. McRoy (Eds.), *Social work practice with the Black family* (pp. 115–132). New York: Longman.

Chestang, L. (1976). Environmental influences on social functioning: The Black experience. In P. Cafferty & L. Chestang (Eds.), *In the diverse society* (pp. 57–74). Washington, DC: National Association of Social Workers.

Children's Defense Fund (1986). *Welfare and teen pregnancy: What do we know? What do we do?* Washington, DC: Children's Defense Fund.

Cloward, R., & L. Ohlin (1960). *Delinquency and opportunity.* Glencoe, IL: Free Press.

Coser, L. (1967). *Continuities in the study of social conflict.* New York: Free Press.

Curry, G. D., & I. A. Spergel (August 1992). Gang involvement and delinquency among Hispanic and African-American adolescent males. *Journal of Research in Crime and Delinquency, 29*(3), 273–291.

Erikson, E. (1959). The problem of ego identity. In G. Klein (Ed.), *Psychosocial issues* (pp. 101–164). New York: International University Press.

Erikson, E. (1968). *Identity: Youth and crisis.* New York: W. W. Norton.

Farley, R. (1980). Homicide trends in the United States. *Demography, 17,* 177–188.

Fox, J. R. (January–February 1985). Mission impossible? Social work practice with Black urban youth gangs. *Social Work, 30,* 25–31.

Franklin, C. W. (1994). Men's studies, the men's movement, and the study of Black masculinities: Further demystification of masculinities in America In R. G. Majors & J. U. Gordon (Eds.), *The American Black male: His present status and his future* (pp. 3–20). Chicago: Nelson-Hall.

Freeman, R. (1990). The Black family's life cycle: Operationalizing a strengths perspective. In S.M.L. Logan, E. M. Freeman, & R. G. McRoy (Eds.), *Social work practice with the Black family* (pp. 55–72). New York: Longman.

Gang manual (1993, 1995). Santa Rosa, CA: National Law Enforcement Institute.

Gangs in schools: Breaking up is hard to do (1990). Malibu, CA: National School Safety Center.

Garbarino, J., K. Kostelny, & N. Dubrow (April 1991). What children can tell us about living in danger. *American Psychologist, 4,* 376–383.

Getzel, G. S., & R. Masters (1986). Social work practice with families of homicide victims. In C. Germaine (Ed.), *Advances in Clinical Practice* (pp. 7–16). Silver Spring, MD: National Association of Social Workers Press.

Gibbs, J. T. (1988). *Young, Black, and male in America: An endangered species.* Waco, TX: Auburn House Publishing Company.

Gibbs, J. T. (1989). Black adolescents and youth: An update on an endangered species. In R. L. Jones (Ed.), *Black adolescents* (pp. 3–27). Berkeley, CA: Cobb and Henry.

Gibbs, J. T. (1994). Anger in young Black males: Victims or victimizers? In R. G. Majors & J. U. Gordon (Eds.), *The American Black male: His present status and his future* (pp. 127–144). Chicago: Nelson-Hall.

Gilbert, R., & C. Tyehimba-Taylor (1994). *The ghetto solution.* Waco, TX: WRS Publishing.

Goleman, D. (September 2, 1986). The roots of terrorism are found in brutality of shattered childhood. *New York Times.*

Grier, W., & P. Cobbs (1968). *Black rage.* New York: Basic Books.

Gross, T. (1995). Fresh air: Interview with a family from Philadelphia, Pennsylvania, on gang violence. National Public Radio.

Hagedorn, J. M. (November 1991). Gangs, neighborhoods, and public policy. *Social Problems, 30*(4), 529–542.

Harvey, A. R. (December 1994). Symposium communication. In *Healing the effects of violence on African-American children and youth: An Afro-centric perspective.* New York: Black Task Force on Child Abuse and Neglect.

Hayes, W., & C. H. Mendel (1973). Extended kinship in Black and white families. *Journal of Marriage and the Family, 35,* 51–57.

Kunjufu, J. (1985). *Countering the conspiracy to destroy Black boys,* Vol. I. Chicago: African American Images.

Kunjufu, J. (1986). *Countering the conspiracy to destroy Black boys,* Vol. II. Chicago: African American Images.

Kunjufu, J. (1990). *Countering the conspiracy to destroy Black boys,* Vol. III. Chicago: African American Images.

Kunjufu, J. (1995). *Countering the conspiracy to destroy Black boys,* Vol. IV. Chicago: African American Images.

Le Blanc, A. D. (August 1994). Gang girl: The making of a street feminist. *New York Times Magazine,* Section 6, pp. 26–33, 46, 49, 53.

Lewis, M. (1988). *Herstory: Black female rites of passage.* Chicago: African American Images.

Lewis, R. (December 1994). Symposium communication. In *Healing the effects of violence on African-American children and youth: An Afro-centric perspective.* New York: Black Task Force on Child Abuse and Neglect.

Logan, S. (1981). Race, identity, and Black children: A developmental perspective. *Social Casework, 62,* 47–56.

Logan, S.M.L., E. M. Freeman, & R. G. McRoy (1990). Race, ethnicity, culture, social class, and gender issues. In S.M.L. Logan, E. M. Freeman, & R. G. McRoy (Eds.), *Social work practice with the Black family* (pp. 115–132). New York: Longman.

Loury, G. C. (Spring 1985). The moral quandary of the Black community. *Public Interest,* 9–22.

Majors, R. G. (1994). Conclusions and recommendations: A reason for hope—an overview of the new Black movements in the United States. In R. G. Majors & J. U. Gordon (Eds.), *The American Black male: His present status and his future* (pp. 299–316). Chicago: Nelson-Hall.

Majors, R. G., & J. M. Billson (1992). *Cool pose: The dilemmas of Black manhood in America.* New York: Lexington Books.

Majors, R. G., R. Tyler, B. Peden, & R. Hall (1994). Cool pose: A symbolic mechanism for masculine enactment and coping by Black males. In R. G. Majors & J. U. Gordon (Eds.), *The American Black male: His present status and his future* (pp. 245–260). Chicago: Nelson-Hall.

Mancini, J. (1980). *Strategic Styles: Coping in the inner city.* Hanover, NH: University Press of New England.

Martin, E. P., & J. M. Martin (1978). *The Black extended family.* Chicago: University of Chicago Press.

May, R. (1972). *Power or innocence: A search for the source of violence.* New York: W. W. Norton.

McCord, W., J. Howard, B. Friedberg, & E. Harwood (1969). *Lifestyles in the Black ghetto.* New York: W. W. Norton.

McRoy, R. G. (1990). Cultural and racial identity in Black families. In S.M.L. Logan, E. M. Freeman, & R. G. McRoy (Eds.), *Social work practice with the Black family* (pp. 97–111). New York: Longman.

Morrisey, P. G. (1990). Black children in foster care. In S.M.L. Logan, E. M. Freeman, & R. G. McRoy (Eds.), *Social work practice with the Black family* (pp. 133–147). New York: Longman.

Moyers, B. (January 1995). *What can we do about violence?* New York: Public Broadcasting Services.

National Education Association (NEA) (1987). *Black Concerns Study Committee report.* Washington, DC: NEA.

Norton, D. (1976). Residential environment and Black self-image. In P. Cafferty & L. Chestang (Eds.), *In the diverse society* (pp. 75–89). Washington, DC: National Association of Social Workers.

Oliver, W. (September 1989). Black males and social problems. *Journal of Black Studies, 20*(11), 15–39.

Perkins, U. E. (1987). *Explosion of Chicago's Black street gangs: 1900 to present.* Chicago: Third World Press.

Poole, E. (August 1991). Kids and guns. *New York Magazine.*

Prothrow-Stith, D. (1991). *Deadly consequences.* New York: HarperCollins.

Public Health Reports (May–June 1991). *Forum on youth violence in minority communities: Setting the agenda for prevention,* 225–279.

Rodgers, A., & L. J. Tartaglia (1990). Constricting resources: A Black self-help initiative. *Administration in Social Work, 14*(2), 125–137.

Rubin, N. (July 1994). The community of helping hands. *New York Newsday.*

Schwartz, R. E. (July 1982). Children under fire: The role of the schools. *American Journal of Orthopsychiatry, 3,* 409–419.

Spergel, I. A. (June 1984). Violent gangs in Chicago: In search of social policy. *Social Service Review, 8*(2), 199–226.

Spergel, I. A. (March 1986). The violent gang problem in Chicago: A local community approach. *Social Service Review, 6*(1) 94–131.

Statistical Abstract of the United States (1991) (111th ed.). Washington, DC: U.S. Department of Commerce.

Tannenbaum, F. (1938). *Crime and community.* New York: Ginn.

Tidwell, B. J. (1990). Research and practice: Challenges and opportunities. In S.M.L. Logan, E. M. Freeman, & R. G. McRoy (Eds.), *Social work practice with the Black family* (pp. 259–272). New York: Longman.

Williams, L. F. (1990). Working with the Black poor. In S.M.L. Logan, E. M. Freeman, & R. G. McRoy (Eds.), *Social work practice with the Black family* (pp. 169–192). New York: Longman.

Wilson, A. N. (1990). *Black-on-Black violence: The psychodynamics of Black self-annihilation in service of white domination.* New York: Afrikan World Infosystems.

PART TWO

Creating and Promoting Positive Change

The six chapters composing Part Two of this book are in some ways an extension of the theme(s) addressed in Part One. Self-help is used in Part One as the organizing focus, whereas in Part Two select systemic problems that plague Black families and children are used as the organizing focus. Nevertheless, the underlying emphasis is on building strength and empowerment. On the whole, these chapters represent a concerted effort to acknowledge and build on the resiliency of the human spirit. They also represent a growing recognition that to make an active contribution to the upliftment of humanity, professional helpers and educators must begin to write and live a new and different story about Black families and children.

Crawley's chapter challenges the reader to begin this renewed process of writing, teaching, and practicing from an African-centered perspective. Crawley proposes this alternative perspective as an empowered means of understanding and working with Black families and children. The focus is primarily on examining the implications of an African-centered framework for developing social programs and services for Black American families. She concludes by encouraging stronger educational preparation and culture-specific practice and intervention strategies.

According to Linda Chavez (Love is colorblind, *USA Today*, March 29, 1995, p. 11), racial politics have made it increasingly difficult for white families to adopt African American, Hispanic, and mixed-race children. These children, she claims, languish in foster care systems that sometimes places more emphasis on the color of these children's skin than on finding them good homes. Although this issue is not as simple as

Chavez claims, no one would disagree that all children need and deserve loving homes. The crux of the matter regarding transracial adoptions concerns the development of healthy self- and racial identity. One could identify at least three major positions on this issue. One position unequivocally opposes transracial adoption as a form of genocide. The second position supports the practice to the extent that the agency staff, adopted children, and their parents are exposed to ongoing culture-specific materials and information. The third position states that children adopted by white families grow up emotionally healthy, comfortable with their racial identity, committed to their adopted families, and capable of living in Black, white, and integrated communities. Somehow, Chavez believes successfully placing children of color with white families will further the goal of achieving a color-blind society.

McRoy, in her chapter, helps us to see that the issue is much more complex than simply helping children to deny their cultural and racial heritage. Her focus is on identity development of Black children and youth in out-of-home care. Each year, it is estimated that about 750,000 children will be admitted to juvenile facilities and 200,000 to child welfare facilities. Black children are disproportionately admitted to these facilities, and services are provided by a predominantly white professional staff and foster care providers. Actually, more than 40 percent of the children awaiting adoption are African American. McRoy addresses the unique needs of these children to develop positive racial self-feelings in racially dissonant contexts. Factors that influence the development of racial identity are identified, and specific issues for children in out-of-home care are discussed. McRoy concludes by presenting implications for practice.

Denby's chapter on family preservation extends McRoy's discussion of out-of-home care. As indicated previously, out-of-home placement rates for African American children are alarming. Despite these rates, however, African American families employ many strategies to build, strengthen, and preserve the family unit. Denby, in her chapter, presents an African American Family Preservation Model. The model is developed through preservation program values. Application of the model is demonstrated by a case vignette that illustrates seven practice principles.

The number of black single-parent families has been growing at a phenomenal rate over the past twenty years. Although the needs of all single-parent families are similar, some concerns are unique to Black single parents. In her chapter, Logan discusses the life-cycle concerns of parents and children. She further describes structural concerns female single-parent families must contend with on a daily basis. Finally, within an ecological system framework, practice principles and strategies are identified and illustrated.

The Black church continues to be the hub of the Black community. It has evolved from a rich history of self-help. Brashears and Roberts not only describe the dynamics of the church in terms and language similar to those used to describe family functioning but suggest that the Black church is a surrogate family to its members. Although other models exist, Brashears and Roberts describe an innovative social service program in a Black church in the Midwest. This approach to strengthening families is appealing to and advancing in the more progressive areas of the country. This program includes a social worker member of the church who provides case management and family support services to members of the church community, including services to homebound and institutionalized members and to families experiencing a traumatic life-cycle transition. The authors encourage the social work community and other helping professionals to explore the untapped resources to be found within natural environments such as churches.

7

Effective Programs and Services for African American Families and Children: An African-Centered Perspective

BRENDA H. CRAWLEY

A race is like a man. Until it uses its own talents, takes pride in its own
history, and loves its own memories it can never fulfill itself completely.
    —John W. Vandercook

This chapter examines the issue of using an African-centered framework for developing social programs and services for Black American
families and how such services might make a difference in their lives. It
is not new to ask whether dominant culture-based education, programs,
services, or paradigms are useful and functional for all citizens. Certainly, it is recognized that great cultural and ethnic diversity exists and
that history has shown that not all groups benefit equally from social or
psychological policies, programs, and services developed on
Western/Euro-American models and norms (Bradbury & Browne,
1986; Center on Budget, 1986; Kenyetta, 1983; Korchin, 1980). And no
one seriously questions that the most persistent and pervasive racial,
ethnic, and cultural issues in the United States pertain to Black Ameri-

can–white American relations (Hanson, 1992; Karenga, 1985; Sue, 1983).

Concerns about African American families have consistently been a part of the landscape of these issues. African American families have always faced the daunting tasks of raising their children and ensuring the survival of the family in the hostile and racist environment of the United States (Crawley, 1988; Kenyetta, 1983). Social scientists of various persuasions have traced Black Americans' individual, family, group, and community survival through stages of acculturation, assimilation, accommodation, and integration strategies throughout their history. Conspicuous by its absence is the stage of full equality. This is especially of note in a democracy that touts itself as synonymous with the application of egalitarian principles of governance for all people. The historical as well as present experiences of African American families belie this view.

A Perspective on the African American Experience

Currently, one does not have to seek far to locate a litany of deplorable conditions in the lives of many African Americans (Riley, 1986). There is a steady and seemingly unrelenting media meal composed of variations on the following statistics (Morganthau et al., 1992, p. 20).

- Black children are three times more likely than whites to live in a single-parent household; 43.2 percent of all African American children live in poverty.
- African Americans now account for 28.8 percent of U.S. AIDS cases. Blacks constitute 52 percent of women with the disease, and black children represent 53 percent of all pediatric AIDS cases.
- Homicide is the leading cause of death for African American males between age 15 and 34. Nearly half of all U.S. murder victims are Black.
- In 1989, 23 percent of all African American men ages 20 to 40 were either in prison or on probation or parole. By one study, one-fifth of all Black males between ages 15 and 34 have criminal records.

There is no dearth of explanations and causal postulates for this complex social crisis. Jeffries and Brock (1991) and Wilson (1978, 1987), among others, cite shifts in the industrial and manufacturing bases of the U.S. economy. These shifts are characterized by a move to (1) a service-based economy, (2) globalization of the economy, and (3) a technologically based economy. These shifts have had profound impacts on the financial viability of African American workers and their families. Karenga (1985) takes the position that the political culture causes as well as aids and abets racism in the United States. And not just the political culture but the political economy as well contributes to racism—in short, the total political milieu contributes significantly to the complex social crisis facing African Americans and their families. The authors of a *Newsweek* article clearly state their causal bias as "poverty, crime, drugs and the disintegration of family and community," as though these conditions exist abstractly apart from the operations of the social structure and its functions—that is, religion, government and politics, the economy, education, *and* family (Morganthau et al., 1992, p. 20). Others have identified racism per se as the systemic disease that pervades all of U.S. society, damaging African American individuals, families, groups, and communities in myriad ways (Lamar, 1992; Lowy, 1991; Markowitz, 1993; Safran, 1991). As is the case with complex social issues, causal truths are to be found in all of these perspectives, as well as in other plausible hypotheses (Crawley, 1988; Malveaux, 1988; Rolison, 1991).

For example, it has been posited that the United States is experiencing massive moral and value decay, sexual immorality and promiscuity, pervasive crime and violence (domestic abuse, child abuse, elder abuse, street crime, suite crime—what is euphemistically labeled "white-collar crime"), and pervasive substance misuse and abuse (including over-the-counter, prescription, and illegal drugs, alcohol, and tobacco) and that *all* families are affected (Staples, 1978; Streeter, 1986). If this is a plausible characterization of society, then Black American families would not find themselves outside of these conditions. Rather, they would find that these problems exacerbate a milieu of inequality, economic hardship, and racism.

An Evolving African-Centered Perspective

The long-term history of slavery, racism, discrimination, prejudice, negative natural and social "science" research, biased media portrayals, and struggles for full equality has made it clear to a sufficient number of African Americans that prevailing Western/Euro-centered perspectives, philosophies, and paradigms are ill suited for describing, explaining, understanding, and remedying their conditions and promoting positive self-identity. History records that time after time whether using acculturationist, assimilationist, accommodationist, or integrationist strategies for surviving and thriving, questions have always arisen that keep a focus toward African-inspired, focused, and centered ideas, values, and visions (Asante, 1988; Crawley & Freeman, 1993; Kunjufu, 1985, 1986). The opening quote to this chapter bespeaks the inexorable and reoccurring quest for full identity and wholeness of self, family, and community that resurfaces the African points of origin in Black Americans' history. A prime example of this is the flight by over a quarter of a million "Island blacks" from the Carolinas to northern Florida to preserve their heritage, particularly as it is expressed in the Gullah language (Dunn, 1987).

Additionally, one has only to reflect on movements to return to Africa, perpetuation of idioms in language, Pan-Africanist philosophies and movements, and references to Africa as the motherland. These ideas and threads in one form or another have been woven throughout the history of persons of African descent since their arrival on these shores. The point is not that every person of African descent accepts or adheres to these currents of consciousness, beliefs, and actions but rather that these threads have been and remain viable in and vital to the African American experience. Nowhere is this more evidenced than in current expressions of African-inspired, African-focused, and African-centered expressions in several spheres: African-centered schools and socialization for Black children (Crawley & Freeman, 1993; Oliver, 1989; Petrie, 1991); African-centered perspectives on history (Keto, 1989); Afrocentric philosophy (Abarry, 1990; Asante, 1988; Oyebade, 1990); African-inspired celebrations such as Kwanza and rites of passage for girls and for boys; and Afrocentric perspectives and approaches in psychotherapy, organizational theory, mental health theorizing, and psychology.

Another excellent example of evolving African American consciousness is the rise of the vibrant Afrocentric philosophical thinking that challenges the hegemonic Eurocentric stranglehold on worldview perspectives (Asante, 1988; Oyebade, 1990). As should be expected, African-centered thinking has migrated into the mainstream. It now occupies a position that allows its tenets to be incorporated into areas such as educational and social programs and services (Black Voices, 1991; Petrie, 1991). According to various authors and researchers, an African-centered perspective (especially as expressed in the Afrocentric paradigm) is useful in social and educational services (Asante, 1991; Kunjufu, 1986; Oliver, 1989).

A synopsis of an African-centered/Afrocentric framework is provided by Crawley and Freeman (1992, p. 17):

> "Afrocentricity as an intervention paradigm" and as "a way of life" facilitates a more holistic and healthy perspective for understanding African American aspirations, strengths, and potential (Oliver, 1989, p. 23). In addition to serving as an intervention paradigm, Afrocentricity as a way of life is a worldview encompassing one's cultural milieu—perceptions, interpersonal relationships, language, communication, and family dynamics, to name a few elements.
>
> Oliver (1989) views the Afrocentric perspective as absolutely essential to the existence of African American people in America. In the face of America's historical and persistent cultural imperative of "White superiority and Black inferiority," Black Americans are continually encouraged to use dysfunctional cultural adaptations.

Oyebade (1990) states that "Afrocentricity is thus a search for those values that will make man to relate to man in a humanistic way and not in an imperialistic or exploitative way" (p. 237). Abarry (1990) avows that Afrocentricity is "complex and multidisciplinary, the concept embodies a humanistic philosophy, a scholarly methodology, and a model of practical action" (p. 123). Oliver (1989) has carefully woven all three of these strands into a tapestry for intervention into the socialization of Black males; indeed, he also cites how Black American scholars are increasingly promoting "Afrocentricity as an intervention paradigm to facilitate the transformation of Blacks from a state of dependence to a state of independence and self-reliance" (p. 23).

Other theorists, researchers, and professionals have focused on these areas: Phillips (1990) describes NTU psychotherapy as "based on the core principles of ancient African and Afrocentric worldview, nurtured through African American culture, and augmented by Western techniques of Humanistic psychology" (p. 56). Azibo (1989, 1991) advances a metatheory of the African personality against the backdrop of Afrocentric reasoning (1991, pp. 38–39). Schiele (1991) posits that organizational theory can be reconceptualized using the Afrocentric paradigm; the critical difference that separates Afrocentric and mainstream organizational theories is an understanding of the ontological differences between the two (p. 147). Finally, Asante (1991) cogently identifies how the Eurocentric dominance in education "imposes Eurocentric realities as 'universal'; i.e., that which is white is presented as applying to the human condition in general, while that which is non-white is viewed as group-specific and therefore not 'human'" (p. 172). He submits a credible case for the use of the Afrocentric paradigm in and throughout the educational system for the multicultural education of all students. Thus, he advocates that the Eurocentric paradigms should constitute only a part of multiple worldviews presented in the classroom—First Nations', Asian, Afrocentric/African-centered, and other people's worldviews are all to be presented. The issue is not one of competition by these "views" but rather that the Eurocentric view should assume a place alongside of, rather than one of dominance over, the others.

As with any cultural (r)evolution, not everyone accepts the viability of an African-centered/Afrocentric perspective or paradigm as relevant. Dr. Kenneth Clark, who vigorously opposes classroom environments designed exclusively for young African American males, "wearily expressed concern the other day not just about the potential reemergence of schools that are intentionally racially segregated [Black male students only] but also about separating students on the basis of their sex" (cited in Roberts, 1990, p. 44). As a member of the "materialist camp," Hazzard-Gordon (1991) believes that first and foremost, contributions must be made to "solving the problem of black male unemployment by gainfully employing all black males over the age of 18, and [then] the positive psychological intent of Afrocentricity will be accomplished" (p. 22). Hooks (1991) appears to use the euphemism "black nationalist responses" to suggest that such responses are "unproductive" (p. 51).

Differing voices on the usefulness of African-centered paradigms are as it should be in a pluralist society. Just as the current cornucopia of humanistic Western/Eurocentric paradigm-based social programs and services is not for everyone, so it cannot be that all Black Americans in need of social programs and services should receive African-centered ones. *Rather, it must be strongly advocated that the absence of Afrocentric-based programs and services precludes freedom of choice for African American families.* At present there are only Euro/American-centered options. As has been noted, a sufficient number of Afrocentrically oriented scholars, professionals, and theorists—including myself—have laid the groundwork for the use of an African-centered framework in the provision of educational, psychological, and social programs and services. Direct service providers, supervisors, and administrators can integrate an African-centered framework into their organizational structures through elements of their (1) program and service design, (2) practice and intervention strategies, and (3) staff training programs. The remainder of this chapter underscores the viability of using an African-centered frame of reference in social programs and services for Black American families.

Design of Social Programs and Services

The design of social programs and services begins with some philosophical underpinnings that determine mission, purpose, goals, and objectives statements. The design also includes a conceptual paradigm that informs the nature of the organizational culture (Gortner, Mahler, & Nicholson, 1987). The usual Western/Euro-American conceptual paradigm of organizations "concentrate[s] on the factors affecting organizational productivity: how fast, how plentifully, and how well something is produced or, in the case of human service organizations, how well and how efficiently people are processed, sustained, or changed" (Schiele, 1990, p. 147). Schiele indicates that "from an Afrocentric perspective, organizational and group survival replaces productivity as the overriding concern" (1990, p. 150). The raison d'être of the organization becomes client-centered outcomes rather than maintenance of the organization. This means the activity of workers is committed to the organization's life so clients or consumers are served and a rapid change or turnover in client population does not occur.

The current structures of most social programs and services, including those specifically targeted to African Americans, are not designed to support the use of the seven African-centered principles of Nguzo Saba. It is probably safe to assert that at present, only a handful of the agencies serving African American families have heard of the Nguzo Saba value system, much less thought of designing and offering services based on these value principles. Even though the litany of problems and ills plaguing numerous African American families continues to spiral out of control, few seek fundamental alternatives to the Euro-American-centered value paradigms for service delivery.

√ Nguzo Saba is an Afrocentric value system that can assist efforts to "rescue and reconstruct Black lives in their own image" (Oliver, 1989, p. 27). The seven foundation values are as follows (Oliver, 1989, pp. 27–32):

- *Umoja* (Unity)—To strive for and maintain unity in the family, community, nation, and race

- *Kujichagulia* (Self-Determination)—To define ourselves, name ourselves, create for ourselves, and speak for ourselves instead of being defined, named for, and spoken for by others
- *Ujima* (Collective Work and Responsibility)—To build and maintain our community together and make our sisters' and brothers' problems our problems and to solve them together
- *Ujamma* (Cooperative Economics)—To build and maintain our own stores, shops, and other businesses and to profit from them together
- *Nia* (Purpose)—To make our collective vocation the building and developing of our community in order to restore our people to their traditional greatness
- *Kuumba* (Creativity)—To do always as much as we can, in the way we can, in order to leave our community more beautiful and beneficial than we inherited it
- *Imani* (Faith)—To believe with all our hearts in our people, our parents, our teachers, our leaders, and the righteousness and victory of our struggle

If, as Oliver and other scholars and professionals report, African American socialization and development are best facilitated by adherence to African-centered values and paradigms, then it is incumbent on more social agencies to investigate and incorporate these into the design of programs and services for African American individuals, families, and communities. Yet as pointed out later in the section on staff training, the lack of education and the miseducation of social workers and other human services professionals regarding African-centered paradigms, theories, and research severely impact their capacity to develop well-rounded and relevant social programs and services for African American families. Three brief references help illustrate this point. First, Kunjufu (1985) tells us that the absence of the use of rites-of-passage observances and ceremonies precludes the availability of powerful rituals that can positively influence the development and socialization of African American families and individuals.

Second, Oliver points out that "Ujima encourages Black parents and adults to define maturity and manhood in terms of actions that contribute to the progress and development of Black people" (1989, p. 29), whereas "Nia is a critical element of Afrocentric socialization because of the emphasis this value places on making Black youth aware of the oppression that Africans and African Americans have experienced" (1989, p. 31). Social programs and services rarely, if ever, see it as being in the African American family's interest to emphasize these matters of critical importance to Black Americans. As such, they miss the opportunity to use "the Nia value, [which] encourages African American parents to instill in Black youth a commitment to devote their lives to eradicating those structural pressures and cultural conditions that prevent African Americans from achieving economic and political parity" (Oliver, 1989, p. 31).

A third reference comes from the nosology of Black/African personality disorders. For example, Azibo (1989) speaks of the personality disorder of "psychological misorientation, [which] is the most fundamental state of disorder in the Black personality [and] refers to operating without an African-centered belief system" (p. 184). Programs and services designed to routinely use the "nosological system prevalent in Euro-American psychology (DSM-III [Diagnostic and Statistical Manual])" (currently DSM-IV) but to never use Black psychological nosological referents and systems will certainly have gaping holes in the design and structure of their program and service delivery systems (Azibo, 1989, p. 173).

Practice and Intervention

If, as pointed out in the previous section, the absence of African-centered/Afrocentric perspectives bodes ill in the design and structure of social programs and services, their absence in intervention and practice must be considered malignant. For example, the usual Western thrust is on the individual (and individualism)—"I think, therefore I am" (Crawley, 1988; Crawley & Freeman, 1993). Such detachment is dangerous for low- and modest-income African American family members in crisis, in need of treatment, and often in need of multiple services. The individual under such conditions needs a strong support system among family members. Thus, intervention and practice strategies that are designed to emphasize group and family strengths and interdependencies—that is, the person as part of her or his collectivity—would likely better serve African American families (Urban Research Review, 1986).

Equally important, however, is the professionally trained helper's perspective on human nature, as well as his or her views on socialization issues and development tasks—in short, on human behavior in the social environment. So critical are these topics in determining the helper's intervention and practice strategies that the profession of social work requires a year of coursework covering human behavior in the social environment. Knowledge-driven practice requires an ontological understanding of humans in general, as well as of their specific ethnic and cultural milieus. The remainder of this section looks first at some socialization and development issues of African Americans that ultimately affect their family's lives and second at African-centered tenets of human nature.

Crawley and Freeman (1993), in their "proactive positive analysis of the life themes and views of both younger and older African American males," point out that typical developmental theories and research fail to include aspects of critical psychosocial developmental tasks and socialization issues for African Americans (p. 15). This gross negligence results from (1) the norming of developmental and socialization research and theories on dominant-group subjects (2) using Western/Euro-American values and philosophical underpinnings and (3) ignoring African-centered perspectives as a way to understand the developmental and socialization experiences of African American males in particular and of the group in general. Over the life span, issues of racism, discrimination, prejudice, and social injustice weave themselves throughout the growth, development, and socialization of African Americans (see Crawley & Freeman, 1993). The impact of these experiences and issues on the African American family is well documented (Chestang, 1980; Oliver, 1989; Riley, 1986; Staples, 1987).

Practitioners who are not trained in understanding the specific developmental and socialization needs of Black Americans or those whose understanding is limited to some general sense that racism and social injustices are random occurrences cannot provide competent and adequate interventions or practice in working with Black families, individuals, or groups. Workers must have knowledge of the lifelong, pervasive presence and impact of the full range of experiences—racism, discrimination, prejudice, and social injustice—on African American lives. Workers additionally must recognize the lifelong skills and responses that must be developed to successfully negotiate daily life in the United States (Safran, 1991). As Kenyetta (1983) and the Urban Research Review (1986) point out, Black American parents and families know all too well the overt and covert training they must provide to their children for proper and successful development. For Kenyetta and the Review, it is the strengths of Black American families that make this complex training possible. As Kenyetta states it, "The black family has had to be smart, tough, and flexible to survive the assault of white racism" (1983, p. 17).

Practitioners must focus unrelentingly on using the "resourcefulness, resilience, and adaptability of the black family" as part of their intervention and practice (Kenyetta, 1983, p. 17). They must also be able to conceptualize interventions from a syncretistic framework (Crawley & Freeman, 1993). A syncretistic framework means practitioners will at first glance appear to draw upon disparate knowledge sources—for example, use of Madhubuti's (1990) and Akbar's (1991) conceptualizations of Black American malehood, which stand in stark contrast to the Euro-American pathologizing and demonizing of this group; Oliver's (1989) use of the seven Nguzo Saba principles as guides to the socialization of healthy African American children; use of Hill's (1972, 1987a) and Urban Research Review's (1986) identified Black family strengths across *all* family forms, such as those headed by two parents, one parent, and grandparent; use of an African-centered personality diagnostic system (Azibo, 1989), as well as the Euro-American-centric DSM-IV (Diagnostic and Statistical Manual); and recognition and use of the "heroic, disciplined efforts of community organizations to [create] better conditions [for Black communities]" (Childs, 1986, p. 16).

Second, practitioners' practice interventions should be informed by African-centered views on human nature. Ultimately, underlying assumptions about human nature inform professional practice. Six African-centered philosophical tenets offer views on human nature and behavior that can be used to structure intervention and practice with African American families (Schiele, 1991, p. 147):

1. Human beings are conceived collectively.
2. Human beings are spiritual.
3. Human beings are good.
4. The affective approach to knowledge is epistemologically valid.
5. Much of human behavior is nonrational.
6. The axiology or highest value lies in interpersonal relations.

It is not so much the case that these tenets are wholly lacking in Western and Euro-American philosophical and ideological thinking but rather that historically the dominant faces of individualism, science as religion, human nature as intrinsically evil, and rationalism as supreme have prevailed. So much have these tenets dominated Euro-American thinking that some recent social science efforts have been directed at radically deconstructing the major paradigms in which they are rooted.

Several of these tenets are especially relevant to intervention and practice strategies in working with Black American families. For example, tenets one, two, three, four, and six find congruence in numerous examples of Black American efforts to assist their families. From the examples cited here, professionals can learn how to support and work with Black American families.

- Hill (1972, 1987a) has consistently acknowledged the good and "powerful assets" African American families possess for handling difficulties in living (p. 18).
- Black families believe in family life, and they cling to family ties.
- Black families believe in work, and they work hard.
- Black families believe in achievement, and they seek the education that makes achievement possible.
- Black families have strong belief systems, and they rely on their churches to support family life.
- Black families have always shown the will and the skill to adapt family roles to meet changing situations (Hill, 1987a, p. 18).

The unrelenting use of these strengths as a practice perspective on Black American families would consistently guide practitioners in providing empowerment opportunities for these families. Of special note would be an emphasis on self-help (see Chapter 2).

Practitioners can best provide empowerment opportunities for African American families through the combined use of the value principles of Nguzo Saba, adherence to the African-centered tenets of human nature and behavior, and the perpetual use of the strengths of African American families described here. The use of these combined factors would guide the employment of self-help and structural changes as a means to intervention and practice. To use these combined factors is to recognize that "the black family grew out of a complex combination of African traditions, Christian beliefs, and adjustments made to slavery" (The American Black Family, 1987, p. 26). For decades, the least focused upon aspect of helping Black American families has been the African component. By reintegrating this aspect through use of the burgeoning African-centered/Afrocentric knowledge base in the social science, philosophical, theory development, research, and practice spheres, better interventions and practices can be made available.

Several examples may suffice to illustrate this last point. The Nguzo Saba principles of Kujichagulia, Ujima, and Imani permeate the many self-help efforts directed both at and by African American families. Efforts include, but are not limited to, religious, fraternal, and communal organizations; projects such as teach-ins; scholarship programs in public housing complexes; sweat-equity projects, and so forth (Halicki, 1988; Levine & Collins, 1986; National Center for Neighborhood Enterprise, n.d.; Paige, 1986; Payton, 1986; Poole, 1986). One of the best examples of an African-centered African American family's self-help effort has been the House of Umoja. An African American couple concerned about youth and growing gang activity in their Philadelphia community "literally extend[ed] their family and home to embrace the gang members. Dialogue sessions soon led to the formation of an inter-gang council to resolve disputes nonviolently. Umoja also channeled the energies of these youths by forming small businesses. Results can be measured: Gang deaths dropped from 32 in 1974 to only one or two in recent years (Hill, 1987b, p. 20). One religious group described its outreach program in support of African American families and others as necessary because "we [Blacks] must learn to practice the sense of belonging to one another" (Hill, 1987b, p. 20). This clearly indicates the Umoja and Imani principles.

Professionally driven interventions, which is one way of speaking about knowledge-driven practice, cannot happen appropriately if the practitioner is not informed by the totality of a group's perspective and experiences. Repeated use of dominant-group perspectives and paradigms in interventions and practice with Black American individuals, families, and communities continues to result in the same deviant, inferiority, and pathology foci. It cannot be otherwise. At present, a sufficient critical mass of an African-centered knowledge base exists, which should become required learning for professionally trained helpers. As the next section shows, there are numerous ways in which currently miseducated practitioners can learn to integrate African-centered materials into more holistic ways of serving African American families.

Staff Training

No aspects of African-centered perspectives and paradigms can reach African American families as clients if social workers are not educated in African-centered philosophy, history, theory, research, and practice. The references for this chapter list many sources practitioners can access. I have integrated Afrocentric materials throughout my human behavior in the social environment courses. Among the options for student assignments is one that allows students to read one of several books and to respond to a set of questions. The books are *Afrocentricity* by Molefi Asante, *The Africa centered perspective of history* by C. T. Keto, and *Understanding an Afrocentric world view: Introduction to an optimal psychology* by L. Myers. Some of the questions are: How would you define Afrocentricity, describe the historical development of the Afrocentric paradigm, identify the author's seminal idea regarding Afrocentricity; how do you relate Afrocentricity to social work practice—provide at least three examples; why is it important for social workers to be exposed to (learn about) another worldview; discuss your reaction to doing this assignment (why did you choose to do this particular assignment, what has it meant to you, how do you think it will affect your practice); and what, if any, recommendations do you make for modifying this assignment in the future?

Overall, student response to the assignment has been favorable. Students were keenly interested in learning another worldview; some students expressed anger at having been educated with myopic vision; some students gained deeper insight into the horrific negative impact of the hegemonic Euro-American perspective, which pathologizes the daily life challenges of Black Americans; a few students found the book they selected to be difficult reading. In short, all students indicated they benefited enormously from being exposed to a different way of viewing the human experience, regardless of whether they found it a difficult or a not-too-difficult assignment.

Practitioners already in the field must also become knowledgeable about African-centered scholarship. The same postgraduation learning opportunities they have used for updating knowledge and skill apply here—workshops, conferences, in-service training, self-directed learning, summer institutes, and the like. In addition to these sources of learning, all major U.S. cities have bookstores whose primary focus is African American and African-centered books, games, videos, cassettes, and other learning resources. Practitioners can acquaint themselves with the stores' inventory. It should not be difficult for practitioners to recognize this content area as part of their educational evolution.

Social work education's history has followed the pattern of using dominant-group research and scholarship and then evolving over time in response to the civil rights movement to using cultural group–specific knowledge—Black Americans, Native Americans, Asian Americans,

Hispanics/Latinas, and Latinos. As reflective of the larger society's experiences, social work education evolved to a focus on cultural sensitivity and subsequently on multiculturalism. Social work education is slowly evolving to a recognition of African-centered perspectives and paradigms as the next steps in the African American experience. This is precisely the point of this chapter. Practitioners cannot continue to intervene and practice as though African-centered perspectives are not a part of the knowledge and experiential milieu.

Just as social workers learned the importance of culturally sensitive practice, they will learn the importance of African-centered frames of reference for practice. It will become clear that just as it is valuable to use culturally relevant pictures, reading materials, and other visual and audio resources to let African American clients know they are welcome, and just as workers know to use culturally sensitive communication and mannerisms as cues of acceptance and rapport building, the essence of their knowledge base must come to recognize the paradigm shift from complete reliance on Euro-American/Western–dominated social science thinking and results to embracing African-centered thinking and scholarship. As Crawley (1991) pointed out, recently women came to experience having the "critical mass of [their] scholarship" included in the training of social workers (p. 2). So, too, will African Americans.

Summary and Conclusion

The homogenization of U.S. society has not happened. Few in this era of multiculturalism, cultural diversity, and "political correctness" expect the nation to return to a melting-pot orientation as a means to ensure acceptance and inclusion for all its citizens. For African Americans, there is a spotty record of acceptance and inclusion as full citizens. Rather, as pointed out, numerous paradigm shifts have been tried—acculturation, assimilation, accommodation, and integration. None of these has achieved the goal of full economic, social, and political equality. Although there has been some noteworthy progress over the centuries, for numerous Black Americans the glaring statistics reported in the Morganthau et al. (1992) and Riley (1986) sources, as well as daily in current media sources, reflect the fact that much work remains.

For those affected by the grim data and whose lives are severely tested and challenged by economic, psychological, and interpersonal crises, social services are frequently touted as the remedy. Social services, however, flow out of the dominant ideologies and paradigms that create and sustain the structural barriers to opportunities and experiences of self-help and development. As discussed earlier in this chapter, African American families have been subject to centuries of survival and "thrival" in the oftimes oppressive and hostile climate of U.S. racism and segregationist practices.

Decades of social services have not proven adequate to significantly alter the life conditions of many low- and modest-income–level African American families. It cannot be expected that social programs and services will substitute for needed structural, societal-level changes. Social programs and services can, however, help to ameliorate personal crises, as well as create opportunities for personal development, change, and empowerment. Thus, it is important that social programs and services reflect an ideology and paradigm, as well as a worldview, that values the client group. This has not been the case for social programs and services used with African American families. As pointed out in this chapter, an African-centered approach to social program and services design, to intervention and practice modalities, and finally to the education and training of social workers (and other human services professionals) would (1) provide greater consumer choice; (2) offer Black families a way of being conceptualized that does not pathologize their struggles, challenges, and life experiences; and (3) provide a framework that allows clients to connect to a vital sphere of their identity—that is, being of African descent.

References

Abarry, A. (1990). Afrocentricity. *Journal of Black Studies, 21*(2), 126–144.

Akbar, N. (1991). *Visions for Black men.* Nashville, TN: Winston-Derek Publications.

The American Black family: Looking back (1987). *American Visions, 2*(6), 26–27.

Asante, M. (1988). *Afrocentricity.* Trenton, NJ: Africa World Press.

Asante, M. (1991). The Afrocentric idea in education. *Journal of Negro Education, 60*(2), 170–178.

Azibo, D. A. (Spring 1989). African-centered theses on mental health and a nosology of Black/African personality disorder. *Journal of Black Psychology, 15*(2), 173–214.

Azibo, D. A. (Spring 1991). Towards a metatheory of the African personality. *Journal of Black Psychology, 17*(2), 37–45.

Black Voices (September–October 1991). *Utne Reader,* 50–61.

Bradbury, K., & L. Browne (March–April 1986). Black men in the labor market. *New England Economic Review,* 32–42.

Center on Budget and Policy Priorities (1986). Falling behind: A report on how Blacks have fared under Reagan. *Journal of Black Studies, 17*(2), 148–172.

Chestang, L. (1980). Character development in a hostile environment. In M. Bloom (Ed.), *Life span development* (pp. 40–50). New York: Macmillan.

Childs, J. (Summer 1986). Policy implications of current research on the Black community. *Social Policy,* 16.

Crawley, B. (1988). Black families in a neo-conservative era. *Family Relations, 37*(4), 415–419.

Crawley, B. (March 1991). Infusion of women of color content into the core curriculum. Paper presented at the Council on Social Work Education Thirty-Seventh Annual Program Meeting, New Orleans, Louisiana.

Crawley, B., & E. Freeman (1993). Themes in the life views of older African American and younger African American males. *Journal of African American Male Studies, 1*(1), 15–29.

Dunn, W. (March 24, 1987). Island Blacks strive to save their heritage. *USA Today,* 8A.

Gortner, H., J. Mahler, & J. Nicholson (1987). *Organization theory: A public perspective.* Chicago: Dorsey Press.

Halicki, T. (April 1988). *The forgotten farmer: The national voter,* 13–15.

Hanson, J. (1992). Dubuque: A future of racial peace or strife? *Crisis, 99*(1), 17–18, 32.

Hazzard-Gordon, K. (1991). In P. Petrie, Afrocentrism in a multicultural democracy. *American Visions, 6*(4), 21–22.

Hill, R. (1972). *The strengths of Black families.* New York: Emerson Hall Publishers.

Hill, R. (August 1987a). The Black middle class defined. *Ebony, 30,* 32.

Hill, R. (1987b). Building the future for Black families. *American Visions, 2*(6), 16–25.

hooks, bell. (September–October 1991). The chitlin circuit. In Black voices. *Utne Reader,* 50–52.

Jeffries, J., & R. Brock (1991). African-Americans in a changing economy: A look at the 21st century. *Crisis, 98*(6), 22–32.

Karenga, M. (1985). Political culture and resurgent racism in the United States. *Black Scholar, 16*(3), 21–35.

Kenyetta, M. (1983). In defense of the Black family: The impact of racism on the family as a support system. *Monthly Review, 34*(10), 12–21.

Keto, C. (1989). *The Africa centered perspective of history.* Blackwood, NJ: K. A. Publications.

Korchin, S. (1980). Clinical psychology and minority problems. *American Psychologist, 35*(3), 262–269.

Kunjufu, J. (1985). *Countering the conspiracy to destroy Black boys,* Vol. 1. Chicago: African American Images.

Kunjufu, J. (1986). *Countering the conspiracy to destroy Black boys,* Vol. 2. Chicago: African American Images.

Lamar, J. (February 1992). The problem with you people. *Esquire,* 90–94.

Levine, A., & D. Collins (August 4, 1986). When tenants take over. *U.S. News & World Report,* 11–13.

Lowy, R. (1991). Yuppie racism: Race relations in the 1980s. *Journal of Black Studies, 21*(4), 445–464.

Madhubuti, H. R. (1990). Black men obsolete, single, dangerous? *Afrikan American families in transition: Essay in discoveries, solution, and hope.* Chicago: Third World Press.

Malveaux, J. (1988). Race, class, and poverty. *Black Scholar, 19*(3), 18–21.

Markowitz, L. (July–August 1993). Walking the walk. *Networker, 17*(4), 19–31.

Morganthau, T., M. Mabry, F. Washington, V. Smith, E. Yoffe, & L. Beachy (April 6, 1992). Losing ground. *Newsweek,* 20–22.

Myers, L. (1988). *Understanding an Afrocentric world view: Introduction to an optimal psychology.* Dubuque, IA: Kendall/Hunt Publishing Company.

National Center for Neighborhood Enterprise, 1367 Connecticut Avenue, N.W., Washington, DC (n.d.). This organization is committed to Black Americans' financial and community development through self-help. It publishes a newsletter.

Oliver, W. (September 1989). Black males and social problems. *Journal of Black Studies, 20*(1), 15–39.

Oyebade, B. (1990). African studies and the Afrocentric paradigm: A critique. *Journal of Black Studies, 21*(2), 233–238.

Paige, R. (February 28, 1986). The other crisis in rural America: *Black land loss. North American Farmer,* 8.

Payton, R. (May 3, 1986). Operation Reachback: The poor helping each other. *Washington Afro-American,* 1.

Petrie, P. (August 1991). Afrocentrism in a multicultural democracy. *American Visions, 6*(4), 20–26.

Phillips, F. (Fall 1990). NTU psychotherapy: An Afrocentric approach. *Journal of Black Psychology, 17*(1), 55–74.

Poole, I. (August 13, 1986). Self-help programs aid at Blacks solving economic, family problems. *Washington Times,* 17–19.

Riley, N. (1986). Footnotes of a culture at risk. *Crisis, 93*(3), 23–29, 45–46.

Roberts, S. (November 12, 1990). School plan for Blacks draws fire. *New York Times.*

Rolison, G. (1991). An exploration of the term *underclass* as it relates to African-Americans. *Journal of Black Studies, 21*(3), 287–301.

Safran, C. (May 28, 1991). What it's really like to be Black. *Woman's Day,* 60, 62–65.

Schiele, J. (December 1991). Organizational theory from an Afrocentric perspective. *Journal of Black Studies, 21*(2), 145–161.

Staples, R. (1978). The Black family revisited. In R. Staples (Ed.), *The Black family: Essays and studies* (2d ed.) (pp. 13–18). Belmont, CA: Wadsworth.

Staples, R. (1987). Black male genocide: A final solution to the race problem in America. *Black Scholar, 18*(3), 2–11.

Streeter, R. C. (Producer and Director) (1986). *The vanishing family—Crisis in Black America* [film]. New York: Carousel Film and Video.

Sue, S. (May 1983). Ethnic minority issues in psychology: A reexamination. *American Psychologist*, 583–592.

Toldson, I., & A. Pasteur (1975). Self-discovery: Implications for using Black art forms in group interaction. *Journal of Negro Education, 44*(2), 130–138.

Urban Research Review (1986). Strong Black families: Research findings. Washington, DC: *Howard University Institute for Urban Affairs and Research Publication, 1*(1), 1–2, 5.

Wilson, W. (1978). *The declining significance of race.* Chicago: University of Chicago Press.

Wilson, W. (1987). *The truly disadvantaged.* Chicago: University of Chicago Press.

8

Racial Identity Issues for Black Children in Foster Care

RUTH G. MCROY

> Teaching a child strategies to deal with racism, and the negative feelings about being Black that racism incurs, is very helpful. But nothing can substitute for the love, care and training that the child needs from birth onward.
>
> —**James P. Comer**

Although the number of children in foster care decreased by 50 percent from about 500,000 to about 242,000 between 1977 and 1982, recent estimates suggest that at present there may be as many as 450,000 children in care (NACAC, 1992). By the mid to late 1990s, it is estimated that the number may increase to over 550,000 (Morton, 1990). In many states about half of the children in care are children of color, in some states this number is even higher. For example, in New York almost 90 percent of the children in care are children of color. In states such as New Jersey, Maryland, and Louisiana, more than 50 percent of the children in care are African American (Stehno, 1990).

Lindsey (1991) reported that parental income is the best single predictor of whether a child of any age will be removed from his or her biological parents and placed in foster care or be left at home and receive supportive services. Once placed, studies have shown that children of color tend to remain in care longer and receive fewer services than white children, and their families have fewer contacts with workers than do white families (Close, 1983). For example, studies of the New York foster care system have reported that workers were less likely to arrange visitations for Black children than for white children (Gurak, Smith, & Goldson, 1986; Stehno, 1990).

The availability of foster care placements with African American families is also an issue. As the number of children entering foster care has increased, agencies have been confronted with a shortage of foster families of all races, but especially of African American families. In Chicago, for example, Black babies often remain in hospitals and in temporary shelters while awaiting placement with a foster family. The low pay for foster parents, inadequate minority recruitment efforts, and the complex problems many children in care are experiencing (e.g., crack-exposed babies, HIV-positive children, and emotionally disturbed children) are all deterrents to families choosing to provide foster care (Stehno, 1990).

In many states the number of African American children in foster care far exceeds the number of African American foster families; thus, African American children are often placed in transracial foster care. Many of these children remain with white families, often separated from their siblings, with limited contact with their birth families or extended families for several years before they are either returned to their families or placed in adoption. In a growing number of court cases, white foster families are seeking to adopt Black children whom they have fostered since infancy (McRoy, 1993). In many of these instances, few if any attempts have been made to initially work toward seeking placements for these children within their extended family before resorting to transracial foster care.

This chapter focuses on the situation of Black children growing up in foster care with white families. I examine factors influencing racial identity for these children, and a case illustration is presented. Suggestions for practice with transracial foster families and Black children in care are provided.

Issues for African American Children in Foster Care

According to a recent study of African American children in the foster care system (National Black Child Development Institute, 1989), Black children enter care at an average age of seven and spend an average of almost two years in care. During this period they may have had more than two caseworkers, have changed schools, and have moved at least two times (Pinderhughes, 1991). Thus, not only have these children been removed from their families of origin, they have also experienced a number of losses and transitions to different environments, even different cultures, from those to which they were accustomed (McDonald et al., 1992). A review of the literature on foster care reveals much attention to adjusting to grief and loss (Aldgate, Maluccio, & Reeves, 1989; Fahlberg, 1981) but almost no attention to the unique racial identity issues to which children of color must also adjust.

According to the Child Welfare Institute, foster care goals include the following: to continue socialization of the child, to facilitate overcoming developmental delays or help to overcome emotional trauma resulting from previous abuse and neglect, and to help the child develop skills in family living that will essentially prepare the child for return to the birth family or for adoptive placement (Morton, 1990). When children are placed in completely different cultural contexts from those to which they are accustomed, foster parents have additional racial and cultural socialization issues to address. It is important to acknowledge the uniqueness of the Black experience and to recognize that Black identity is much more than simply not being white (Logan, 1981).

Racial identity is defined as "one's self perception and sense of belonging to a particular group. It goes beyond the notion of racial self-identification and includes how one differentiates between oneself and members of other groups and the extent to which an individual has acquired behaviors specific to the particular racial group" (McRoy, 1990, p. 98). Children become aware of racial differences as young as three years of age (McRoy & Zurcher, 1983; Mussen, Conger, & Kagan, 1969; Proshansky, 1966), and they are able to distinguish between color and hair texture. Their attitudes toward "being Black" are influenced by the racial attitudes and race socialization message they received from their caretakers. For example, if children are raised in positive, nurturing foster care environments, it is possible that they have received positive socialization messages and feel positively about their appearance and racial identity.

The following four variables are among the factors that influence the child's adjustment and development of racial identity in a new foster care situation: racial environment and attitudes of the foster family and peers, and race of other children in care; age of the child; race socialization experiences; and stage of racial identity development. Each is discussed briefly.

Racial Environment

A number of contextual factors including the immediate family, school, the community, and broader society influence one's self-awareness and one's ethnic self-description. If African American children are growing up in an environment in which they are in the majority, they will define themselves in terms of others in the environment and may exhibit group preference (Rotheram & Phinney, 1987). However, if they are growing up in a racially dissonant environment in which African Americans are in the minority, they may express less emphasis on their differentness and may even exhibit outgroup (white) preference behavior.

African American children who come into foster care settings are most likely to come from low-income, single-parent families of origin (Lindsey, 1991). With the added stresses of limited financial and affective support and in some instances abuse or neglect, many may have been exposed to very few, if any, role models other than those in their community and family. They may have been exposed to chaotic family situations in which parents were out of control because of alcohol or drug abuse. Black children who have been removed from this environment may be placed in a foster home that is completely different from their family of origin. As a result of the shortage of African American foster families, they are likely to be placed with a white family residing in a predominantly white or racially integrated neighborhood. They may shift from almost daily contact with only Blacks to very limited or no contact with Blacks. Both their previous experiences and their new experiences with whites and Blacks will influence their adjustment. It is also important to note that racial identity issues may become even more complex in foster care situations in which the child may be moving from home to home and the racial socialization attitudes and behaviors may vary greatly, just as the parenting styles may vary.

Age of the Child

The age of the child will influence the understanding of racial differences and of one's own racial identity. For example, until children cognitively develop the sense of constancy or permanence, usually around age seven, and are able to understand the permanence of their racial classification, they assume that by putting on a blonde wig they can become white (Semaj, 1985). Once they mature cognitively, they begin to understand the permanence of their racial background.

The age and cognitive development stage of the child at the time of placement will make a difference in terms of his or her race socialization experiences. Infants or toddlers who receive loving, nurturing care from white foster care providers are likely to generalize to other whites the positive experiences they have had within their foster home. They are likely to feel positively about whites and may tend to feel very anxious and cautious when around Blacks, especially if they experienced abuse at the hands of Blacks. These feelings will continue unless the child has positive parental or family visiting experiences and receives positive messages about Blacks from foster parents. If Black children spend much of their early years in a white foster home, they may express a desire to be adopted by the foster family or another white family. In fact, some white foster parents report that Black toddlers reared only around whites express alarm and signs of insecurity when left in a room with unfamiliar Blacks. When left in a room with unfamiliar whites, the toddlers appeared much more comfortable and showed fewer signs of distress. These toddlers are likely to have had negative early experiences with Blacks in their families of origin and have learned to equate whites with positive, nurturing experiences.

Racial Socialization

Studies of Black parenting have revealed the functional value of racial socialization in preparing Black children to survive life in a race-conscious and often racist-oriented society (Peters, 1985). Black parents have often experienced prejudice and racism themselves and must find a way to convey to their children culture-specific values, attitudes, and behaviors.

Black children who come into foster care during middle childhood or adolescence may have already developed distinctive racial attitudes. Some may feel very suspicious toward whites and may express their discomfort and dislike over being placed in a white family. They may have difficulty adjusting to any family because of their age and previous experiences, but they will especially have problems with a white family if they have not had positive interactions with whites. Moreover, if placement with a white family means they may be moving from a predominantly Black or integrated school and neighborhood to a predominantly white school and neighborhood, they may have even more adjustment difficulties. They may express a desire to be placed with a Black family to enable them to remain in a familiar neighborhood and school.

Although only limited research attention has been given to issues of racial identity in white foster families, studies of transracial adoptions have revealed the presence of color-blind children (Simon & Alstein, 1977) and color-blind parents (Rosenthal et al., 1991). In these studies children and parents were likely to report various adjustment problems in the areas of child behavior, learning disabilities, discipline, and school issues, but they rarely commented on the issue of race. The failure to comment on race is very significant, as many of the criticisms of transracial adoptions stem from the fact that Black children need to have a strong racial identity and must develop survival skills to live in a race-conscious society (Chestang, 1972; Jones & Else, 1979; Ladner, 1977; McRoy & Zurcher, 1983; National Association of Black Social Workers, 1972; Small, 1984). Longitudinal research is needed to assess outcomes for Black children living in transracial foster care as well as for adoptions. Are parents and children using denial of differences as a means of dealing with discomfort associated with issues of race, or are parents and children not understanding racial issues? (Rosenthal et al., 1991).

Stage of Racial Identity Development

A number of authors have proposed various models of racial identity development (Cross, 1987; Parham & Helms, 1985; Phinney, Lochner, & Murphy, 1990). For example, Phinney, Lochner, and Murphy (1990) have developed a model of adolescent ethnic identity development that consists of three stages. Stage one, ethnic identity diffusion/foreclosure, suggests that the adolescent has either diffused identity, in which he or she seems to have no interest in his or her ethnicity, or foreclosure, in which one's ethnic self-attitudes are influenced by others. Often, these youths may judge themselves by white norms and tend to view themselves negatively. Phinney and colleagues suggest, moreover, that adolescents with foreclosed identity may be at risk for a poor-self-concept. An experience with racism or increased awareness of the value of minority culture often leads to the second stage, an intense immersion through ethnic identity search. In this stage, ethnic identity search/moratorium, the encounter experience may prompt adolescents to a heightened awareness of both their racial identity and the impact of prejudice and racism on their lives. The final stage, ethnic identity achievement, occurs when one can internalize and accept belonging to a distinct ethnic group. Ethnic identity has a real meaning for youths, and they are now much more likely to learn ways of dealing with both majority and minority cultures.

A Black child in a white foster home may develop a diffused or foreclosed identity depending upon his or her experiences prior to coming into care, age at placement and experiences while in care. If the child is biracial (one Black and one white birth parent), racial identity issues may be even more complex. For example, some "racially mixed" young people may find themselves overidentifying with either their white or their Black parent. Some may find they are rejected by both Black and white peers. Gibbs (1989) has found that many may experience diffusion or identity foreclosure or the assumption of a negative identity characterized by overidentifying with the negative stereotypes of lower-income Blacks.

Although there has been some research on mixed-race or biracial transracially adopted children, again little has been written on biracial children in transracial foster care. Biracial children are typically considered Black, as in our society race categories are often assumed based upon phenotypic characteristics rather than percent of Black genes (Chimezie, 1975; Jones & Else, 1979; Small, 1984). However, it may be difficult for white families to help these children to accept the reality that they may be viewed as Black. Some studies of transracial adoptive families with mixed-race children have suggested that some white parents raise these children to believe they can be whatever they want to be. McRoy and Zurcher (1983) found that some children in their study tended to deny the significance of race completely or were likely to define themselves racially as "half white," "mixed," "part white," or Mexican. These categories tended to emphasize their kinship with whites or denied their actual identity entirely by identifying "Mexican" as a group they found to be more socially acceptable to Blacks.

Case Illustration

Clearly, research attention needs to be given to the many variables that may affect the child's racial identity in a foster care situation. For example, this case illustrates the many dilemmas a child can experience:

After repeated allegations of physical abuse by her mother and boyfriend, Mary—an 11-year-old medium-brown–complexioned African American female with short, brown, braided hair—was placed, with her two younger brothers, with the Silsbys, a white foster family. The Department of Human Services, operating under a new state law that stipulated that race should not be a primary consideration in making foster and adoptive placements, placed the children in a white foster home. The Silsbys soon became overwhelmed with the care of all three children in addition to two other foster girls already in their home. Mary's two younger brothers were sent to a Black foster home, and the 11-year-old girl remained with the Silsbys. The two white foster siblings in the home were blonde, blue-eyed girls ages 9 and 11. The family lived in a middle-income, predominantly white community, and the girls attended a neighborhood elementary school. Prior to removal from her family of origin, Mary had lived in a predominantly Black community and had attended a predominantly Black school.

Mary had learned in her old neighborhood that whites were not to be trusted. She refused to let her foster mother touch her hair and was antagonistic about everything she tried to do for her. Her new foster siblings seemed afraid of Mary and told their foster mother they thought Mary might steal from them. They asked their foster mother why Mary was so dark and why her skin turned so ashy after her bath. The foster mother explained that Mary was a "brown" girl and that she was just like them, so they should ignore her skin color and different hair texture. "All you girls must be friends," she said. "There are no differences between people." One day Mary ran home from school in a rage, exclaiming that the kids had called her a "Nigger." She said she would never go back to that school again. The foster mother told her that some kids are prejudiced but not to worry—she was just as good as anyone who was white and not to let their taunts bother her. Mary began to have many behavioral problems at school and was acting out at home. After her first six weeks in the foster home and attending the new school, Mary received failing grades in all of her classes, and she began skipping school. The foster mother called the worker to complain about the behavioral problems and academic difficulties at school.

Mary had developed feelings of cultural paranoia and a basic distrust of whites while living in her home environment. These attitudes were reinforced as she entered a racially dissonant context in foster care. Already experiencing feelings of loss, abandonment, and rejection, she was placed in a situation in which she felt even further rejected by peers at school. The foster mother did not realize that dismissing Mary's pain and fears and saying "she is just as good as anyone white" suggested perhaps unknowingly, that Mary's concerns were unwarranted and that she is okay, as she is equivalent to the white standard.

However, these subtle communication messages and not-so-subtle experiences with racism may have had a very negative impact on Mary's behavior. For workers and foster parents who are unaware of the impact of racial identity on children, all of Mary's problems may be attributed solely to her physical abuse, removal from her home, separation from her siblings, and placement in a foster home. It is important to note the significance of racial differences for children and to include this as a very important component in assessment of foster children, as well as in assessment and training for all foster parents. It is difficult enough for any child to be removed from his or her family of origin and placed in a completely different home with a different set of parents. For Black children placed in racially dissonant foster homes and communities, the adjustment can be even more complex.

Implications for Practice

As more and more African American children come into care, agencies must seek more same-race foster families for children to minimize some of the traumas children must experience. Research suggests that African American children remain in foster care longer than other children. Therefore, agencies should seek the most adaptive, nurturing environment possible. Foster families should be sought that are sensitive to a child's racial identity issues, as well as to the impact of being Black in a race-conscious society. Time in care should be minimized, and attempts should be made to improve the situations of birth families so reunification can occur (Morton, 1990) and to consider kinship care whenever possible.

To accomplish these goals, agencies must hire more culturally competent workers. Several recent studies have documented that the majority of workers are white, and many families of color may not pursue adoptive or foster parenting because of the culturally insensitive application procedures and attitudes of workers (McRoy, 1990; NACAC, 1992; Rosenthal et al., 1991). Developing culturally competent and proficient protective services, family preservation, adoption, and foster care staffs is essential, especially as their clientele is increasingly people of color. Black children entering foster care have already experienced severe emotional and often physical trauma, grief, and loss through no fault of their own. They should not have to risk being placed through a system that is culturally insensitive to their unique racial socialization needs. U.S. children must learn to adapt to a society that is often racist and race-conscious. They not only need nurturing, support, and understanding as they come to grips with being separated from the only family they have ever known; they also need to be placed in a context in which their cultural needs can be addressed appropriately.

Many white families that are currently providing foster care for Black children may espouse color-blind attitudes toward children in their care. However, this attitude suggests a rejection of a reality for children of color. They have some experiences that are similar to those of children in all racial groups, but in many ways children of color experience the world differently because of a societal history of racial oppression. Differentness does not suggest inferiority and should not be interpreted as an anomaly of the white norm. Instead, differences between racial groups are culturally relevant and should be acknowledged.

It is important that foster care program staff and foster families receive training in cultural sensitivity, grooming, cross-cultural communication, and race socialization issues for Black children. They need to be aware of the unique challenges faced by Black children and to learn ways to help children develop positive racial self-feelings. They might be given resource lists that include an emphasis on Black churches, organizations, and beauticians to help with hair care and skin care. Families must confront their own racial attitudes and stereotypes through self-awareness exercises to be able to appropriately raise Black children in their care. Initial training, as well as ongoing foster parent training, must address cultural differences in communication, understanding, and dealing with experiences of racism and the affective development of Black children. White foster parents should seek opportunities for the family to have substantive contact with other Black adults and children to provide Black role models and to increase understanding of and sensitivity to racial issues. They might become involved in Black churches or volunteer to assist with a predominantly Black scout troop or children's group.

Agencies can facilitate these linkages by working closely with community or social groups—such as Black fraternal organizations, community centers, churches, or groups of Black professionals—to invite groups of foster families parenting Black children to attend activities and educational programs. In one community a Black social organization awarded college scholarships to several Black children who were growing up in foster care and involved these youths in discussion forums on contemporary youth issues. These contacts may also serve as a mechanism to recruit more Black foster and adoptive families, provide information about the needs of children in care, recruit more volunteers for client advocacy programs and other support organizations such as Big Brothers and Big Sisters or Court Appointed Special Advocates, and collaboratively develop respite programs and resources that might serve to support and preserve families of color and decrease the need for foster care.

Summary and Conclusion

As an old African proverb states, "It takes a whole village to raise a child." We, as social workers, educators, and child advocates, must join foster families as they seek to provide care for the many children entering the child welfare system. Families that have assumed these often difficult parenting responsibilities deserve to be applauded for their commitment. The community should also be called upon to help strengthen birth families whose children are at risk for abuse and neglect. As we enhance the cultural competence and experiences of staff and families, we increase the likelihood of stability and improved parenting ability of foster parents.

References

Aldgate J., A. Maluccio, & C. Reeves (1989). *Adolescents in foster families.* Chicago: Lyceum Books.

Chestang, L. (1972). The dilemma of biracial adoption. *Social Work, 17,* 100–105.

Chimezie, A. (1975). Transracial adoption of Black children. *Social Work, 20,* 296–301.

Close, M. M. (1983). Child welfare and people of color: Denial of equal access. *Social Work, 19*(4), 13–20.

Cross, W. E. (1987). A two-factor theory of Black identity: Implication for the study of identity development in minority children. In J. S. Phinney & M. J. Rotheram (Eds.), *Children's ethnic socialization* (pp. 117–133). Newbury Park, CA: Sage Publications.

Fahlberg, V. (1981). *Helping children when they move.* London: British Agencies for Adoption and Fostering.

Gibbs, J. T. (1989). Black American adolescents. In J. T. Gibbs, L. N. Huang, & associates (Eds.), *Children of color: Psychological interventions with minority youth* (pp. 179–223). San Francisco, CA: Jossey Bass.

Gurak, D. T., D. A. Smith, & M. F. Goldson (1986). *The minority foster child: A comparative study of Hispanic, Black and white children.* New York: Hispanic Research Center of Fordham University.

Jones, C. E., & J. F. Else (1979). Racial and cultural issues in adoption. *Child Welfare, 58*(6), 373–382.

Ladner, J. (1977). *Mixed families: Adopting across racial boundaries.* New York: Anchor Press.

Lindsey, D. (1991). Factors affecting the foster care placement decision: An analysis of national survey data. *American Journal of Orthopsychiatry, 61*(2), 272–281.

Logan, S. L. (1981). Race, identity, and Black children: A developmental perspective. *Social Casework, 62*(1), 47–56.

McDonald, T., R. Allen, A. Westerfelt, & I. Piliavin (1992). What we know about the effects of foster care. *Focus, 14*(2), 22–34.

McRoy, R. G. (1990). An organizational dilemma: The case of transracial adoptions. *Journal of Applied Behavioral Science, 25*(2), 145–160.

McRoy, R. G. (1993). Attachment and racial identity issues: Implications for child placement decision making. *Journal of Multicultural Social Work, 3*(3), 59–75.

McRoy, R. G., & L. A. Zurcher (1983). *Transracial and inracial adoptees: The adolescent years.* Springfield, IL: Charles C. Thomas.

Morton, T. (Summer 1990). *The future of foster care: Ideas in action.* Atlanta, GA: Child Welfare Institute.

Mussen, P. H., J. Conger, & J. Kagan (1969). *Child development and personality* (2d ed.). New York: Harper and Row

National Association of Black Social Workers (1972). Position statement on transracial adoption. Paper presented at the National Association of Social Workers Conference, Nashville, Tenn.

National Black Child Development Institute (NBCDI) (1989). *Who will care when parents can't? A study of Black children in foster care.* Washington, DC: NBCDI.

North American Council on Adoptable Children (NACAC). (1992). Adoption at the federal level. In *Adoptalk* (newsletter), p. 5. St. Paul, MN: NACAC.

Parham, T. A., & J. E. Helms (1985). The relationship of racial identity attitudes to self-actualization of Black students and affective states. *Journal of Counseling Psychology, 32*, 431–440.

Peters, M. F. (1985). Racial socialization of young Black children. In H. P. McAdoo & J. L. McAdoo (Eds.), *Black children: Social, educational and parental environments* (pp. 159–173). Beverly Hills, CA: Sage Publications.

Phinney, J. S., B. T. Lochner, & R. Murphy (1990). Ethnic identity development and psychological adjustment in adolescence. In A. R. Stiffman & L. E.

Davis (Eds.), *Ethnic issues in adolescent mental health* (pp. 53–72). Newbury Park, CA: Sage Publications.

Pinderhughes, E. E. (1991). The delivery of child welfare services to African American clients. *American Journal of Orthopsychiatry, 61*(4), 599–605.

Proshansky, H. (1966). The development of intergroup attitudes. In L. W. Hoffman & M. L. Hoffman (Eds.), *Review of child development research.* New York: Sage Publications.

Rosenthal, J. A., V. Groze, H. Curiel, & P. A. Westcott (1991). Transracial and inracial adoption special needs children. *Journal of Multicultural Social Work, 1*(3), 13–32.

Rotheram, M. J., & J. S. Phinney (1987). Ethnic behavior as patterns as an aspect of identity. In J. S. Phinney & M. J. Rotheram (Eds.), *Children's ethnic socialization: Pluralism and development* (pp. 201–218). Newbury Park, CA: Sage Publications.

Semaj, L. T. (1985). Afrikanity, cognition and extended self-identity. In M. B. Spencer, G. K. Brookins, & W. R. Allen (Eds.), *Beginnings: The social and affective development of Black children* (pp. 173–183). Hillsdale, NJ: Lawrence Erlbaum Publishers.

Simon, R. J., & H. Alstein (1977). *Transracial adoption.* New York: John Wiley & Sons.

Small, J. W. (1984). The crisis in adoption. *International Journal of Social Psychiatry, 30*(1, 2), 129–142.

Stehno, S. M. (1990). The elusive continuum of child welfare services: Implications for minority children and youths. *Child Welfare, 69*(6), 551–562.

9

Resiliency and the African American Family: A Model of Family Preservation

RAMONA W. DENBY

> I will lift up mine eyes unto the hills, from whence cometh my help.
> My help cometh from the Lord, which made heaven and earth.
> —Psalms 121: 1–2

Within the past decade there has been a major proliferation of family preservation programs. Nationally, between 1982 and 1988 the number of such programs increased from 20 to 333 (National Resource Center on Family-Based Services, 1988). Current attention is concentrated on the evaluation of these programs for their effectiveness, cost efficiency, and client appropriateness. Absent, however, is a focus on the need for more cultural specificity in these programs.

As researchers explore ways to improve the delivery of family preservation services, credence must be given to culturally specific family preservation models. Further, if such models are to inform service delivery, they must begin by establishing a value base. This chapter presents an African American–centered value system from which family preservation programs should address the needs of African American families. Clues to the discovery of effective family preservation models for African Americans are found in an examination of strategies already employed by this group. These strategies maintain strong, healthy, and intact families.

The following sections provide (1) a definition of family preservation, (2) discussion of cultural competence in relation to family preservation, (3) discussion of African American family values, and (4) discussion of family preservation values. The points outlined earlier serve as a framework for the proposed model, which has been developed through a synthesis of family preservation program values and African American family values. A case vignette demonstrates elements contained in the proposed model and suggests practice principles.

Family-Based Initiatives

What Is Family Preservation?

Cole and Duva (1990) cite a growing body of research, successful program models, increased numbers of children in foster care, and federal legislation as factors influencing the development and expansion of family preservation services. These researchers describe family preservation services as "a unique and powerful set of interventions at the point of a family crisis that is likely to result in the imminent removal of a child from the home" (1990, p. 1).

Family preservation program characteristics cited by Cole and Duva (1990) include immediate response to referrals, revolving availability of services, family centered intervention, intensive intervention, in-home therapeutic services, limited treatment objectives vis-à-vis the crisis endured by the family, multiple services (i.e., counseling, concrete assistance, advocacy, information, and referral), short-term intervention, and small caseload size. Noticeably missing from these program characteristics is the acknowledgment of culturally based services.

Culturally Specific Family Preservation Models

Why is there a need for culturally specific programming? What is the relevance of such programming to an African American Family Preservation Model? These and similar questions are easily answered through an examination of out-of-home placement rates. The population of children and adolescents who have been placed outside their natural homes because of maltreatment, delinquency, mental health problems, or developmental disabilities is astronomical—and increasing. Nationally,

429,000 children were in out-of-home care at the end of 1991, a 4.1 percent increase from 1990 and a 64 percent increase since 1982 (Merkel-Holguin & Sobel, 1993). More alarming is the rise in the rate of children-of-color placement since 1982, particularly African American children, for whom the out-of-home placement rate rose 46.7 percent between 1982 and 1989 (Merkel-Holguin & Sobel, 1993). In 1989, 30.6 percent of the children who entered out-of-home care were African American (Merkel-Holguin & Sobel, 1993).

Although troubling, these figures alone do not signify the need for culturally specific programming. Experience and available research have shown that services to African American families and children are generally not provided in a culturally sensitive context or by culturally competent practitioners (Logan, Freeman, & McRoy, 1990; also see Chapter 7 and Chapter 12). Together these factors justify the development of culturally driven models of practice.

The cultural context of the population served by family preservation programs must be reflected in the programs' values, philosophies, and service delivery. Such a reflection would consider the varying needs of service populations. Indeed, it has been suggested that the models of traditional family preservation programs have been developed based on the community workings and characteristics of nonurban, white populations and have not yet demonstrated their effectiveness in communities of color (Frankel, 1990). Family preservation models that are culturally specific to African Americans are ones in which:

- Program values and philosophies have been developed in accordance with the values espoused by African Americans.
- Services are prescribed according to these values.
- Workers are well grounded in their knowledge of the African American value base.
- Intercultural diversity is recognized.
- Workers respect and acknowledge the African American value system as viable.

When considering culture, it is also significant to note that African Americans are not a monolithic group. "Intercultural variations" caused by geographic region, religion, and socioeconomic status must be considered. Williams and Wright (1992) proposed the use of a "sociocultural" theoretical framework that takes into account intercultural variations. Service delivery models (e.g., family preservation programs) that employ a sociocultural theoretical framework in working with African American families (1) consider the historical, cultural, social, economic, and political forces endured by African Americans; (2) consider the diversity within African American families; and (3) assume that African Americans have carryovers of African culture (Williams & Wright, 1992). By not discounting the diversity in African American family life, a core set of values exists.

African American Families: A Framework of Values

It is sometimes forgotten that most African American families live and prosper as intact units. "On any given day, fully 75 percent of African-American people will be found living in families of one kind or another" (Billingsley, 1990, pp. 90–91). What can be learned from these families? How can family preservation programs devise a value base that is more applicable to African Americans? This section highlights key characteristics, values, and strategies already employed by African American families that help to strengthen and preserve the family unit. The values presented are the culmination of an extensive review of current knowledge about African American families. Figure 9.1 displays a collection of African American values and characteristics as cited by numerous scholars in the literature. The five areas discussed have been taken from Figure 9.1 and chosen for their specific relevance to family preservation programming.

Childrearing.   Among the many strategies that African Americans have successfully employed to strengthen the family unit is their approach to childrearing. Three aspects of African American childrearing are offered as examples of successful strategies to preserve the family unit: (1) shared parenting, (2) pride in children, and (3) "nurturing firmness" in discipline.

An African cultural residual employed by African American families is the use of "collective" or "shared" parenting (Carson, 1981; Hall & King, 1982; Hays & Mindel, 1973; Hill, 1977; Martin & Martin, 1978; Stack, 1974; Sudarkasa, 1988). This occurrence is exemplified in the extensive use of the entire family in childrearing, the use of older siblings in caregiving, and intergenerational support-giving (usually grandmother or aunt to a younger mother). Researchers have noted that such a practice is a direct carryover from African tribal life, whereby the general orientation was that of "we" as opposed to "I" (Franklin & Boyd-

Figure 9.1 Values, Characteristics, and Belief Systems That Have Sustained African American Families

Billingsley, 1968, 1992	Boykin, 1983	Christopherson, 1979	Gary et al., 1983	Hill, 1971	Martin & Martin, 1985	McAdoo, 1988	Nobles, 1976, 1979, 1988	Scanzoni, 1971 Staples, 1994	Stack, 1974 Aschenbrenner, 1973
• Value of learning, knowledge, education, and skill development • Deep spiritual values • Quest for self-governance • Service to others • Cooperative economics, politics, and social goals • Race pride • Strong Black-owned, private enterprises • Family ties	• Spirituality • Harmony • Movement • Verve • Affect • Communalism • Expressive individualism • Orality • Social time perspective	• Love of children • Acceptance of children born out of wedlock • Strong resilience • Adaptability of family coping skills	• Strong kinship bonds • Strong achievement orientation • Parenting skills • Strong religious-philosophical orientation • Intellectual-cultural orientation • Ability to deal with crises • Strong work orientation • Independence • Organization • Active recreation orientation • Appreciation for each other • Adaptability of family roles • Self-expression • Love, kindness, and compassion • Supportiveness and caring	• Strong kinship bonds • Strong work orientation • Adaptability of family roles • Strong achievement orientation • Strong religious orientation	• Elements of extended family 1. Mutual aid 2. Social class cooperation 3. Male-female cooperation 4. Pro-socialization of children • Extension of extended family elements 1. Fictive kinship 2. Racial consciousness 3. Religious consciousness • Institutions of Black helping tradition 1. Black churches 2. Mutual aid societies 3. Fraternal orders 4. Women's clubs 5. Unions 6. Orphanages, senior homes, and hospitals 7. Schools 8. Protest movements 9. Race-consciousness organizations	• Kinship and mutual assistance are more than provision of basic needs	• Strong family ties • Unconditional love of children • Respect for self and others • Assumed natural goodness of children • Legitimation of beingness • Provision of a family code • Elasticity of boundaries • Provision of information and knowledge • Mediation of concrete conditions	• Strong mother-child bonds • Heavy emotional nurturance	• Relationship and kinship ties • Reciprocity • Fidelity to family obligations • Strong commitment to children

Franklin, 1985; Mbiti, 1970; Nobles, 1980). In addition, the notion of shared parenting permeates the biological family to include the practice of "nonblood" relatives caring for, providing for, and rearing children (Boyd, 1982; Hines & Boyd-Franklin, 1982).

A second component of the African American approach to childrearing that has maintained the family unit and is worthy of emulation is the high value placed on children. A family's esteem and worth are often related to the presence of children. Many African American parents consider their children to be their contribution to society. This elevation is necessary because society has devalued, depreciated, and marginalized African American people. As a result, African American families tend to exercise unconditional, positive regard for their children. The existence of children in a family allows African Americans to leave their legacy by transferring "traditions, beliefs, symbols, language, ways of thinking, rules for interacting within Black cultures, and providing a foundation for what it means to be Black" (Dilworth-Anderson, 1992, p. 29). The significance African Americans place on children, family, and family bonds has been noted by several researchers (Bell, 1971; Gary et al., 1983; Nolle, 1972; Scanzoni, 1971; Staples, 1994). Their writings corroborate the sanctity and inherent worth of children in the African American community.

The third aspect of African American childrearing that sustains the family unit is the discipline style nurturing firmness. "Discipline styles among African-American parents are closely scrutinized; yet, they may be among the most positive aspects of African-American childrearing" (Denby & Alford, 1996, p. 1). African American discipline is characterized as firm, caring, and uncompromising. Staples (1994) observed that African American mothers of lower socioeconomic standing combine physical measures with "very high doses of emotional nurturance" (p. 12). Although this combination may prove more effective than a withdrawal of love (often employed by middle-class parents), it is not given merit.

Child discipline in African American families goes beyond the purpose of correcting undesirable behavior. Discipline is largely considered to be a means of socializing children about issues related to race differentials. Staples (1994) noted in his observations of childrearing and parental roles in African American families that parents must socialize their children to adapt successfully to the majority culture's values while simultaneously readying them to know their own ethnicity. Many researchers have observed the strength, creativity, and brilliance employed by African Americans in providing their children with a dual socialization (Brown, 1988; Denby & Alford, 1996; Devore, 1983).

Emphasis on Parenthood (Motherhood).   In addition to childrearing patterns, a theoretical model for preserving African American families would concentrate on the culture's emphasis on motherhood. Like the value given to children, much significance and honor are given to mothers. Discussion of motherhood as an underpinning in African American family life focuses on two main points: (1) centrality of African American motherhood and (2) centrality of grandmothers.

In exploring the meaning of motherhood in the African American culture, Collins (1994) discusses four common themes: women-centered networks, providing as part of mothering, community "other mothers" and social activism, and motherhood as a symbol of power. Women-centered networks—inclusive of mothers, sisters, aunts, godmothers, and grandmothers—have been a force, as well as an unchanging presence, in African American family life. Such networks fulfill varied roles: nurturer, financial provider, teacher, caregiver, and community and family stabilizer. These roles are indicative of the self-reliance, resourcefulness, and strength that are inherent in Black motherhood.

Second, the centrality of grandmothers is critical in bolstering African American family functioning. Flaherty, Facteau, and Garner (1994) found seven key functions of grandmothers in their study of multigenerational African American families: managing, caretaking, coaching, assessing, nurturing, assigning, and patrolling. Grandmothers are often the glue that holds generations of family members together. They are referred to for guidance in both major and minor family matters. Such eminence is not granted to the grandmother simply because of African Americans' regard and respect for elders but also because she epitomizes endurance, wisdom, and spirituality.

Emphasis on Parenthood (Fatherhood).   Juxtaposed with the role of motherhood, the parameters of fatherhood are broad in the African American community. Uncles, ministers, deacons, elders of the church, and male teachers can all be viewed as father figures. These men play a significant part in solidifying the foundation of African American communities.

Contrary to popular belief, many biological fathers embrace their fatherly duties with sincerity and thoroughness. In his discussion of father-child interaction in the African American family, J. McAdoo (1988) noted that given economic and social supports, African American fathers welcome the responsibilities of childrearing: "Black fathers, like fathers of all ethnic groups, take an equal part in the childrearing decisions in the family. Their expectations for their child's behavior in the home also appear to be similar given socioeconomic status patterns. . . . [The father's] predominant relationship and interaction pattern appears to be nurturant, warm, and loving toward his children" (p. 266).

In the case of the dubious father who may require extra incentive to fulfill his rightful responsibilities, elders or male fictive kin fill in the gaps by encouraging and redirecting him toward familial matters of importance. They also serve as role models, caretakers, tutors, and informal counselors for the youth of the community. Unselfish efforts such as these are performed to facilitate interest and shore up successful possibilities for young people who are victims of social, economic, and educational disenfranchisement. Several African American men's groups have initiated service projects to help improve the economic and social plights of deprived children and families. The Black Masons, for instance, have a long-standing reputation for their charitable activities (Martin & Martin, 1985). Other groups of similar distinction include 100 Committed Black Men, the Elks, Male Africentric Rites of Passage Programs, and African-American Church Groups. In addition, African American fraternities (Alpha Phi Alpha, Omega Psi Phi, Kappa Alpha Psi, and Phi Beta Sigma) extend their purview in the form of graduate chapters so members can continue their service to humankind beyond undergraduate studies through altruistic deeds and scholarship enhancement. Big-brother mentoring and man-to-man "rap sessions" offered by these fraternal organizations provide opportunities for cathartic release and curative redirection.

Racial Pride and Strong Ethnic Identity. Building racial pride, self-respect, and a strong sense of racial identity are key components in cultivating the family unit. In a study of young African American children and parents, Peters (1985) noted that "racial identity undergirds every parent's child-rearing philosophy" (p. 165). Harrison (1985) noted that a major task for African Americans in the family environment is to socialize children to acquire a positive attitude toward their ethnicity. African American families realize that cultural preservation begins with family preservation. Research has noted the positive results of instilling African American consciousness and self-pride within the African American community (Fox & Barnes, 1971; Hraba & Grant, 1970; Lipscomb, 1975; McAdoo, 1970; Ward & Braun, 1972). Similarly, McAdoo (1985) countered claims that African American children do not value themselves because of negative environmental messages and found, to the contrary, that children felt competent and valued and believed they were perceived positively by their mothers. By instilling a strong sense of ethnic pride, Black families communicate to their children that they matter and that they are important to their communities and families.

Communalism.   A discussion of African American family characteristics that help to enhance the family system is incomplete without mention of the strong sense of communalism that is prevalent in most African American families. Much has been written about the nature of communalism in the African American family (Billingsley, 1968; Gutman, 1976; Hill, 1972; Ladner, 1971, 1973; Martin & Martin, 1978, 1985; McAdoo, 1981; Nobles, 1986; Staples, 1971). This discussion of communalism focuses on two points: (1) family support structures and (2) community support structures.

Two key elements in family support structures that enrich African American families are kinship networks and egalitarian family units. African American families tend to rely on kinship ties in maintaining the family unit. Many researchers have discovered the importance of kin networks in the African American family (Allen, 1979; Angel & Tienda, 1982; Hays & Mindel, 1973; Hofferth, 1984; McAdoo, 1980; Stack, 1974). Strong kinship networks provide not only such concrete necessities as child care, finances, and transportation but also provide emotional support that acts as a buffer to outside stressors and eventually helps to preserve the family unit. The flagrant use of kin in the African American family has also been described as use of a "mutual aid system." It has been noted that the contemporary mutual aid system in African American families "continues to absorb needy and dependent members, using few, if any formal services to support the family" (Dilworth-Anderson, 1992, p. 30). The use of kin networks not only preserves and supports the family but is also a prevention mechanism employed in the African American culture to avoid intervention by official agencies into families.

Although shared roles between husbands and wives may be a relatively new phenomenon within the dominant, middle-class culture, this egalitarian practice has been an enduring tradition in African American families (Hill, 1973; Scanzoni, 1971; Willie, 1976). The sharing of roles lessens the pressures associated with raising a family and ultimately promotes family cohesion and strength.

The second point related to the use of communalism involves community support structures within the African American culture. Indigenous community support structures have assisted African American families in ensuring that the family remains intact. These resources, also referred to as mediating structures, help families withstand the impact of stresses brought on by the larger community (Leigh & Green, 1982). Although some question the viability of contemporary African American community support structures, evidence suggests the existence of a strong, capable, and nurturing community. Billingsley (1992) postulates that African Americans constitute a community in four ways: (1) Geographically, most Blacks live in neighborhoods in which most of their neighbors are Black; (2) there is a shared set of values; (3) most Black people strongly identify with their heritage; and (4) there is a set of institutions and organizations that grew out of the African American heritage, that identify with that heritage, and that serve primarily African American people and families (pp. 71–73).

Resiliency Through Spirituality.   One final value found within the African American culture that has a lasting legacy in strengthening the family unit is spirituality. Spirituality can assume multiple meanings; for example, spirituality can be manifested in a belief structure of perpetual optimism and the ability to recover from adversity. African Americans' undaunted belief in "a better day" is said to be based on a strong religious orientation. Such a belief system sustains the family unit, because this belief is transferred and transposed onto children. Likewise, spirituality leads to parental hopefulness, which is undergirded by love, support, and commitment to children.

A more concrete example of spirituality is that of the African American church. This institution is viewed as a major ingredient in preserving the family. The church often serves as a vehicle of renewal and solace. In addition to providing spiritual guidance, church activities (e.g., church "welfare" programs, libraries, nurseries, preschools, Saturday and Sunday schools) intensify the bonding and solidarity of African American families (Scott & Black, 1994).

Traditional Family Preservation Program Models: A Framework of Values

Although there are several family preservation program models, an overall value structure can be identified. Program values are essential because they are the vehicle by which service delivery, program design, and workers' behaviors are assessed (Rapp & Poertner, 1992). Ronnau and Sallee (1993) obtained several family preservation program values from various sources (e.g., the Child Welfare League of America, the Behavioral Sciences Institute, and the National Resource Center on Family-Based Services) (cited in Ronnau & Marlow, 1993, pp. 540–541):

- People of all ages can best develop, and their lives can best be enhanced, with few exceptions, by remaining with their family or relying on their family as an important resource.
- The family members' ethnic, cultural, and religious background, values, and community ties are important resources to be used in the helping process.
- The definition of *family* is varied, and each family should be approached as a unique system.
- Policies at the local, state, and national levels should be formulated to strengthen, empower, and support families.
- The family members themselves are crucial partners in the helping process.
- Family members should be recognized as being in charge in order to resolve their own problems and avoid dependence on the social service system.
- The right and dignity to privacy of all family members should be respected.
- Families have the potential to change, and most troubled families want to do so.

From this value base, five aspects have been chosen to demonstrate how traditional family preservation values can be synthesized with African American family values to form a more culturally specific value base: (1) a strengths perspective, (2) an empowerment perspective, (3) resource building, (4) belief in change and (5) emphasis on family.

Strengths Perspective.   Many family preservation programs are premised on the belief that there are inherent strengths, capabilities, and "positives" in all individuals and families. Such strengths are utilized in planning interventions with the family.

Empowerment Perspective.   Family preservation programs emphasize to families that their services are different from traditional services in which, for various reasons, a family may have developed feelings of hopelessness and distrust. Families are advised that family preservation services are implemented to reduce the need for intervention by child welfare, juvenile justice, and mental health systems as opposed to being an extension of these service systems (Cole & Duva, 1990). Family preservation emphasizes a family's ability to self-direct its life and to assume its inherent power to make necessary changes.

Resource Building.   Another key value inherent in family preservation programs is the belief in resource building. Families are taught how
to use resources (outside the family preservation agency) to function in-
dependently from the agency.

Belief in Change.   Another fundamental conviction held by family
preservation programs upon which services are predicated is the belief
that all families have the desire and ability to change their situation positively.

Emphasis on Family.   Finally, family preservation service delivery is
governed by the principle that "family is the fundamental resource for
nurturing children" (Kolb, 1993, p. 9). Family preservation program values also consider that the definition of family varies and should be defined
by the family unit itself.

An Integrated Value Framework:
The African American Family Preservation Model

This section integrates traditional family preservation values with those
of African American families to propose a content model more germane
to African American culture. To intervene more effectively in preserving the African American family, practitioners should operate from this
value base.

1. *Recognize African American childrearing patterns as a viable
   family strength.* In the spirit of a strengths perspective, a basic assumption that should be made is that African American childrearing patterns are healthy. In providing treatment to enhance family
   functioning, it is paramount that the family be validated and supported in its role as disciplinarian. Practitioners should not en-
   dorse the use of physical measures. Instead they should validate
   the family in its intent, which is to provide firm, uncompromising,
   nurturing discipline that helps to socialize children as the family
   wants them to be socialized.
2. *Recognize African American motherhood and fatherhood as essential to defining family.* Traditional family preservation models correctly suggest that service delivery should emphasize the family as
   a whole. Indeed, all family members are equal partners in produc-
   ing needed family change. However, with the emphasis placed on

motherhood and the women-centeredness of many African American families, it behooves practitioners to take full advantage of the role of women in preserving the family unit. Intervention must be derived from knowledge about the roles women play in the family structure. A mother-centered base thus becomes relevant. Ownership for family change remains collective, but the power inherent in the status of woman or mother should be considered.

Family preservation workers should expand their definition of fatherhood vis-à-vis the African American community, to include all community men who actively strive to uplift and restore the potential of the family unit. Aggressively seeking assistance from African American male groups would be a viable course of treatment. Acknowledgment and affirmation of the capacities of African American men regarding their families would also broaden a family's perspective and prevent it from feeling relegated to standards inconsistent with its cultural background. In essence, the great value of African American men as a resource in sustaining the family unit has been underestimated by practitioners (Hines & Boyd-Franklin, 1982; Hyde & Texidor, 1994; Logan, 1983; Nobles, 1978, 1988). More emphasis should be placed on this commodity as a catalyst for positive change. Planful intervention should maximize the influential power these men have in working with the family.

3. *Recognize that empowerment must focus on racial identity and pride and on overcoming the pressures associated with racism.* A family preservation program model that is more culturally relevant and addresses the needs of African Americans would include provisions of empowerment pertaining to issues of racial identity and overcoming race-related obstacles. "Given the power blocks created by oppression and the powerlessness which results in the lives of Black clients, empowerment as a goal and process of interventions is of great significance in social work practice with Black clients" (Weaver, 1982, p. 101). African American families should be empowered to create a family climate that buffers them from the effects of race-related pressure that may be threatening the survival of the family unit. The sense of self-determination achieved through racial pride is an area in which intervention can be planned.

4. *Increase usage of indigenous support structures, and decrease reliance on external structures.* It is widely acknowledged that resource building is crucial in family preservation programming. It

should be recognized that indigenous support structures have a strong history of maintaining African American families. The use of such support structures should take precedence over external, official structures.

5. *Recognize the ability to change as having a spiritual link.* Practitioners must recognize that African American families may attribute the ability to effect change in their circumstances as relating to a spiritual source. Although the assumption that the family can change is appropriate, it can be suggested that families cannot only persevere but that African American families have a documented history that suggests they will do so. "Black families are survivors in a hostile environment" (Devore, 1983, p. 528).

Application of the Model

Case Illustration

To illustrate how an African American family preservation model can be applied, a case vignette detailing a family situation is offered. The vignette is followed by a listing of practice principles that serve as a guide to interpreting the family dynamics from an African American value base.

Ms. Jones is a family therapist with a small, private, nonprofit family preservation agency. This agency is contracted to receive referrals from the local Department of Social Services. During a biweekly unit meeting, Ms. Jones is assigned the following referral:

• • •

Vernita Jefferson, African American, age 28, is the mother of Michael, 12, Lamar, 10, Camille, 4, and DaShaun, 2. The family has been referred following a report that Lamar received a "whipping" from an aunt after allegedly stealing athletic shoes from a sporting goods store located in the neighborhood mall. Ms. Jefferson's children are considered at great risk for placement because there is a history of substantiated reports of neglect, the family is without a permanent residence (they are living with Ms. Jefferson's sister), and Ms. Jefferson uses drugs. Upon assessment of the family, one of the caseworker's most salient notes contained this observation: "The mother appears to lack control over her own children, often deferring discipline of the boys to her sister, whose choice of discipline techniques appears somewhat harsh, unreasonable, and inappropriate. Although the mother's sister is not appropriate in her choice of discipline techniques, she does seem vital to the family's support structure, given the mother's current drug use and devalued status." Ms. Jones notes, among many things, that intervention with this family will center around counseling all adults and caretakers about the inappropriateness of corporal punishment, working with the mother to take responsibility in her role as mother, and lessening the mother's dependency on her sister.

Practice Principles

An integrated family preservation model would require that a practitioner effect change in the following manner.

• • •

Principle #1:   Before any intervention, Ms. Jones should begin by assessing her current knowledge of this family's culture. Questions to consider include: From what value base is the family operating? Is what I know about this family based on fact? Do I have the skills and knowledge base to effect change in this culture? Is my approach to this family informed by its cultural influences?

Principle #2:   Instead of assuming that negativity and destruction exist in the family's discipline style, exploration and subsequent acceptance, if appropriate, of the family's intent should be pursued.

Principle #3:   In lieu of lessening the mother's perceived dependency on her sister for assistance in disciplining, consideration of the family's cultural reality is needed. Acceptance of the importance of the extended family's role in the rearing of the children should be communicated to the family.

Principle #4:   Although paternal figures are not mentioned specifically, it should not be assumed that none exist. An assessment of paternal involvement (as defined by the family) should be made. A support network that includes these individuals should be accessed.

Principle #5:   Skills should be developed that promote the family's ability to effectively discipline the children. Such skill can be developed by using indigenous parent training classes and support groups that validate the family in its attempt to socialize its children.

Principle #6:   Care should be taken not to relegate Ms. Jefferson to a "devalued" status because of her drug use. The family may still regard her as a contributing member, given her status as mother.

Principle #7:   Indigenous community support should be galvanized in planning service provision (e.g., church-run drug counseling programs, fraternal orders for mentoring youth, church-operated benevolent funds for concrete assistance, and self-help community groups for skill development and general support).

• • •

A grim case vignette was constructed purposefully to demonstrate that even in the midst of great despair, with proper intervention a troubled family can remain intact. The practice principles offered here are intended to generate thought about the various resources available in situations such as that presented in the case vignette. Moreover, the vignette is given to elucidate the use of themes contained in the African American Family Preservation Model. It should not be inferred that implementation of these practice principles alone will completely resolve the problem, but the principles possess great applicability to culturally specific practice.

Summary and Conclusion

In a period in which congressional cuts of social programs are seemingly commonplace, preserving the family unit is the treatment of choice for many direct service providers. Family preservation initiatives that operate from an African American value base and provide a range of therapeutic and concrete services are more likely to be effective in sustaining African American families than ones that are void of cultural consideration.

References

Allen, W. R. (1979). Class, culture and family organization: The effects of class and race on family structure in urban America. *Journal of Comparative Family Studies, 10,* 301–313.

Angel, R. J., & M. Tienda (1982). Determinants of extended household structure: Cultural pattern of economic need? *American Journal of Sociology, 87,* 1360–1383.

Aschenbrenner, J. (1973). Extended families among Black Americans. *Journal of Comparative Family Studies, 4,* 257–268.

Bell, R. (1971). The related importance of mother and wife roles among Black lower class women. In R. Staples (Ed.), *The Black family: Essays and studies* (2d ed.) (pp. 248–255). Belmont, CA: Wadsworth.

Billingsley, A. (1968). *Black families in white America.* Englewood Cliffs, NJ: Prentice-Hall.

Billingsley, A. (1990). Understanding African-American family diversity. In J. Deward (Ed.), *The state of Black America* (pp. 85–108). New York: National Urban League.

Billingsley, A. (1992). *Climbing Jacob's ladder: The enduring legacy of African-American families.* New York: Simon and Schuster.

Boyd, N. (1982). Family therapy with Black families. In E. Jones and S. Korchin (Eds.), *Minority mental health* (pp. 227–249). New York: Praeger.

Boykin, A. W. (1983). The academic performance of Afro-American children. In J. Spence (Ed.), *Achievement and achievement motives* (pp. 321–371). San Francisco: Freeman.

Brown, A. (Spring 1988). Duality: The need to consider this characteristic when treating Black families. *The Family, 8,* 88.

Carson, N.H.D. (1981). *Informal adoption among Black families in the rural south.* Unpublished Ph.D. dissertation, Northwestern University, Chicago.

Christopherson, V. (1979). Implications for strengthening family life: Rural Black families. In N. Stinnett, B. Chesser, & J. Defrain (Eds.), *Building family strengths: Blueprints for action* (pp. 63–73). Lincoln, Neb.: Lincoln University Press.

Cole, E., & J. Duva (1990). *Family preservation.* Washington, DC: Child Welfare League of America.

Collins, P. H. (1994). The meaning of motherhood in Black culture. In R. Staples (Ed.), *The Black family: Essays and studies* (5th ed.) (pp. 165–173). Belmont, CA: Wadsworth.

Denby, R., & K. Alford (1996). Understanding African-American discipline styles: Suggestions for effective social work intervention. *Journal of Multicultural Social Work, 4*(3).

Devore, W. (1983). Ethnic reality: The Life Model and work with Black families. *Social Casework: The Journal of Contemporary Social Work, 64,* 525–531.

Dilworth-Anderson, P. (Summer 1992). Extended kin networks in Black families. *Generations, 16,* 29–32.

Flaherty, M. J., L. Facteau, & P. Garner, (1994). Grandmother functions in multigenerational families: An exploratory study of Black adolescent mothers and their infants. In R. Staples (Ed.), *The Black family: Essays and studies* (5th ed.) (pp. 195–203). Belmont, CA: Wadsworth.

Fox, D., & U. Barnes (April 1971). Racial preference and identification of Blacks, Chinese, and white children. Paper presented at the American Educational Research Association Meeting, New York, New York.

Frankel, H. Family-centered, home-based services (1990). Quoted in S. M. Stehno, The elusive continuum of child welfare services: Implications for minority children and youths. *Child Welfare, 69,* 551–562.

Franklin, A. J., & N. Boyd-Franklin (1985). A psychoeducational perspective on Black parenting. In H. P. McAdoo and J. L. McAdoo (Eds.), *Black children* (pp. 194–210). Newbury Park, CA: Sage Publications.

Gary, L., L. Beatty, G. Berry, & M. Price (1983). *Stable Black families: Final Report, Institute for Urban Affairs and Research.* Washington, DC: Howard University.

Gutman, H. (1976). *The Black family in slavery and freedom, 1750–1925.* New York: Pantheon.

Hall, E., & G. King (1982). Working with the strengths of Black families. *Child Welfare, 61*, 536–544.

Harrison, A. O. (1985). The Black family's socializing environment. In H. P. McAdoo and J. L. McAdoo (Eds.), *Black children* (pp. 174–193). Newbury Park, CA: Sage Publications.

Hays, W. C., & C. H. Mindel (1973). Extended kinship relations in Black and white families. *Journal of Marriage and the Family, 35*, 51–57.

Hill, R. B. (1971). *The strengths of Black families.* New York: Emerson Hall.

Hill, R. B. (1972). *The strengths of Black families.* New York: Emerson Hall.

Hill, R. B. (1973). *Strengths of Black families.* New York: National Urban League.

Hill, R. B. (1977). *Informal adoption among Black families.* Washington, DC: National Urban League.

Hines, P., & N. Boyd-Franklin (1982). Black families. In M. McGoldrick, J. K. Pearce, & J. Giordano (Eds.), *Ethnicity and family therapy.* New York: Guilford.

Hofferth, S. L. (1984). Kin networks, race, and family structure. *Journal of Marriage and the Family, 46*, 791–806.

Hraba, J., & G. Grant (1970). Black is beautiful: A reexamination of racial preference and identification. *Journal of Personality and Social Psychology, 16*, 398–402.

Hyde, B. L., & M. Texidor (1994). A description of the fathering experience among Black fathers. In R. Staples (Eds.), *The Black: Essays and studies* (5th ed.) (pp. 157–164). Belmont, CA: Wadsworth.

Kolb, L. (Spring 1993). Family preservation in Missouri. *Public Welfare, 51*, 8–19.

Ladner, J. (1971). *Tomorrow's tomorrow.* New York: Anchor Press.

Ladner, J. (1973). *The death of white sociology.* New York: Vintage Books.

Leigh, J. W., & J. W. Green (1982). The structure of the Black community: The knowledge base for social services. In J. W. Green (Ed.), *Cultural awareness in the human services* (pp. 24–37). Englewood Cliffs, NJ: Prentice-Hall.

Lipscomb, I. (May 1975). Parental influences in the development of Black children's racial self-esteem. Paper presented at the meeting of the American Sociological Association, San Francisco, California.

Logan, S. (1983). *Black fathers as nurturers.* New York State Sociological Association (From *Sociological Abstracts, 1983*, Abstract no. 15,718). Chicago: University of Chicago Press.

Logan, S., E. Freeman, & R. McRoy (Eds.) (1990). *Social work practice with Black families.* New York: Longman.

Martin, J. M., & E. P. Martin (1978). *The Black extended family.* Chicago: University of Chicago Press.

Martin, J. M., & E. P. Martin (1985). *The helping tradition in the Black family community.* Silver Spring, MD: National Association of Social Workers.

Mbiti, J. S. (1970). *African religions and philosophies*. Garden City, NY: Anchor.

McAdoo, H. P. (1980). Black mothers and the extended family support network. In L. Rodgers-Rose (Ed.), *The Black woman* (pp. 125–144). Beverly Hills, CA: Sage Publications.

McAdoo, H. P. (Ed.) (1981). *Black families*. Beverly Hills, CA: Sage Publications

McAdoo, H. P. (1985). Racial attitude and self-concept of young Black children over time. In H. P. McAdoo and J. L. McAdoo (Eds.), *Black children* (pp. 213–242). Newbury Park, CA: Sage Publications.

McAdoo, H. P. (1988). Transgenerational patterns of upward mobility in African-American families. In H. P. McAdoo (Ed.), *Black families* (2d ed.) (pp. 148–168). Newbury Park, CA: Sage Publications.

McAdoo, J. L. (1970). *An exploratory study of racial attitude change in Black preschool children, using differential treatment*. Ph.D. dissertation, University of Michigan, Ann Arbor (University Microfilms 71-468).

McAdoo, J. L. (1988). The roles of Black fathers in the socialization of Black children. In H. P. McAdoo (Ed.), *Black families* (2d ed.) (pp. 257–269). Newbury Park, CA: Sage Publication.

Merkel-Holguin, L. A., & A. J. Sobel (1993). *The child welfare stat book 1993*. Washington, DC: Child Welfare League of America.

National Resource Center on Family-Based Services (1988). *Annotated directory of selected family-based programs*. Iowa City: School of Social Work, University of Iowa–Oakland Campus.

Nobles, W. W. (1976). *A formulative and empirical study of Black families*. Washington, DC: U.S. Department of Health, Education, and Welfare.

Nobles, W. W. (1978). Africantry: Its role in Black families. In R. Staples (Ed.), *The Black family: Essays and studies* (pp. 19–26). Belmont, CA: Wadsworth.

Nobles, W. W. (1979). *Mental health support systems in Black families*. Washington, DC: U.S. Department of Health, Education, and Welfare.

Nobles, W. W. (1980). African philosophy: Foundations for Black psychology. In R. Jones (Ed.), *Black psychology* (pp. 23–36). New York: Harper and Row.

Nobles, W. W. (1986). *African psychology: Toward its reclamation, reascension and revitalization*. Oakland, CA: Black Family Institute.

Nobles, W. W. (1988). African-American family life: An instrument of culture. In H. P. McAdoo (Ed.), *Black families* (2d ed.) (pp. 44–53). Newbury Park, CA: Sage Publications.

Nolle, D. (1972). Changes in Black sons and daughters: A panel analysis of Black adolescents' orientation toward their parents. *Journal of Marriage and the Family, 34*, 443–447.

Peters, M. F. (1985). Racial socialization of young Black children. In H. P. McAdoo and J. L. McAdoo (Eds.), *Black children* (pp. 159–173). Newbury Park, CA: Sage Publications.

Rapp, C. A., & J. Poertner (1992). *Social administration: A client-centered approach.* New York: Longman.

Ronnau, J. P., & C. R. Marlow (1993). Family preservation, poverty, and the value of diversity. *Families in Society: The Journal of Contemporary Human Services, 74,* 538–544.

Ronnau, J., & A. L. Sallee (1993). *Towards a definition of family preservation: Approach, model, or policy?* Las Cruces: Department of Social Work, New Mexico State University.

Scanzoni, J. (1971). *The Black family in modern society.* Boston: Allyn and Bacon.

Scott, J. W., & A. Black (1994). Deep structures of African American family life: Female and male kin networks. In R. Staples (Ed.), *The Black family: Essays and studies.* (pp. 204–213). Belmont, CA: Wadsworth.

Stack, C. (1974). *All our kin: Strategies for survival in a Black community.* New York: Harper and Row.

Staples, R. (1971). Toward a sociology of the Black family: A theoretical and methodological assessment. *Journal of Marriage and the Family, 33,* 119–138.

Staples, R. (1994). Changes in Black Family structure: The conflict between family ideology and structural conditions. In R. Staples (Ed.), *The Black family: Essays and studies* (5th ed.). (pp. 11–19). Belmont, CA: Wadsworth.

Sudarkasa, N. (Summer 1988). Reassessing the Black family: Dispelling the myths, reaffirming the values. *Sisters 1,* 1, 22–23, 38–39.

Ward, S. H., & J. Braun (1972). Self-esteem and racial preference in Black children. *American Journal of Orthopsychiatry, 42,* 644–647.

Weaver, D. R. (1982). Empowering treatment skills for helping Black families. *Social Casework: The Journal of Contemporary Social Work, 63,* 100–105.

Williams, S. E., & D. F. Wright (1992). Empowerment: The strengths of Black families revisited. *Journal of Multicultural Social Work, 2,* 23–36.

Willie, C. (Ed.) (1976). *The family life of Black people.* Columbus, OH: C. E. Merrill.

10

Strengthening Family Ties: Working with Black Female Single-Parent Families

Sadye L. Logan

> A single woman who is raising children is not alone if she has a family. Having relatives and friends is critical. One person alone cannot raise a child. Two people are not enough to raise a child. Children need everybody, so you must seek out everybody.
> —**Toni Morrison**

During the past 20 years, the number of Black families headed by women has more than doubled, and today nearly half of all Black families are without a father in the home (Dworkin, 1986; Hill, 1990). Available evidence suggests that this structure will be permanent for most, if not all, of these families. Despite the general recognition that all Black single-parent families are not beset by debilitating problems and needs, research findings still speak to the impact of single parenthood on the psyche of the children, as well as on their quality of life. What is different about this reporting is the shifting emphasis away from the negative aspects of family dynamics. Instead, a more balanced perspective is being presented that depicts families as experiencing both difficulties and an extraordinary resiliency of spirit (Billingsley, 1992; Gary et al., 1983; McAdoo, 1988).

Despite the expanding literature on female single-parent families, very little of this research focuses specifically on strengths-oriented helping strategies for working with Black female single-parent families. Therefore, it is our intent in this chapter to provide guidelines for service providers working with Black female single-parent families that are culture-specific and strengths-oriented. The family life cycle and ecostructural principles will serve as an organizing framework.

Family Life-Cycle Issues Within an Ecostructural Framework for Black Single Parents

Most theorists conceptualize family life cycles in terms of predictable developmental stages (Carter & McGoldrick, 1988). Generally, these stages reflect the norms of white middle-class two-parent families. Seldom, if ever, are special issues such as remarriage or single parenting addressed in the context of the family life cycle. Carter and McGoldrick (1988) believe the life processes of these families are so complex that they are best viewed and analyzed as additional stages in the family life cycle. Of course, factors resulting in single parenthood dictate specific tasks for the family. For example, if single parenthood results from divorce, separation, or death, families mourn their losses and then restabilize. If it results from out-of-wedlock childbearing or adoption, families must negotiate new and often complex roles.

Figures 10.1 and 10.2 provide a visual depiction of issues and concerns of Black female single-parent families. The depiction in Figure 10.1 serves a threefold purpose: One, it highlights various aspects of Black single parenthood; two, it anchors the discussion along critical dimensions of family life; and three, it focuses intervention at the interface between the family and the various environments in which the family intersects.

Figure 10.2 extends the level of conceptual understanding about family dynamics. It provides useful information about family strengths, as well as about stressors, from an internal, intergenerational, spiritual, developmental, and ecological perspective. *Internally,* information is reflected on the horizontal axis in terms of meanings, relationships, and patterns that describe the family. *Intergenerationally,* information is reflected on the horizontal axis in terms of the patterns and ways of being in the world that have evolved over time. *Spiritually,* information is also

Figure 10.1   The Ecostructural Environment of
Black Female Single-Parent Families

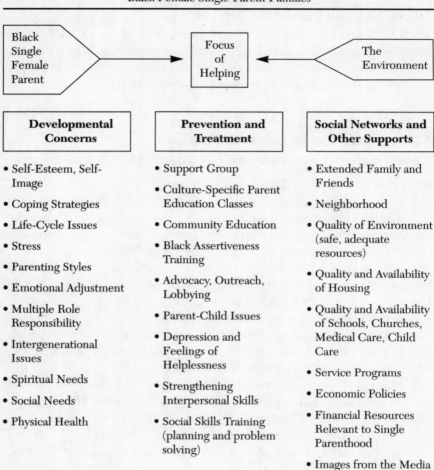

reflected on the horizontal axis in terms of the family's search for a sense of meaning and a morally fulfilling relationship with the universe and the purpose and meaning for being. *Developmentally,* information is reflected on the vertical axis in terms of the experiences and shifting patterns of the family over their time together. *Ecologically,* information is depicted within a social and cultural context and reflects the transactions between families and their environments. The horizontal flow in families

Figure 10.2   Social-Emotional "Map" for Assessing Single-Parent Families

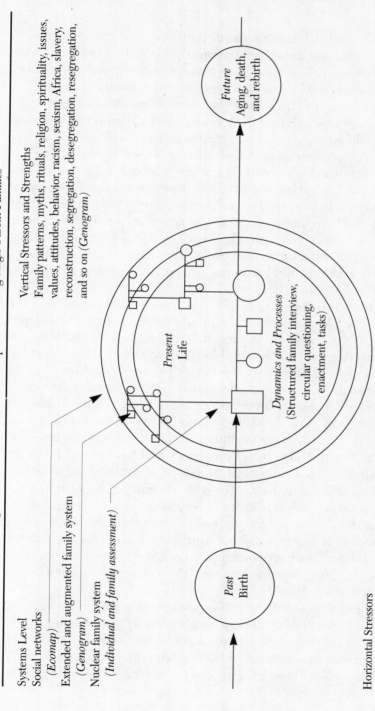

Systems Level
Social networks
  (*Ecomap*)
Extended and augmented family system
  (*Genogram*)
Nuclear family system
  (*Individual and family assessment*)

Vertical Stressors and Strengths
Family patterns, myths, rituals, religion, spirituality, issues, values, attitudes, behavior, racism, sexism, Africa, slavery, reconstruction, segregation, desegregation, resegregation, and so on (*Genogram*)

Present Life

Dynamics and Processes
(Structured family interview, circular questioning, enactment, tasks)

Future
Aging, death, and rebirth

Past
Birth

Horizontal Stressors
Life-cycle transitions, war, the economy, education, polity, care and support, early death, longevity, acute and chronic illness, good mental and physical health, and so on. (*Timeline*)

Source: Adpated from S. Logan, 1990. "Diversity Among Black Families: Assessing Structure and Function," in S. Logan, E. Freeman, and R. McRoy, eds., *Social Work Practice with Black Families: A Culturally Specific Perspective*, pp. 73–96 (New York: Longman).

includes both predictable and unpredictable life-cycle events. The vertical flow is transmitted across generations through stories and emotional triangles (Bowen, 1978). The figure also suggests a variety of practice tools that may be used by practitioners in assessing family dynamics.

The vast majority of Black female single parents with children under 18 range in age from 18 to 44 (McAdoo, 1988). Within this wide age span, life-cycle issues for the parents range from adolescence to late adulthood. The phenomenon of teenage parenthood has helped to create a distinguishing characteristic of the life cycle of female single Black parents, whose life cycles are generally more truncated. This means families have less time to resolve the developmental tasks of each stage. Often, individuals are required to take on new roles and responsibilities before they are developmentally capable of doing so. Essentially, a truncated life cycle means important family transactions—such as leaving home, having children, and becoming grandparents—occur earlier than predicted (Hodgdinson, 1991).

Despite the stress that is generally inherent in early parenthood and in related life-cycle changes, with support there are stories that depict varying degrees of success. Parents acknowledge the difficulties but also the joy in growing up with their children and recognize the support and understanding the children's youthful grandparent(s) provide.

For the female single parent, three major life tasks must be negotiated: (1) self-concept and identity concerns, (2) establishing satisfactory social relationships, and (3) managing multiple roles. Self-concept and identity issues present similar yet different concerns for young as well as older adults. For the adolescent, pregnancy and parenthood make the expected adolescent psychosocial processes of establishing a mature identity more difficult and stressful. The attempt to reconcile the demands of parenting with the desire to be young and carefree is a major concern for the adolescent parent. For the older parent, this can be a time of uncertainty and doubt about worthiness and overall capabilities. Generally, for more mature women the concern is reconciling who they believe people think they are with who they would like to be (Logan, Freeman, & McRoy, 1990).

Single mothers, especially younger mothers, often have a conflictual or no relationship with the father of their children (Crackenberg, 1981). Loneliness and depression are often problems for socially isolated mothers experiencing emotional cutoffs from family and friends (Kissman & Allen, 1993). This feeling of loneliness is also a result of the virtual unavailability of eligible Black men (Billingsley, 1992). Coupled with the overwhelming demands of multiple roles, single mothers often struggle to establish satisfactory social relationships, which include nurturing social supports, meeting new friends, and dating. Moreover, attempts to establish an ongoing quality relationship with a significant other create undue stress for the mother, especially in those situations in which the children are older and the significant other becomes a permanent part of the family's household or visits more than frequently (Kissman & Allen, 1993; McAdoo, 1985; Mendes, 1979). Children, especially adolescents, sometimes become resentful and uncooperative. Based on my practice, it has been shown that these friendships are sometimes viewed by the children as a threat to their relationship with their mother. Other conflicts involve the children's resentment at being disciplined by another man who is not their natural father. However, through support groups, friends, family, and parenting classes, parents learn ways to respond effectively to their children's concerns without neglecting their own needs.

Special Life-Cycle Needs of Children

It has been estimated that almost half of all children born today will spend at least one year living with their mother only (Pittman, 1985). According to the experts, most of these children will be living in poverty (Lewin, 1992; U.S. Bureau of the Census, 1985). Although it is important to note that not all one-parent families are impoverished, mother-headed families earn less than 50 percent of the wages earned by male single-parent families, even when the women work full-time (U.S. Bureau of the Census, 1985). Scarce financial resources also have a direct impact on the nature and quality of parental decisions regarding child care. Take, for example, a situation involving a young mother who leaves her six-year-old home alone for one hour watching television until it is time to join a neighbor child for the walk to school. Such situations can easily become the rule rather than the exception. This situation may occur because the mother reasons that the funds required to provide before-school services can better be used as money for food (Lewin, 1992). Overall, the monetary situation for most single mothers is severe, particularly for those who rely on child support to supplement the family's income. These mothers rely on either extended family or public support to survive financially.

Researchers also report that although children in female single-parent families are likely to have more behavior and academic problems than children in two-parent families, there is a lack of research evidence to support this contention. Sparse data exist that cite single parenthood as the sole cause of the problem (Lewin, 1992).

As mothers struggle to manage the demands of multiple roles, their children often share in this responsibility. Although this is sometimes problematic for the child, it is a family's strength. Mothers sometimes unwittingly, though, encourage their children, especially the oldest child, to assume more household chores than is appropriate. This may be done through encouraging the child to assume parenting responsibilities for younger children, to substitute as a companion for the mother, or to share in confidences inappropriate for the child's level of development (Weiss, 1979). With appropriate support, however, such role-sharing arrangements can be fairly functional in many families. Through this process children often develop important skills, competence, and self-esteem. Regular family meetings, task negotiation, and clear definition of roles and role expectations help both parent and child in facilitating this process. Overall, the parent, not unlike the child, needs affirmation and support to counter negative stereotypes about life experiences in single-parent families.

The Sociopolitical Context of Structure and Functioning: Guidelines for a Strengths Assessment

The responsibility of parenting is all-encompassing. Despite the commonly held assumption that the best environment for raising children is one with two parents, it has been shown the one-parent family units, when not overwhelmed by poverty, are as effective as two-parent families. Cashion (1982) describes the concerns of the one-parent unit as more transitional than psychological. Such findings suggest viewing one-parent units on a continuum from high adaptive functioning to very low adaptive functioning (see Figure 10.3). This type of conceptualization makes it possible to better understand family dynamics and to more clearly identify interventions that may range from prevention to treatment (see Figure 10.1). Preceding any form of intervention, however, an assessment of the family's strengths and concerns provides useful guideposts for the work that is to follow. At a minimum, a strengths-oriented assessment should include the following:

171

Figure 10.3 Levels of Functioning in Black Female Single-Parent Families

High Functioning	Medium Functioning	Low Functioning	Malfunctioning
• Effective discharge of parental responsibilities	• Usually effective in discharging parental responsibility	• At risk for family disruption—parent not fully in charge	• Social agency, not parent, in charge as authority figure
• Boundaries clear and appropriate	• Boundaries usually clear and appropriate	• Boundaries diffuse	• Boundaries rigid, disengaged
• Communications clear	• Communications clear	• Socially isolated	• Socially isolated
• Outside social contacts	• Outside social contact	• Limited or no demonstration of affection	• Lacking in affection and caring
• Caring and loving at all times	• Parent employed or in training	• Unemployed	• Unemployed
• Parent gainfully employed	• Caring and loving most of the time	• Communication unclear	• Communication occurs through yelling and name calling

  I. An understanding of how the family lives together (positives and negatives) through exploring six life domains
   A. Recreation and socialization
     1. What do they do for fun, individually or as a unit?
     2. How are children viewed, parented, and integrated into the family functioning?
   B. Self-image
     1. To what extent were dreams deferred?
     2. How does the family feel about itself (racial identity)?
     3. How does the family think it is viewed by others?
   C. Guidance
     1. What is the coping philosophy?
     2. Are the Black church and other spiritual and cultural organizations relied on as important resources?
   D. Family cooperation
     1. Who does the family depend on for support?
     2. To what extent is role sharing practiced?
   E. Health (mental and physical)
     1. What are the family's cultural beliefs and patterns regarding health issues?
     2. Is the family generally flexible, in touch with feelings, motivated, and able to follow through?
   F. Economics
     1. What is the level of satisfaction with the physical setting of home and neighborhood?
     2. What is the level of satisfaction with financial resources?
     3. What resources are available but not being utilized?
     4. What would raise the level of satisfaction in all of these areas the least and the most?
 II. An understanding of the family wants and needs, examined in the context of the life domains
   A. What do you want to change?
   B. What difference will that make?
   C. What will you need to make that change happen?
   D. What will you need to sustain the change (keep it going)?
III.   Tools for connecting with the family's strengths (see Figure 10.2)
   A. Constructing a family tree.
   B. Constructing a strengths-oriented family genogram (see Compton and Galaway, 1994). (Here the author's intent is to specifically construct a genogram in which the emphasis is on strength rather than deficits.)

C. Looking at family albums.

D. Constructing an ecomap (see Compton and Galaway, 1994).

E. Using good basic listening skills.

F. The worker's subjective experience of the family: common interests, beliefs, values, and so on.

Two cases serve as examples of a strengths-oriented assessment and intervention. These cases also reflect both ends of the continuum—a high functioning family and a family at risk for possible placement of all of the children.

The Todd Family

The Todd family can be viewed as high functioning. This family consists of a 33-year-old divorced mother and her four children: Renee (15), Matt (10), Rodney (7), and David (5). The children are doing well in school and at home. The mother is employed as an aide in a nursing home. She uses food stamps to supplement the family's income. She is a member of the neighborhood church, has a girlfriend from childhood who she views as a good friend, and has a male companion who occasionally sleeps over but has his own place. The extended family consists of her mother, six siblings (Paul, Robert, David, Rachael, Thomas, and Edith), two distant uncles, and one aunt. Ms. Todd is closer to some of her siblings than to others.

Sometimes Ms. Todd is frustrated with her work situation. She always wanted to be a nurse but had to leave school when she became pregnant with Renee. Her desire is to fulfill this dream one day. In addition to this disappointment, the family lives and copes with the daily ups and downs of most families: broken household items, high telephone bills with threats of cutoff notices, a car that constantly overheats, and a grandma whose diabetic condition is becoming chronic. But according to Ms. Todd, "We are doing the best we can. We have good days and bad days, but we manage. The most important thing we have is that sense of family and our faith that things will all work out."

The Martin Family

The second family under consideration is the Martin family. As indicated earlier, the Martin family can be viewed as being close to the extreme end of the continuum of functioning. Ms. Martin (37) is a never-married single parent. She has four children: Tony (13), Gail (9), George (8), and Richie (6). She is currently receiving services from a local family service agency based on a referral from her public assistance social worker. Three of Ms.

Martin's children had been placed in a residential group home for three and one-half years while she received treatment for substance abuse. During this period the youngest child was allowed to stay with the mother, because it was felt that she should not be separated from her mother because of her age. The other children had been reunited with their mother seven months prior to the referral to the family agency.

Ms. Martin lives a fairly isolated existence. She has an aunt who she views as a role model. The aunt is a well-respected community leader and disapproves of her niece's lifestyle. There is an older sister from whom she feels estranged. The sister is an office manager with a prestigious publishing company. Ms. Martin describes their relationship as tense. The sister is critical of her parenting skills and lifestyle.

The family was referred for help because of Tony's disruptive behavior in school. Actually, all of the children are experiencing some kind of academic concern. Ms. Martin describes Tony as a very helpful child but is at a loss to understand his behavior at school. At home Tony helps with general housework: cooking, cleaning, washing clothes, and supervising his younger siblings. Ms. Martin feels frustrated by the school's complaints and sees returning Tony to residential care as the only solution.

Discussion of Cases

Despite the different issues presented by both families, the strengths perspective maintains that all people have strengths, abilities, and resources for coping, problem solving, and change (see Logan's Introduction to Part Two). The practitioner approaches both families with this and the other assumptions undergirding a strengths orientation. She or he engages the family without judgment, with no preconceived notions about what needs "fixing" and how it should be "fixed." The practitioner comes with respect for the families and with faith in their abilities to change their situation. Utilizing selected information from the ecostructural diagram (Figure 10.1) and the social-emotional map (Figure 10.2), the practitioner joins each family around its motivation for help (How are you hoping I can help you?). For Ms. Todd, help would come in terms of relief from stress. For Ms. Martin, help would occur in terms of changing Tony's disruptive behavior. To solve both of these concerns, the focus would be on what both families want from the helping process (goals).

Once goals have been established, many questions would be asked to stimulate the families' ideas about possible exceptions to these concerns or ways to solve the problems. These families need affirmation that they can solve their concerns. This is best accomplished by helping them to explore other contexts in which they have been successful. For both parents, caring for their children is a central drive in their lives, coupled with their will to survive, to persevere. These qualities require courage and tenacity. Affirming these qualities creates the necessary bridge for moving beyond feelings of apathy and helplessness.

Within this context the search continues for exceptions (When is (or was) the concern less?) or solutions to concerns. In this process the practitioner moves from the role of expert to that of coach (DeJong & Miller, 1995; Shazer et al., 1986). This stance not only acknowledges both families as the experts on their own lives but also supports self-determination and strengths as the foundation upon which lasting change is built. Ms. Todd captures the essence of this stance in summarizing her life situation. She reminds us that it is always helpful to assume that everyone has positive intentions and is doing the best they can at any given moment in time.

Overall, this level of intervention suggests a proactive approach to service delivery. A proactive stance would move one beyond the family as a unit of attention to include external factors—programs, policies, and punitive ideologies. For example, unlike countries that provide an allowance for all mothers, in the United States families must meet eligibility requirements for AFDC benefits that are so low that more than 50 percent of the children receiving benefits live in poverty (Shore, 1986).

With the recognition that assessment is an ongoing, complex process, this discussion is not intended to be comprehensive. The intent is to illustrate the central role of a strengths perspective in framing our view of people and our practice. Additionally, this discussion provides a context for proposing a variety of strengths-oriented principles.

Strengths-Oriented Practice Principles

The previous discussion not only addresses the complexities of parenting for Black single mothers. It is obvious that a strengths-oriented, solution-focused approach provides useful guidelines for moving beyond the deficit perspective and working more effectively with Black single-parent families. Essentially, a more effective approach requires certain modifications in the practitioner's frame of reference.

The first set of modifications concerns avoidance of assumptions, and the second set of modifications concerns practice strategies. The importance of self-understanding and self-knowledge is emphasized more and more as a critical component of effective helping (Keeney, 1990; Lackie, 1983). Included within this self-understanding are value clarification and identification of prejudices and biases. Many practitioners are inadvertently influenced by the pervasive comparison of Black single-parent families with two-parent families of other ethnic groups and with the label "dysfunctional" families. Additionally, the emphasis in the literature on single parenthood resulting from divorce, separation, and widowhood skews the practitioner's perception of this client group. Although Black female single parenthood exists as one of the identified categories, there is an increasing number of never-married Black single mothers whose needs are different in some ways than they were previously described (Billingsley, 1992).

Self-aware practitioners who are sensitive to external factors adversely affecting the quality of life of Black single mothers and their children are better prepared to enter the clients' world as a helper. Additionally, several assumptions regarding practice strategies would enhance workers' effectiveness. The first assumption concerns the need for a broad perspective that incorporates concerns regarding the families' spiritual, psychological, and physical worlds. An ecological systems orientation would not only assist practitioners in organizing and thinking clearly about complex data but would also focus intervention at the point of exchange between the families and their environment (see Figure 10.1). As suggested in the diagrams, equal attention is directed toward understanding family functioning, aspects of the environment, and the transaction between the two.

Translating this approach into action means the helper must keep in mind that problems and needs in one area of the family's life directly influence other aspects of functioning. For example, when Ms. Martin experienced problems with substance abuse, it affected her ability to parent, exacerbated feelings of hopelessness and helplessness, caused her to be unable to work or to look for work, and nearly caused her to become homeless.

As discussed in Chapter 5, substance abuse frequently leads to a total breakdown in single-parent families. In such situations, helpers must cope with unlimited demands and fewer resources. Within this context, intervention could range from prevention to treatment, as discussed earlier. The focus of helping must involve action-oriented practice activities.

From the perspective of family functioning, practice principles are concerned with supporting and strengthening the executive functions and establishing generational boundaries (McAdoo, 1985; Welter, 1982). Strategies for supporting the executive system may include the use of professional help along with:

1. Providing respite care for mothers with young children through natural networks such as churches and other community social groups
2. Cultivating nurturing social support networks and support groups, which may include family-of-origin members or a partner or significant other
3. Providing material resources through the church, fraternal organizations, and related groups
4. Holding regularly scheduled family meetings to process daily family activities
5. Assigning age-specific family chores
6. Redefining the role of the "parental" child, thereby creating an exchange that is normative and not a burden for the child
7. Planning creative, timesaving devices (developing a schedule for family members) for managing household tasks (cleaning, ironing, cooking)
8. Seeing the family as a unit for a time-limited basis in addressing unclear role expectations and troublesome parent-child issues
9. Affirming the family's structure as viable and acceptable

Strategies for strengthening generational boundaries might include:

1. Negotiating contracts with older children regarding use of time for household chores, schoolwork, and social activities.
2. Encouraging mothers' assertiveness with children through modeling, role-play, and reading materials
3. Affirming mothers' role as ultimate family decisionmaker
4. Encouraging adult socialization experiences for the mother
5. Encouraging peer-group socialization experiences for the children
6. Identifying off-limit family and parental issues and concerns for the children

Strategies for strengthening or changing contextual concerns (social and political contexts) might include:

1. Initiating a community needs assessment developed for and by Black single mothers
2. Organizing parental cooperatives or a network of babysitters to provide respite care
3. Organizing food cooperatives to ensure healthy eating habits

4. Advocating for welfare reform and other policy changes, including greater wage equity
5. Exploring and identifying opportunities for educational training and other job-enhancement options
6. Empowering single mothers to organize service cooperatives or resource groups and to speak on their own behalf regarding program and policy issues
7. Enhancing communication between the children's school and the home

Strategies for providing individual support might include:

1. Identifying specific times for refreshing oneself and restoring energy through culture-specific related activities
2. Affirming self-worth and self-esteem through culture-specific emphasis on issues related to grooming, identity, reading materials, and general survival in an often hostile environment
3. Discussing issues related to dating and a social life in general
4. Discussing future goals related to education, work, social life, health, finances, and relationship to children

These suggested strategies suggest a multidimensional approach to intervention, as well as an expanded attitude toward helping on the part of the practitioner. This attitude incorporates a stance that views the Black female single parent as a respected human being—someone with the capability of contributing to society and the community and of taking control over her role as an effective parent.

Summary and Conclusion

Black female single-parent families as a group present unique strengths, needs, and issues. Although their needs and concerns are complicated by the complexity of and variability within each family grouping, it is imperative that awareness be maintained of the sociopolitical context that shapes the quality of home and family life in very destructive ways for this category of families. In addition to contextual concerns, other important factors need to be taken into account when assessing and intervening in Black female single-parent households; for example, the quality and availability of support from extended family members, life-cycle issues that are unique for Black female single mothers, and the influence of culture and ethnicity on sibling subsystem role responsibility.

In recognition of the need to be proactive in working comprehensively with Black female single-parent families, a variety of creative strategies have been suggested. As the helper, we must recognize and respect behaviors single parents have used in coping with family issues, but we must also teach them other behaviors that will not only enhance previous ways of problem solving but also introduce new options. Taken as a starting point, these practice principles must be implemented within an ecostructural framework. This focus allows for a broader definition of the needs and concerns and multiple starting points for assessment, planning, and intervention.

References

Billingsley, A. (1992). *Climbing Jacob's ladder: The enduring legacy of African American families.* New York: Simon and Schuster.

Bowen, M. (1978). *Family therapy in clinical practice.* New York: Aronson.

Carter, B., & M. McGoldrick (1988). *The changing family life cycle* (2d ed.). New York: Gardner Press.

Cashion, B. G. (1982). Female-headed families: Effects on children and clinical implications. *Journal of Marital and Family Therapy, 8,* 83–91.

Compton, B., & B. Galaway (1994). *Social work processes.* Pacific Grove, CA: Brooks/Cole.

Crackenberg, S. (1981). Infant irritability, mother responsiveness, and social support influence on the security of infant-mother attachment. *Child Development, 52,* 857–865.

DeJong, P., & S. D. Miller (November 1995). How to interview for clients' strengths. *Social Work, 40*(6), 729–736.

Dworkin, B. (March 2, 1986). Family and nations: A Godkin lecture series. *New York Times Book Review,* 9.

Facts on Working Women (July 1985). *Women who maintain families* (Fact Sheet no. 85-2). Washington, DC: U.S. Department of Labor, Women's Bureau.

Fox, M. F., & S. Hesse-Biber (1984). *Women at work.* Palo Alto, CA: Mayfield Publishing.

Gary, L. E., L. A. Beatty, G. L. Berry, & M. D. Price (1983). *Stable Black families: Final report.* Washington, DC: Howard University.

Hill, R. B. (1990). Research on African-American families: A holistic perspective. In W. L. Reed (Ed.), *Assessment of the status of African-Americans,* Vol. I (pp. 31–48). Boston: University of Massachusetts Press.

Hodgdinson, H. L. (1991). What ever happened to the Norman Rockwell family? In D. Bishop (Ed.), *The changing American family* (pp. 1–6). Providence, RI: Manisses Communications Group.

Keeney, B. (1990). *Improvisational therapy.* New York: Guilford Press.

Kissman, K., & J. A. Allen (1993). *Single parent families.* Newbury Park, CA: Sage Publications.

Lackie, B. (1983). The families of origin of social workers. *Clinical Social Work Journal, 12,* 309–321.

Lewin, T. (November 9, 1992). Single mothers work, worry and do their best. *Kansas City Star,* D1, D5.

Logan, S. (1990). Diversity among Black families: Assessing structure and function. In S. Logan, E. Freeman, and R. McRoy (Eds.), *Social work practice with Black families: A culturally specific perspective* (pp. 73–96). New York: Longman.

Logan, S., E. Freeman, & R. McRoy (1990). Treatment considerations for working with pregnant Black adolescents, their families, and their partners. In S. Logan, E. Freeman, and R. McRoy (Eds.), *Social work practice with Black families: A culturally specific perspective* (pp. 148–168). New York: Longman.

McAdoo, H. (1985). Strategies used by Black single mothers against stress. *Review of Black Political Economy, 14*(2–3), 153–166.

McAdoo, H. (Ed.) (1988). *Black families* (2d ed.). Newbury Park, CA: Sage Publications.

Mendes, R. (May 1979). Single-parent families: A topology of lifestyles. *Social Work, 24,* 193–200.

Pittman, K. (1985). *Preventing children having children.* Washington, DC: Children's Defense Fund.

Shazer, S., I. K. Berg, E. Lipchik, E. Nunnally, A. Molnar, W. Gingerich, & M. Weiner-Davis (1986). Brief therapy: Focused solution development. *Family Process, 25.*

Shore, B. (May 1986). NASW preliminary report: Single heads of households. Paper presented at the National Association of Social Workers National Conference on Women's Issues, Atlanta, Georgia.

U.S. Bureau of the Census (1985). *Money, income and poverty status of families in the U.S., 1984.* Washington, DC: U.S. Government Printing Office.

Weiss, R. (Fall 1979). Growing up a little faster: The experience of growing up in a single-parent household. *Journal of Social Issues, 35,* 97–111.

Welter, J. S. (June 1982). A structural approach to the single parent family. *Family Process, 21,* 203–205.

11

The Black Church as a Resource for Change

FREDA BRASHEARS

MARGARET ROBERTS

> Because the minister and the church could gratify social and psychological needs, he and the institution were very powerful.
>
> —James P. Comer

Social work practice in the church is rarely mentioned in the professional literature. It is well documented that social work is based largely on Judeo-Christian theology (Day, 1989; Dolgoff & Feldstein, 1984; Johnson & Schwartz, 1988; Morris, 1986; Skidmore, Thackeray, & Farley, 1988), but practice is more typically conducted in a variety of public or private organizational settings other than the church (Skidmore, Thackeray, & Farley, 1988).

Religious organizations, however, do have a long and rich history of providing social services to the poor and downtrodden in the community at large (Day, 1989; Netting, 1984; Skidmore, Thackeray, & Farley, 1988). Individual churches provide concrete emergency services to persons referred to them by other agencies (Abbott et al., 1990; Garland &

Bailey, 1990), and others arrange for therapy from Christian counselors for church members (Smith, 1984). Some churches minister to specific groups through programs such as family life education (Garland, 1985) or Alzheimer patient caregivers support (Filinson, 1988).

In these examples, services are provided either by the church, as an organization, to nonmember recipients or by church staff to members who request help. In the first instance, the church is viewed as a community resource similar to any other public or private service provider, to be tapped by the general citizenry. In the second instance, persons with family or individual problems who may have sought assistance from other social service agencies are given the option of receiving counseling services at their church. Both examples follow traditional service delivery models but use the church as an alternative resource.

This chapter describes an innovative social service program in an African American church in Kansas City, Missouri. The program is innovative in that it uses the informal structure of the natural environment of church-member relationships as the mechanism of response to service needs. Specht (1988) writes that the major function of social work is to help people meet their needs by using elements in their social environment such as family, friends, and social groups. The service program developed from this practice model fits particularly well in an African American church because of the unique role the church has historically played in African American culture and because self-help and informal mutual aid are common responses to need among Black people (Taylor & Chatters, 1986).

The Role of the Church
in African-American Culture

Black Americans are, by many measures, the most religious group in the world (Gallup & Castelli, 1991). In a poll conducted in early 1991, the Gallup organization found that 81 percent of Blacks were church members. The poll also found that even though this large majority claimed membership, there was evidence that religious knowledge was limited to a range of 39 to 65 percent. Yet 78 percent believed religion was important in their lives, and 93 percent felt religion would become more important to them over the next five years. Gallup concluded that the discrepancy between the high percentages of church membership and place of importance of the church and the low percentage of religious knowledge could be attributed to the relatively low percentage of college graduates among African Americans. It is possible, however, to draw other conclusions from these data.

One conclusion could be that African Americans belong to and attend church for reasons other than, or in addition to, religious education. The church has performed many functions throughout African American history besides religious ones. It was part of the underground railroad during slavery, for example, and provided secular education for children when such education was unavailable from any other source (McAdoo & Crawford, 1991). Denied access to institutions and services of the dominant culture, African American people turned to each other. The church often served as the meeting place, and the members as the communication network, where news was passed, financial transactions were completed, and strength of purpose was found.

The significance of the church can be attributed to its position as one of the few institutions within the African American community that is built, financed, and controlled primarily by Blacks (Taylor, Thornton, & Chatters, 1987). Leadership positions denied in the larger community are available in the church. The church may also be one of the few institutions that is owned by Blacks in the psychological sense of ownership, in that it represents the Black cultural self. The Black church serves as a transmitter of cultural history that is unique among religious organizations. Through rituals and traditions, cultural awareness and history of the Black experience are taught. Individual, family, and cultural identity is learned.

It is generally agreed that the church has a prominent place in African American culture and has had an impact upon virtually every aspect of Black American life (Taylor, Thornton, & Chatters, 1987). The church is central to the experience of being Black in the United States. It has provided leadership in the fight against racism and discrimination, and most African Americans indicate that the church has helped the overall condition of Blacks in the United States (Taylor, Thornton, & Chatters, 1987). In addition, the church has been called upon to provide support for families (McAdoo & Crawford, 1991), for educational programs for the prevention of premature parenthood (Allen-Meares, 1989), for after-school tutoring and counseling for school-aged children (McAdoo & Crawford, 1991), and as a source of mental health therapy through the religious experience (Griffith, Young, & Smith, 1984).

Second Baptist Church, Kansas City, Missouri

Second Baptist is the oldest African American Baptist Church in Kansas City. It was founded in October 1863 on the banks of the Missouri River at a spot known as Straggler's Camp and has an unbroken history since that time.

The church has had three locations in its 132-year history. The first building, built in 1898 and paid for by the members, was destroyed by fire in 1926. It was partially rebuilt in 1928 and served the members until 1941. In 1941, the church purchased a "four-story, modern, fully equipped" building—complete with library, gymnasium, pipe organ, grand pianos, oaken benches, and broadloom carpeting (Payne, 1983, p. 28)—which served the members until 1963. In that year, the church purchased another building in which it continues to be located.

Only six pastors have led Second Baptist, three from 1863 to 1895 and three since then. Those since 1895 have been highly educated men with advanced degrees who are prolific writers and have traveled throughout the world. Second Baptist has a history of firsts in Kansas City: the first Black church to have a robed choir; the first Black church to have a vacation bible school; the first Black church to own and operate a summer camp for youth; and the first to sponsor cultural events, particularly music, and that introduced the Midwest to Marian Anderson.

Second Baptist views itself as a large family whose needs are met within itself and in which all aspects of living are recognized and supported. There is a rich tradition of the church caring for its members. In 1911, the Relief Workers Club was organized "to assist in the care of unfortunate members of the church" (Payne, 1983, p. 15). In later years, concrete services were delivered to members of the church and community alike through the church's welfare department and fellowship care committee.

In 1925, the Ever Ready Girls Club was organized to promote growth in Christian character and service through physical, social, and spiritual training. There is a Birthday, Travel, Health, and Happiness Club through which health, fitness and social activities and group travel tours are arranged. The church sponsors recreation teams for youth, Boy Scout troops, an after-school tutorial program, and social activities for all ages.

Second Baptist values education. It serves as a teaching church for local theological seminarians, has a scholarship fund and supportive activities for college student members, and annually recognizes junior and senior high school achievers throughout the Kansas City area.

There are approximately 700 members of Second Baptist, many of whom are related to each other. There are several large, extended families in the membership, some of them third- and fourth-generation members. It is common for three-generation families to be regular and active members together.

Members of Second Baptist tend to represent the middle class and professional groups in the community. There are educators, attorneys, judges, doctors, nurses, social workers, business owners and managers, financial consultants, civil service workers and administrators, and office holders in national and local organizations. Most of the families have some degree of financial well-being, and the church, as an organization, has prided itself on a tradition of being debt free. It is within this cultural milieu that the social service program was developed.

The Social Service Program at Second Baptist

In 1987, a master's-level social worker, who was a member of the church, was added to the church staff in a part-time paid position to assist the pastor in caring for the human needs of the members of the church. The social worker developed a generalist practice of providing direct services to the members of the church and their families, as well as serving as program administrator in the church's organizational structure.

Although office space was available at the church, almost all service delivery was done in the field. The social worker met with people in their homes, while hospitalized, and at the church during other services or activities. Frequently, telephone calls were made and received at the social worker's home in the evening and on weekends. All services were available at no cost to all members of Second Baptist, their family members, and affiliates, regardless of whether they were members of Second Baptist.

Direct services were provided in the following areas:

1. Case management for elderly and disabled members
2. Support services to homebound and institutionalized members
3. Support services to members and families experiencing distress, health crises, and death

4. Family support services
5. Community requests for emergency assistance

Administrative functions included:

1. Development and implementation of educational workshops and materials for members and the community
2. Coordination of social service activities with other organizations and programs within the church
3. Field instructor for social work practicum students and consultant with seminary students in placement at the church for field training

Case Management for Elderly and Disabled Members

The membership at Second Baptist is aging, a common experience among churches (Doka, 1986). Because of this phenomenon, there was a greater demand on the pastor to provide services, which was one of the main reasons a social worker was added to the staff.

The goal of the case management services area was to prevent institutional placement. The social worker developed service plans with individuals to determine their resources and needs. The services necessary to sustain independence at the highest level possible were then arranged. Assistance was given in locating and applying for services from community resources. The service ministries of organized groups in the church were also used to provide in-home services.

Support Services to Homebound and Institutionalized Members

Support services were given through extensive field visiting and arranging for individual church members or church groups to "adopt" shut-in members. Friend-to-friend visiting was done regularly and frequently, holidays and other special days were remembered with gifts throughout the year, and clothing was provided as needed. It was especially critical for the church to provide these services for members without families.

For institutionalized members, the social worker contacted each facility's administrator and social service department to tell them of the church's social service program and interest in the member's care. It appeared that improved care was given to the patients as a result of the increased interest shown by friends and members of the church. The church was available to be appointed legal guardian for those who needed it to prevent them from becoming wards of the state.

Support Services to Families and Members Experiencing Distress, Health Crises, and Death

The social worker visited members during hospitalizations to assess their personal and family needs during the illness. Identified needs were met by the social worker arranging response from family, friends, church members, and church organizations, as well as using community resources. The social worker arranged contact among the patient, family, and hospital social service department in regard to discharge planning. Participation in discharge planning allowed for more complete information to be shared and for services to be provided in a more comprehensive way.

If in-home services or out-of-home placements were required upon discharge, the social worker met with the person to facilitate those arrangements. The family and social worker met for a family conference to discuss the impact of the illness on the family and to make appropriate plans for service provision. The social worker located and contacted out-of-town family members to involve them in the care planning for ill family members. Referral information was given to family members to arrange for needed services, or the social worker arranged for the services directly. Because of the social worker's professional knowledge of community resources and the personal relationship with the recipient families, linkage between the two was facilitated.

Grief counseling and ongoing support were given to ill persons and their families—including the children—during times of illness or imminent death and upon the death of loved ones. Family members were assisted in planning for and handling matters and issues involved in the dying and deaths of their relatives. Many times, the business side of death became a focal point of involvement with families as property needed to be managed, financial arrangements made, and insurance companies, doctors' offices, hospitals, government agencies, funeral homes, and cemeteries dealt with.

Family Support Services

Family support was made available to all families and individuals in the church. Service delivery was done informally, usually with people simply asking for help in locating community resources. Information and referral were provided in such areas as career counseling, employment and educational opportunities, location of child-care facilities, family and individual counseling, and emergency services. Interpersonal counseling with individuals and families was also provided on a limited basis. Most counseling services were provided by the pastor, who had a counseling practice through the church.

Community Requests for Emergency Services

The fellowship care committee was placed under the direction of the social worker. In an effort to better serve the persons requesting assistance, the social worker interviewed them to assess their resources and needs and then referred them to the appropriate agency for response. A social service assessment form was developed, and over time, volunteer members of the committee were trained to conduct the initial interview. Decisions regarding response were made in consultation with the social worker.

Administrative Functions

Organizationally, the social worker served as program administrator for the social services department. Duties included preparing the annual budget and quarterly and annual reports to the church and overseeing general social service program development. The social worker served as chair of the fellowship care committee, held regular meetings to address the functions of the committee, and trained the volunteer members in program procedures. The social worker also served as coordinator of the various worship and missionary groups who had contact with shut-in, ill, or elderly members to see that needs were met in a balanced, inclusive way.

Also in this function, the social worker arranged for educational programming for the membership in areas such as a presentation from a hospice on "Living with Illness" and a panel of community agencies discussing services available for senior citizens. A 52-page guide of approximately 280 resources for seniors was compiled and made available to members of the church. The social worker participated in a career-planning conference for young people at which the focus was on social work and church-related vocations as career options.

Second Baptist is a training church for seminarians, and this role was expanded to include social work students. The social worker served as field instructor for the social work students and as a consultant for the seminary students.

Social Ministry Council

A social ministry council was formed under the leadership of one of the assistants to the pastor. The purpose of the council was to "engage the church corporately, as well as members individually, to utilize their many and varied resources to respond to vital human concerns and needs" (Roberts, 1987, p. 2). The council focused on ministry in the areas of pastoral care and counseling, social service and advocacy, community relations, and public-policy action. Representatives of the various auxiliaries, clubs, departments, boards, and councils, as well as individual members, participated on the council. In effect, the council served as an advisory board to the social service department, giving the program the needed institutional support of the church.

Implications for Social Work Practice

Changing conditions dictate that social work must develop innovative service delivery programs. Public programs have retrenched, relying increasingly on private programs. Program funding methods exert increasing control over the nature and extent of service provision. "Eligibility" for services is determined more and more by diagnostic category or population characteristic, such as physical or mental illness or disability, advanced age, or foster care, for which funding is available. Resources have become so limited that in many areas of practice a triage-type screening is done to determine who will have access to them. As a result, services that assist families and individuals in the struggles of daily living do not exist.

Changing philosophies also dictate that social work must develop innovative programs. Over the last several decades, service provision across the broad spectrum has moved from the community to centralized locations. Service recipients have been expected to go to those locations for assistance. In recent years, there has been a shift in this philosophy to the effect of redirecting service delivery back to the community. Family support advocates have pointed out that the central location settings often turned into bureaucratic, institutionalized agencies that were not user-friendly. Professional disciplines across the board now speak of the need to do community and home-based service delivery. For social work, this movement is a return to historical roots and practice models. Social work, founded in community-centered methods, is in a position to lead the movement for developing new and creative approaches to meeting people's needs.

The practice experience at Second Baptist Church shows that there are untapped resources in the community and that there are new and expanded ways for social work to go about carrying out its mission. The experience underscores the need for renewed emphasis on generalist practice preparation and skill. The human service delivery system as a whole is highly complex and difficult to navigate. Social workers available to people in their natural environments can provide the unique and needed service of assisting persons along that navigation. Second Baptist's experience reveals a need for such practice, an appreciation for the services by the recipients, and a rich and rewarding experience for the practitioners involved.

The Black Church as a Resource for Change

The Black church in the United States is a particularly relevant resource for change because of its rich heritage as a focal point for community activity. Although not all churches have a social outreach ministry such as the one described here, most do have organizations within their structure that are amenable to working together with social workers to meet the needs of their members and the surrounding community. Such organizations may include mission circles, clubs, Sunday School classes, and men's, women"s, and youth groups. Some congregations participate in local, state, and federal political action, and some serve as leaders for economic growth and educational achievement in their neighborhoods.

Engaging the church in social ministry or in the delivery of social work services does not imply a subrogation of the legal principles of separation of church and state or necessarily an attempt to teach religious doctrine through social activism. This is especially true in reference to the Black church in the United States, which is often seen, accurately or not, as the single institution representing the general Black population. When assessing strengths and available resources, social workers should routinely include information regarding the role of the church in the lives of their clients and in the community at large, recognizing and accepting it as an integral, and at times forceful, part of the overall scene.

Summary and Conclusion

This chapter has described an innovative social service program in a Black church in Kansas City, Missouri. The sociohistorical role of the church in Black culture was described, as was a brief history of Second Baptist Church. The program was set in the cultural milieu of a church that is 132 years old with a tradition of supporting its members and families across all areas of life. The program proved to be a successful endeavor for the church as a body, the member recipients, and the member practitioner. The model of generalist practice in the natural environment is one that can be duplicated and should be considered for wider application, particularly in the current times of fewer resources available to meet increasing demand.

References

Abbott, S. D., D. R. Garland, A. Huffman-Nevins, & J. B. Stewart (1990). Social workers' views of local churches as service providers: Impressions from an exploratory study. *Social Work and Christianity*, 17(1), 7–16.

Allen-Meares, P. (1989). Adolescent sexuality and premature parenthood: Role of the church in prevention. *Journal of Social Work and Human Sexuality*, 8(1), 133–142.

Day, P. J. (1989). *A new history of social welfare*. Englewood Cliffs, NJ: Prentice-Hall.

Doka, K. J. (1986). The church and the elderly: The impact of changing age strata on congregations. *International Journal of Aging and Human Development*, 22(4), 291–300.

Dolgoff, R., & D. Feldstein (1984). *Understanding social welfare* (2d ed.). New York: Longman.

Filinson, R. (1988). A model for church-based services for frail elderly persons and their families. *Gerontologist*, 28(4), 483–486.

Gallup, G., Jr., & J. Castelli (June 8, 1991). Religious activity of Blacks is up. *Kansas City Star*, E-11.

Garland, D. R. (1985). Family life education, family ministry, and church social work: Suggested relationships. *Social Work and Christianity*, 12(2), 14–26.

Garland, D. R., & P. L. Bailey, (1990). Effective work with religious organizations by social workers in other settings. *Social Work and Christianity*, 17(2), 79–95.

Griffith, E.E.H., J. L. Young, & D. L. Smith (1984). An analysis of the therapeutic elements in a Black church service. *Hospital and Community Psychiatry*, 35(5), 464–469.

Johnson, L., & C. Schwartz (1988). *Social welfare: A response to human need*. Newton, MA: Allyn and Bacon.

McAdoo, H., & V. Crawford (1991). The Black church and family support programs. *Prevention in Human Services, 9*(1), 193–203

Morris, R. (1986). *Rethinking social welfare.* New York: Longman.

Netting, F. E. (1984). The changing environment: Its effect on church-related agencies. *Social Work and Christianity, 11*(1), 16–30.

Payne, J. A. (Ed.) (1983). *Second Baptist Church 1863–1983.* Available from Second Baptist Church, 3620 East 39th Street, Kansas City, MO 64128, 816–921–2326.

Roberts, M. (1987). Social ministry council: Statement of purpose and organization. Available from Second Baptist Church, 3620 East 39th Street, Kansas City, MO 64128, 816–921–2326.

Skidmore, R. A., M. G. Thackeray, & O. W. Farley (1988). *Introduction to social work* (4th ed.). Englewood Cliffs, NJ: Prentice-Hall.

Smith, K. G. (1984). Developing a Christian counseling ministry in the local church: A proven model. *Social Work and Christianity, 11*(2), 29–45.

Specht, H. (1988). *New directions for social work practice.* Englewood Cliffs, NJ: Prentice-Hall.

Taylor, R. J., & L. M. Chatters (1986). Patterns of informal support to elderly Black adults: Family, friends, and church members. *Social Work, 31*(6), 432–438.

Taylor, R. J., M. C. Thornton, & L. M. Chatters (1987). Black Americans' perceptions of the sociohistorical role of the church. *Journal of Black Studies, 18*(2), 123–138.

Epilogue:
Understanding Help-Seeking Behavior and Empowerment Issues for Black Families

SADYE L. LOGAN

> Let this thought then stay with you: There may be times when you cannot find help, but there is no time that you cannot give help.
>
> —George S. Merrian

Langston Hughes wrote in a poem, "We have tomorrow bright before us like a flame." This sentiment reflects the resiliency and positive coping patterns within African American families. Helping professionals have become more cognizant of this strength but are still struggling with ways of interpreting it as attempts are made to understand help-seeking behavior and ways of managing daily problems-in-living. As indicated throughout this book, Black families make up a significant portion of the caseloads in public social service agencies. Service contacts in many instances are of a nonvoluntary nature. However, a growing trend among Black families in general is to seek professional support for dealing with problems-in-living.

This growing acceptance signals the need for helping professionals to revisit research findings that show that Black families generally do not seek help outside of the family context. The real issues seem to be twofold: one, that a certain amount of confusion still exists regarding the dynamics of Black family life, and two, that a lack of preparedness of service delivery systems still exists in providing quality therapeutic services to Black families and children. These issues are interconnected and lead to a general lack of service effectiveness to this client group.

This chapter builds on the assumption that understanding help-seeking behavior and empowerment issues for Black families will enhance overall service effectiveness. Therefore, it is my intent to discuss those factors that affect service utilization by Black families. The discussion concludes with guiding principles in the form of implications for effective practice with Black families.

Patterns of Service Utilization

The help-seeking literature has given little or no attention to the demographic differences within the Black population or the helping process that affect help-seeking behavior among Black families. Neighbors (1984) reports that most data on help-seeking behavior in the general Black population result from comparative studies on Black and white utilization ratios of various helping facilities. Nearly thirteen years ago, however, a national study entitled the National Survey of Black Americans was conducted. This sample of the general Black population provided for differentiation among various population subgroups along dimensions previously noted (Neighbors & Taylor, 1985).

Based on an analysis of the data from the National Survey of Black Americans, several help-seeking patterns were identified (Neighbors & Jackson, 1984):

1. Women were more likely than men to seek both informal and professional help.
2. Persons with physical health problems were more likely than people with other types of problems to seek both professional and informal help.
3. Respondents with emotional problems were less likely than those with other types of problems to seek both informal and professional help.
4. People with physical problems were less likely than those with other types of problems to seek informal help only.
5. Respondents with emotional problems were more likely than persons with other types of problems to seek no help.

It is evident from these help-seeking patterns that gender, age, and problem type directly influence the help-seeking behavior of Black families. As is consistent with the help-seeking literature, Black women in this study reported receiving more services than men. The disparity in service rate was attributed to what was described as affiliate behavior. In this regard, Black women combined the use of informal networks with professional services. Black men appeared less inclined to talk about their concerns with informal helpers and acquaintances; as a result, they were more likely to be cut off from information about the availability of professional services.

Age, according to the analysis, had the greatest influence on help-seeking behavior. The findings indicated that older Blacks were more consistently nonusers of both professional and informal networks than younger Blacks. This outcome suggests that a considerable number of older Blacks may be in need of help but are experiencing some type of barrier to receiving that help. More recent studies corroborate these findings (Crawley, 1988; Crawley & Freeman, 1992). Therefore, it is extremely important that services are available, accessible, and affordable for older Blacks.

Problem types were grouped into two broad categories: physical and emotional. The respondents were highly consistent in their belief that informal and professional help should be used in dealing with physical health care. They were equally consistent in their stance regarding emotional problems. The data indicated that the participants were less likely to seek informal or formal help for emotional problems and more likely to seek no help at all.

Despite some indication that low-income persons were unlikely to seek any help and were less likely to seek informal help only, income was not very strongly related to patterns of help seeking. As is consistent with other findings regarding help-seeking styles among Blacks, this study also concludes that its most important finding was the large number of respondents who were categorized as users of informal help only or of informal help in combination with professional help.

Within the context of these six help-seeking behaviors, it is important to identify and discuss those factors influencing overall service utilization among Black families. For example, available evidence suggests that service utilization by Black families is influenced by several factors, including the lack of diversity among service staff, the location of the service delivery system, a negative perception of the service system, the manner in which Black families conceptualize problems and needs, and the manner in which Blacks conceptualize strategies for resolving problems. Although the majority of these factors are structural in nature, equally important is the family's perception of the severity of the problem and of the kind of intervention that is most effective in providing relief.

Making Service More Ethnically Sensitive

Despite some progress in efforts to increase the number of Black social service professionals, there is an ongoing call for greater commitment from professional communities to increase and sustain the number of professionals from ethnic groups of color (see Part Two). This point is underscored especially in areas significantly influenced by culture-specific issues and concerns (see discussion in Part Two).

Coupled with the need for more diverse service professionals is the need to make services more accessible to families within the Black community. Accessibility refers not only to the physical location of the services within a catchment area but also to whether the community views the service as having been developed for meeting the needs of white families only. Additionally, many Black families still maintain the view that the primary goals of public social services are to disrupt families and remove children from their families (Logan, 1980; anecdotal evidence).

In addition to the aforementioned areas of concern, issues affecting the conceptualization of problems, needs, and strategies of intervention are primary barriers to service utilization and service effectiveness. These culture-specific issues may also be discussed in terms of sociocultural factors, societal projections, and empowerment issues. The remaining sections of this chapter focus on these concerns.

Impact of Black Culture

The practice and the education community are becoming increasingly aware of factors that are essential to working effectively across cultures (see the entire issue of *Families in Society,* 1992). The demand for culturally competent practice will continue to shape the practice and the education community. This would mean that to practice in an ethnically sensitive context, the practitioner must have a working understanding of a group's history, its value orientation, its family and community patterns, and the deleterious impact of oppression the group may have experienced. For Black families, these visible markers of ethnic-sensitive practice are reflected in Black culture.

The emerging consensus about multiculturalism, ethnicity, and diversity continues to debunk the old controversy that U.S. Blacks have no distinct culture. Instead, there is a much broader acceptance of a positive Black culture. The essence of this distinct culture is directly related to ways of being in the world or to an orientation to the experience of existence. It may also be viewed as ethos or philosophy (Blauner, 1972). For U.S. Blacks, ways of being in this society evolved out of an unnatural process in that Blacks did not enter this country as immigrants but as a group of enslaved strangers with different cultural experiences. Despite the crippling effect of slavery on the social, psychological, and economic growth of U.S. Blacks, ethnic-group identity and a distinctive culture evolved.

Black culture is not unlike other cultures. Essentially, different cultures value common elements within a particular context, which includes region, polity, social class, age, gender, sex, language, and religion. For U.S. Blacks, this context more specifically includes a continuous and unifying stream for Black lifestyles that reflects a combination of Africa, the American South, slavery, racism, poverty, and migration. This stream of life is also expressed in music, family patterns, language, love, religion, and numerous other ways of being in the world. The bottom line is that Black culture refers to the characteristic lifeways of a people—the way they think, feel, and behave (Chestang, 1976; Logan, 1980).

Black English

Within the context of Black culture, Gullah, a creole language, and Black English are important cultural variables that are often overlooked as important factors in the helping encounter. Highlighting Gullah and Black English as important variables of Black culture is not intended to minimize the importance of other variables identified. These have been discussed at length in other contexts (Logan, Freeman, & McRoy, 1990; Pinderhughes, 1992; Solomon, 1976). However, Black English, a major tool in sending and receiving messages in the Black community and the primary mechanism in the helping process, is little understood.

As mentioned earlier, language is one of the many variables that constitute the stream of Black life. Although it is a powerful mechanism for survival in the Black community, as well as a means of gaining power outside the community, it is also a variable that can be viewed as a barrier to effective service delivery. In fact, a large number of Blacks in the inner cities and in parts of the South speak a language that is commonly referred to as nonstandard English. The correct terminology, though, is Black English. Dillard (1972), among other experts who have researched the philological origins of Black English, have concluded that it is a language in its own right. He contends that recognition and acceptance of this culturally different variety of Anglo-Saxon English would result in improved relations between Blacks and whites.

For many inner-city Blacks, their speech pattern reflects a unique lifestyle. It is a way of expressing themselves verbally as well as nonverbally (Draper, 1979). On the verbal level, certain words and expressions carry a distinct meaning for the culture (Cheeks, 1976; Dillard, 1972). For example, if a client says "it's cheer" to the social worker's questions about how things are going, he or she is simply remarking that things are good. However, at another level the meaning could be very ambiguous for an outsider. For example, words are sometimes used to convey the opposite meaning: "bad sounds" (good music), "bad vines" (good-looking clothes). There are other words such as blood, nigger, and splib that Blacks use in a special way with each other but that would be received as insulting and degrading if used by an outsider.

On the nonverbal level, especially in a helping situation, the response may take the form of having little or no eye contact, responding in monosyllables, and stumbling over some words. These individuals are generally described by the helper as inarticulate or unable to verbalize freely. One practitioner, for example, after encountering such a situation, wrote impressionistically that the client was hostile, angry, depressed, and possibly in need of hospitalization. She further wrote, " He uses colloquialisms with which I am unfamiliar. His lack of literacy is disturbing" (Logan, 1990, p. 33).

Of course, this situation is no different than other practice situations in which the helper encounters a cultural barrier: In such instances, a culturally sensitive response dictates that one slow down, listen attentively and respectfully, learn what is considered the norm for this individual, and then intervene with care. What is often at the root of this interchange for the help seeker is the fear of being misunderstood, of not being accepted, or of being considered ignorant—all of which could lead to ineffective or inappropriate service intervention.

The bottom line is that this mode of expression has meaning and relevance for the families involved. It is a language, with its origins in the history of a people—a language that comes into existence as the product of communication among speakers of different linguistic backgrounds (Jones-Jackson, 1987). At the core of this discussion are issues of powerlessness that are exacerbated by societal projections about inferiority and lack of acceptance.

Empowering Black Families

In discussing the help-seeking behavior of Black families, it is important to remain aware of the context. For example ecological realities for U.S. Blacks have always been characterized by economic, social, and political powerlessness. On a day-to-day basis, this powerlessness manifests in terms of inadequate or no housing, unemployment or underemployment, poor or no health care, and inferior or no education (Logan, Freeman, & McRoy, 1990). The lack of these basic human needs not only negatively affects fulfilling family roles and responsibilities but also destroys opportunities for self-enhancement.

These experiences reflect the cultural adaptations of U.S. Blacks to a hostile environment. In U.S. society Blacks generally interact with this hostile environment in two distinct ways: (1) by remaining isolated, with limited contact outside the Black community; or (2) by assuming a bicultural interpersonal style, which means having a great deal of pride in racial identity and embracing diversity but being unable to integrate the two experiences (Atkins, Morten, & Sue, 1983). At best, both forms of adaptation are marginal. They are reservoirs of both strength and conflict. Although biculturalism is generally viewed as one of the positive mechanisms for surviving in a hostile environment, numerous others are less positive. Families experience the fallout from such adaptive methods in terms of homelessness, substance abuse, violence to self and others, and many other debilitating conditions (see Parts One and Two).

Poverty and other systemic problems stress the community system, which is the expected source of support for families. Under the stress of numerous problems and limited or nonexistent resources, the community becomes depressed, and the quality of living diminishes significantly (Williams, 1990). It is within this context that Black families must be supported in assuming more proactive roles in defining and assuming life goals (Billingsley, 1992).

Defining Empowerment

To speak of U.S. Blacks assuming more proactive roles in determining life goals is another way of saying they must gain and maintain mastery over their lives. This is empowerment. It is a process. According to Rapport (1984), some people may experience empowerment as a sense of control, whereas others may experience it as actual control. I contend, however, that the sense of control or an internalized attitude must precede any observable behavior of empowerment. In other words, to move beyond this process as more than mere words it must become an experience. It must be a focal point for thinking about and acting on problems-in-living. Several assumptions undergird this process: (1) that many competencies are already present or possible, (2) that new competencies are learned or relearned in the process of living life, (3) that there are many different ways and means of achieving competencies, and (4) that partnership must replace paternalism.

As indicated earlier, empowerment is essentially an internal process that manifests outwardly. It implies a "goodness of fit" between individual internal resources and external environmental resources (Germain, 1973). The idea of a goodness of fit with the environment suggests the ability to affect, influence, and change the life forces that affect one's life space for one's own benefit (Germain & Gitterman, 1980; May, 1972; Pinderhughes, 1992). Given that this fit is generally nonexistent for Black families, empowerment becomes the approach for realizing this goal.

Implications for Practice

As indicated earlier, a large number of Blacks utilize social networks or a combination of social networks and professional help to deal with problems-in-living. However, it is also evident that Black families across the socioeconomic strata continue to experience increasing amounts of stress and hardship as a result of the social, economic, and political climate of the country. Struggles with issues of powerlessness and equity have been ongoing aspects of Black family life. Black families need support in moving toward a second order of change—that is, in breaking free of a vicious, rigid cycle of toughness, self-defeating messages, negative stereotypes, and ongoing struggles to a stance that provides a place to be in greater control of all aspects of their lives. This place on which to stand must provide choice, power, stress management, and the elevation of self-image and self-esteem.

Attaining this stance, commonly referred to as proactive, is a complex task that will require commitment and long-term work. It can begin with simple individual activities, then move to incorporate more complex activities within larger systems. For example, individual activities may include (1) providing knowledge or information about where and how to secure needed resources such as health and medical care, (2) teaching through role-play and discussing skills of delegating responsibilities to children in a manner that allows them to feel they are a part of a process, and (3) developing support networks to provide affirmation of strengths and competencies. Empowering activities within larger systems may include grassroots involvement in assessing community needs, planning and developing a community resource directory that informs community residents of existing services, developing community support groups for special needs (for example, single parents, sickle cell disease), and creating linkage within the church and fraternal groups (for example, planning and implementing special-needs workshops for adults and children) (Biegel, 1992; Naparstek, Biegel, & Spiro, 1982).

Given the help-seeking responses of U.S. Blacks, it is obvious that a great deal of work needs to be done in terms of service accessibility, availability, and overall effectiveness. Practitioners can begin to change this process by assuming a more proactive stance in addressing these concerns. The first line of action could begin by applying a set of ethnically sensitive questions to one's practice. This list serves as baseline data in working to create a more user-friendly service system for African American families (Hartman, 1990):

- Is my practice based on an understanding that U.S. Blacks are part of current and intergenerational family systems that had their origins in Africa and that these human connections are powerful, persistent, and essential to the ongoing growth and development of the individual?
- Does my practice include, support, and strengthen these important human connections?
- Does my practice involve the family to the fullest extent possible in defining problems and creating solutions, or does it replace a family function in a situation where, with help, the family itself could meet the needs of its members?

- Does my practice move toward separation, hospitalization, or institutionalization only as a last resort? And when separation is required, do I facilitate ongoing family connections?
- Is my practice sensitive to the diversity of family life and flexible in adapting to the different needs of families in terms of culture, race, lifestyles, structures, or life stage?
- In partnership with families, does my practice empower and enhance the family's autonomy, cohesion, competence, spirituality, and self-esteem?
- Is my practice committed to understanding and changing the broader sociopolitical context (eradicating racism) in which the families I see in treatment live?

Such change is not easy and will require ongoing, persistent efforts. For Black families, the position of powerlessness has existed over the life span of this country. It is entrenched and exists on many levels. For example, the social systems in which Black families interact are equally locked into rigid responses to the needs of Black families and communities. The verbal response is usually politically correct, but the action lacks impact. However, the situation is not hopeless; it is one of great promise and provides numerous challenges to families, the country, and human service professionals. The process of change begins with layers of recognition:

1. That the paternalistic approach does not work and should be abandoned (Solomon, 1976; Swift, 1984)
2. That we should not force clients to fit their problems and needs into the framework professionals have created to meet specific needs at a particular point in time (Keeney, 1990)
3. That we should build on clients' strengths and their natural ways of problem solving (Logan, Freeman, & McRoy, 1990; Saleebey, 1992)
4. That strategies of intervention incorporate these natural helping processes (Logan, Freeman, & McRoy, 1990; Saleebey, 1992)

Given this framework, the professional helper's role will be multifaceted. Empowering families begins with a specific attitude on the part of the helper, an expanded attitude that reflects the stance of an empowered helper (Pinderhughes, 1963). An empowered helper enters the family system with preconceived ideas not about pathology but about strength.

The guiding question is not what is wrong with this family but what is right with this family. An empowered helper, however, is only minimally effective if not supported by the service structure. For empowerment to be effective as a service goal, agencies must make a serious commitment at the highest level to quality service. An empowered helper may find it necessary to assume a variety of roles in the helping encounter. These may include resource consultant, teacher or trainer, broker, advocator, sensitizer, mediator, and facilitator. As helpers assume these roles, they must do so from a partisan position. This involves mutuality in all aspects of helping: problem definition, goal setting, and intervention.

With empowerment as a goal, it is a given that powerlessness is the problem. As indicated earlier, for U.S. Blacks this is an ingrained problem that permeates all aspects of Black family life. To address this debilitating condition, the first line of strategy should be to teach families about power dynamics in terms of relationships within the family and between the family and external systems. The use of a strengths orientation in this process affirms the inner resources and resiliency of families and also conveys that helping is a respectful and collaborative process.

Let us take the example of the Seabrook family as an illustration. The family consists of the mother, Mindy, age 27, and her two children, Benny and Debby, age 7. Debby is 10 months older than her brother. Mindy separated from her husband, Stewart, age 30, shortly after Benny's birth. Stewart had a tendency to get drunk and beat up his wife. Since that time, he has had sporadic contact with the family. The family was referred to a local family service agency by the Department of Social and Rehabilitation Services (SRS) for possible neglect. The children were expelled from the Catholic school because of "disruptive and uncontrollable behavior." The children are currently enrolled in public school, but there is similar feedback regarding their behavior (climbing the walls and running out into the streets without any awareness that what they are doing is dangerous).

Since the SRS investigation, the children have lived with their maternal grandmother, and Mindy lives across the street. She watches the children at her mother's house until her mother comes in from work. Mindy is currently unemployed. The conditions for return of the children to Mindy's care are that she change her passive, permissive stance with her children, learn to set limits and boundaries, and create consistency when responding to the children's unacceptable behavior.

The social worker was initially overwhelmed by the challenges presented by the family. The children seemed totally out of control, and the mother vacillated between angry outbursts at the worker, claiming not to know what SRS was wanting from her, to passivity and bouts of depression.

The first line of strategy involved a shift in the worker's attitude about the presenting problem and the mother's behavior as "impossible." Second, the worker moved toward a team-oriented approach of helping. This meant coordinating supporting activities of other service professionals who are involved. In this process, the client and the worker are empowered. Feelings of helplessness and lack of trust by the worker and the client are diminished. The worker also reframed her role as active supporter of the mother in her efforts to use a more assertive parenting style. She no longer saw herself as responsible for changing the mother. Reframing was also utilized in supporting the mother's move from an emotionally reactive stance to an intellectually proactive stance (Kerr & Bowen, 1988). Through the use of a strengths-oriented focus, the mother was helped to see and experience how her behavior, although maladaptive, was her learned way of coping but that it was possible to rechannel that energy in adaptive ways. This meant deciding what was growth enhancing for herself and her children—a task that required conviction and belief in herself.

Several strategies were used in affirming and supporting the mother's self-worth, including restorying as a means of healing old hurts and gaining new perspectives (see Laird, 1989). In this regard, the mother was encouraged to talk about family values, culture, ethnicity, myths, beliefs, and other issues related to family dynamics and to living in a multicultural, multiracial world. Modeling is another useful strategy in this process. This was accomplished through a variety of means: home visits, the use of media, and thoughtful comments. Home visits were used to join the mother in implementing simple tasks and to observe and give feedback and try out different ways of setting limits with the children. Different ways of interacting with the children and others were introduced by such comments as "Have you thought about," "You have a choice," "It might be useful," or "Another way is to." With trust and respect, these strategies provide a sense of worth and power.

Summary and Conclusion

Black Americans are more responsive in seeking help from informal service systems. It is contended that aspects of Black culture and issues of powerlessness mitigate against greater service utilization by Black families. Client empowerment is proposed as a primary goal in responding to families' underutilization of services. To embrace empowerment as a practice goal requires that helpers acquire appropriate and effective practice skills and knowledge on the overall quality of Black life.

References

Atkins, D. R., G. Morten, & D. W. Sue (Eds.) (1983). *Counseling American minorities: A cross-cultural perspective* (2d ed.). Dubuque, IA: William C. Brown.

Biegel, A. (1992). Help seeking and receiving in urban ethnic neighborhoods: Strategies of empowerment. *Prevention in Human Services, 3*(43), 119–143.

Billingsley, A. (1992). *Climbing Jacob's ladder: The enduring legacy of African American families.* New York: Simon and Schuster.

Blauner, R. (1972). *Racial oppression in America.* New York: Harper and Row

Cheeks, D. K. (1976). *Assertive Black puzzle: A Black perspective on assertive behavior.* San Luis Obispo, CA: Impact Publishers.

Chestang, L. (1976). The Black family and Black culture: A study in coping. In M. Sotomayer (Ed.), *Cross-cultural perspectives in social work practice and education* (pp. 76–94). Houston, TX: University of Houston Graduate School of Social Work.

Crawley, B. (1988). The social service needs of elderly Black women. *Affilia, 3*(2), 6–15.

Crawley, B., & E. Freeman (1992). Themes in the life views of older and younger African American males. *Journal of African American Male Studies, 1*(1), 15–29.

Dillard, J. L. (1972). *Black English: Its history and usage in the United States.* New York: Random House.

Draper, B. J. (1979). Black language as an adaptive response to a hostile environment. In C. B. Germain (Ed.), *Social work practice: People and environments* (pp. 267–287). New York: Columbia University Press.

Families in Society: The Journal of Contemporary Human Services (June 1992) 73(6), entire issue.

Germain, C. (June 1973). An ecological perspective in casework practice. *Social Casework, 54*(4), 12–18.

Germain, C., & A. Gitterman (1980). *The life model of social work practice.* New York: Columbia University Press.

Hartman, A. (1990). Family ties. *Social Work, 24,* 195–196.

Jones-Jackson, J. P. (1987). *When roots die: Endangered traditions on the sea islands.* Athens: University of Georgia Press.

Keeney, B. P. (1990). *Improvisational therapy: A practical guide for creative clinical strategies.* New York: Guilford Press.

Kerr, M., & M. Bowen (1988). *Family evaluation: An approach based on Bowen Theory.* New York: W. W. Norton.

Laird, J. (1989). Women and stories: Restorying women's self-constructions. In M. McGoldrick & C. M. Anderson (Eds.), *Women in families* (pp. 427–450). New York: W. W. Norton.

Logan, S. (1980). The Black Baptist church: A social-psychological study in coping and growth. *Dissertation Abstracts International, 41,* 6A.

Logan, S. (1990). Black families: Race, ethnicity, culture, social class and gender issues. In S. Logan, E. Freeman, & R. McRoy (Eds.), *Social work practice with Black families: A culturally specific perspective* (pp. 18–37). New York: Longman.

Logan, S., E. Freeman, & R. McRoy (Eds.) (1990). *Social work practice with Black families: A culturally specific perspective.* New York: Longman.

May, R. (1972). *Power and innocence.* New York: W. W. Norton.

Naparstek, A., D. Biegel, & H. Spiro (1982). *Neighborhood networks for human mental health care.* New York: Plenum Press.

Neighbors, H. W. (1984). Professional help use among Black Americans: Implications for unmet need. *American Journal of Community Psychology, 12*(5), 551–565.

Neighbors, H. W., & J. S. Jackson (1984). The use of informed help: Four patterns of illness behavior in the Black community. *American Journal of Community Psychology, 12*(6), 629–644.

Neighbors, H. W., & R. J. Taylor (1985). The use of social service agencies by Black Americans. *Social Service Review, 59,* 259–268.

Pinderhughes, E. (June 1963). Empowering our clients and ourselves. *Social Casework, 64*(6), 331–338.

Pinderhughes, E. (1992). Legacy of slavery: The experience of Black families in America. In M. P. Mirkin (Ed.), *The social and political contexts of family therapy* (pp. 289–306). Boston: Allyn and Bacon.

Rapport, J. (1984). Studies in empowerment: Introduction to the issue. *Prevention in Human Services, 3*(43), 1–7.

Saleebey, D. (Ed.) (1992). *The strengths perspective in social work practice.* White Plains, NY: Longman.

Solomon, B. (1976). *Black empowerment: Social work in oppressed communities.* New York: Columbia University Press.

Swift, C. (1984). Empowerment: An antidote for folly. *Prevention in Human Services, 3*(43), xi–xv.

Williams, L. F. (1990). Working with the Black poor: Implications for effective theoretical and practice approaches. In S. Logan, E. Freeman, & R. McRoy (Eds.), *Social work practice with Black families: A culturally specific perspective* (pp. 169–192). New York: Longman.

About the Book

With eleven selections designed to reinforce the goal of empowering clients to take charge of their lives, this edited volume serves a twofold purpose. It extends the small but growing body of strengths-oriented literature to include African American families, and it serves as a natural extension of current texts on African American families to provide social workers and the education community with a broader framework for understanding the needs of these families.

Offering both a research orientation and a practice perspective, this book should appeal to social work educators and practitioners involved in family services, health and mental health settings, and child and public welfare.

About the Editor and Contributors

Freda Brashears graduated from the University of Missouri and received her Master of Social Work degree in 1983. She has been practicing social work for twenty-seven years and continues to work toward the development of innovative service delivery programs. She currently provides social work services to families involved with the child welfare system throughout the Kansas City area using an in-home, generalist private practice model. Brashears continues to serve as a consultant to the social services program at Second Baptist Church, Kansas City, Missouri, and provides direct services to members on a referral basis. In addition, Brashears is studying at the University of Kansas School of Social Welfare doctoral program, specializing in analysis of public policy implementation.

Brenda Crawley is director of training for SOS Kinderdorf International, an international humanitarian organization. She is responsible for the development of training programs and training centers for a five-country area in southern Africa. Crawley received her Ph.D. from the University of Illinois at Urbana-Champaign in 1981 and her Master of Social Work degree in 1973. Crawley has had over ten years of university teaching experience as well as experience as a trainer and field representative with the National Council on Aging. Her research and writing focus on older/mature adults, women's issues, black families, and program and policy issues. She has published numerous articles and several training manuals in these areas.

Ramona W. Denby recently received her doctoral degree in social work from the Ohio State University. During her studies, Denby was a National Institute of Mental Health (NIMH) Minority Research Fellow. Through her NIMH training, she engaged in specialized research on minority children's mental health and child welfare issues. These interests led to the study of targeting services to special populations within family preservation programs. Currently, Denby is assistant professor in clinical social work at the University of Tennessee, Knoxville (UTK). She continues to conduct research concerning child welfare and children's mental health through research activities at UTK's College of Social Work, Children's Mental Health Center.

Edith Freeman is a professor at the University of Kansas School of Social Welfare where she teaches graduate practice methods courses. She was a recipient of the First Chancellor's Award for Teaching Excellence in 1989. Her research and writing interests include issues related to children and families, substance abuse prevention and treatment, multiculturalism, community development, and empowerment. Freeman has published six books, numerous articles, and several training manuals in these areas. She also provides consultation and training in these and other areas to staff in community organizations and social agencies.

Shirley A. Hill is an assistant professor at the University of Kansas Sociology Department with an adjunct appointment in Health Services Administration. She earned a master's degree at the University of Missouri in 1978 and a doctorate from the University of Kansas in 1992. She received the Best Dissertation Award from the Medical Sociology section of the American Sociological Association for her research on sickle cell disease and is the author of a book and several articles on caregiving in African American families. Her current research examines the family socialization experiences of African American children, with a special focus on the race, class, and gender dimensions of socialization. She teaches courses on the family, social inequality, and social stratification, and she has an ongoing interest in health care issues and policies and the welfare and development of children.

Jerome Joyce earned his Master of Social Work degree at the University of Kansas in 1988. He is currently employed by the state of Kansas as a staff social worker working with adolescents in residential treatment. He is also an adjunct faculty member at Highland Community College. Joyce's expertise is in educating and counseling African American families, specifically of AIDS victims. Joyce is active in the Baptist Church and serves on its trustee board.

Sadye L. Logan is associate professor in the School of Social Work and associate chair of African and African American Studies at the University of Kansas. She teaches practice method courses and courses on family treatments. She also chairs the foundation practice sequence and is co-director of the Institute for the Study of Black Family Life. She earned a master's degree in social work from Hunter College and a doctorate of social welfare from Columbia University in 1980. Her research interests include families and children, culturally specific services for children and families of color, the psychospiritual dimensions of practice and education, addictive behaviors, and racial identity development. Logan has written and published extensively in these areas. She has also addressed them through consultation, workshops, local, national, and international presentations, and professional organizations.

Ruth G. McRoy holds the Ruby Lee Piester Centennial Professorship in Services to Children and Families and is the director of the Center for Social Work Research at the School of Social Work at the University of Texas in Austin. She also holds a joint appointment at the U.T. Center for African and

African American Studies. McRoy received her bachelor's degree and master's degree in social work from the University of Kansas. She received her Ph.D. degree from the University of Texas in 1981 and went on to accept the University of Texas Outstanding Dissertation Award. McRoy's research interests include: open, transracial, Black, and special-needs adoptions and emotionally disturbed adopted children and adolescents; cross-cultural relationships; racial identity development; treating alcoholic clients; and homelessness. McRoy recently completed a study for the Texas Department of Protective and Regulatory Services on adoption disruptions and dissolutions in the state of Texas. She has co-authored four books, written numerous articles and essays, and presented many invited papers at national and international conferences.

Sarah G. Mitchell graduated from Williams College and received her Master of Social Work degree from Hunter College School of Social Work in New York City. While obtaining her degree, Mitchell developed a keen interest in urban violence and its effects on adolescent development. Mitchell has extensive child welfare experience in foster care as well as preventive services. She currently works as a clinical social worker with adolescents and their families who have been referred for counseling from the Brooklyn Family Courts' Mediation and Diversion program.

Margaret N. Roberts is associate pastor at Second Baptist Church, Kansas City, Missouri. She received a Master of Divinity degree in theology from Central Baptist Theological Seminary. Roberts is also a doctoral candidate at the St. Paul School of Theology, majoring in ethics and social change.

Harrison Y. Smith is a professor in the Department of Social Work, College of Health and Human Services, Eastern Michigan University. In addition to his nine years of practice, for the past twenty-six years Smith has authored many scholarly publications, including studies of the roles and responsibilities of faculty field liaisons, the use of mental health supervision as a means of quality assurance, and social work with disenfranchised minority children in predominantly majority public schools. Smith's current scholarly interest is in an area he conceptualizes as "community management." It involves creating community self-reliance through interdisciplinary and interprofessional training and developing community-based urban leadership role models.

Index

Abarry, A., 116
Acquired Immune Deficiency
Syndrome (AIDS), 6–7, 31,
53–54, 59–60, 65
family caregiving, 7, 54, 55–59,
63–65
persons with (PWAs), 53, 54, 55,
56, 57, 62, 63–65, 113
social services, 54, 60–65
Adolescent development, 88–90
parenthood, 168
Adopt-a-family programs, 101
Adoption, 33–34
transracial, 110, 132, 136
AFDC. *See* Aid to Families with
Dependent Children
*Africa centered perspective of history,
The* (Keto), 125
African American family, 3(n1). *See*
also Black family
African American Family
Preservation Model, 110, 145,
155–159 African-centered
consciousness. *See*
Afrocentricity
African-centered values, 2, 3(n2). *See
also* Afrocentricity; Values
African heritage, 2, 9–10, 11(fig.), 12.
See also Afrocentricity; Values
Afrocentric, 3(n2). *See also*
Afrocentricity
Afrocentricity, 16–17, 114–118
in education, 97, 98, 115, 117

in social services practice, 35,
117–123, 127
See also Empowerment; Helping
tradition; Self-development;
Values
Afrocentricity (Asante), 125
AIDS. *See* Acquired Immune
Deficiency Syndrome
Aid to Families with Dependent
Children (AFDC), 76, 77
Akbar, N., 122
Alcoholics Anonymous, 79
Alcoholism, 69, 75, 76
Alienation, 84, 89, 93
Alpha Phi Alpha (fraternity), 151
Alpha Psi (fraternity), 151
American Medical Association, 43
Ancestors, 2, 12
Anderson, Marian, 184
Arendt, Hannah, 87
Asante, Molefi, 116, 125
Aschenbrenner, J., 148(fig.)
Assimilation, 27, 72(fig.)
Azibo, D. A., 116, 120

Baraka, I., 15
Bassuk, E. L., 67, 74
BCCC. *See* Black Community
Crusade for Children
Beacon Program (Rheedlen Center),
96–97
Belief system. *See* Afrocentricity;
Values

213